So You Think You Know Gettysburg?

Volume 2

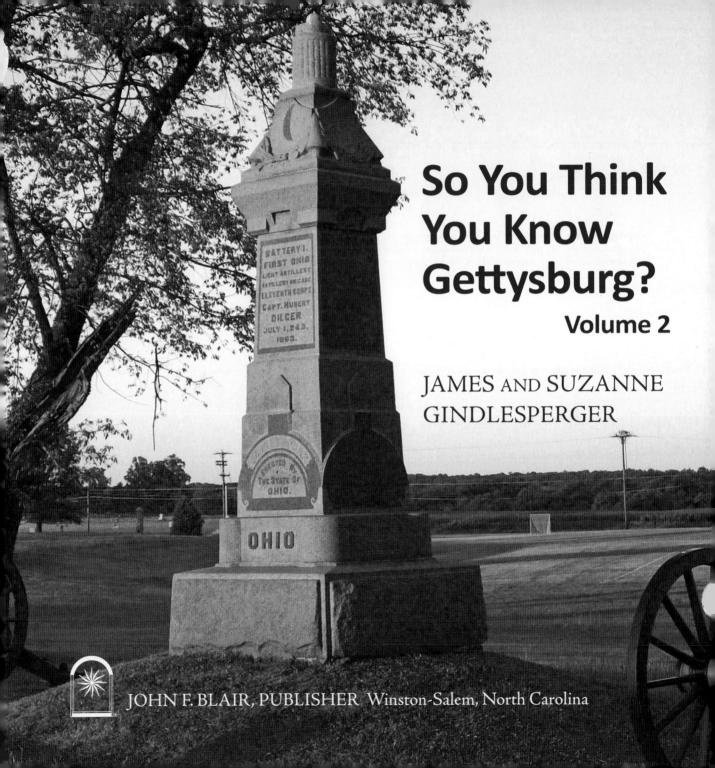

So You Think You Know Gettysburg?

Volume 2

JAMES AND SUZANNE
GINDLESPERGER

JOHN F. BLAIR, PUBLISHER Winston-Salem, North Carolina

Published by
JOHN F. BLAIR,
PUBLISHER
1406 Plaza Drive
Winston-Salem, North Carolina 27103
www.blairpub.com

Printed in South Korea

COVER IMAGE
Cushing's Battery, near the focal point of Pickett's Charge and the scene of horrific hand-to-hand fighting on July 3, 1863

MAPS BY BILL TRUNINGER
BOOK DESIGN BY DEBRA LONG HAMPTON

Library of Congress Cataloging-in-Publication Data

Gindlesperger, James, 1941–
   So you think you know Gettysburg? : the stories behind the monuments and the men who fought one of America's most epic battles / James and Suzanne Gindlesperger.
      p.   cm.
   Includes index.
   ISBN 978-0-89587-374-3
   1. Gettysburg National Military Park (Pa.)—Tours. 2. Gettysburg, Battle of, Gettysburg, Pa., 1863 3. United States—History—Civil War, 1861–1865—Monuments. I. Gindlesperger, Suzanne. II. Title.
   E475.56.G744 2010
   973.7'349—dc22

                2009045842

10 9 8 7 6 5 4 3 2 1

To those whose stories
these monuments represent:

Thank you.

THE MUFFLED DRUM'S SAD ROLL HAS BEAT
THE SOLDIER'S LAST TATTOO.
NO MORE ON LIFE'S PARADE SHALL MEET
THAT BRAVE AND FALLEN FEW.

THE 20TH MAINE REG'T
3D BRIG, 1ST DIV, 5TH CORPS,
COLONEL
JOSHUA L. CHAMBERLAIN
CAPTURED AND HELD THIS
POSITION ON THE EVENING
OF JULY 2D, 1863, PURSUING
THE ENEMY FROM ITS FRONT
ON THE LINE MARKED BY
ITS MONUMENT BELOW.
THE REG'T LOST IN THE BATTLE
130 KILLED AND WOUNDED
OUT OF 358 ENGAGED.
THIS MONUMET MARKS THE
EXTREME LEFT OF THE UNION
LINE DURING THE BATTLE OF
THE 3D DAY.

"In great deeds, something abides. On great fields, something stays."

Brevet Major General
Joshua Lawrence Chamberlain
Dedication speech for
Twentieth Maine Infantry
Monument, October 3, 1889

Gettysburg Battlefield   July 1 – 3, 1863

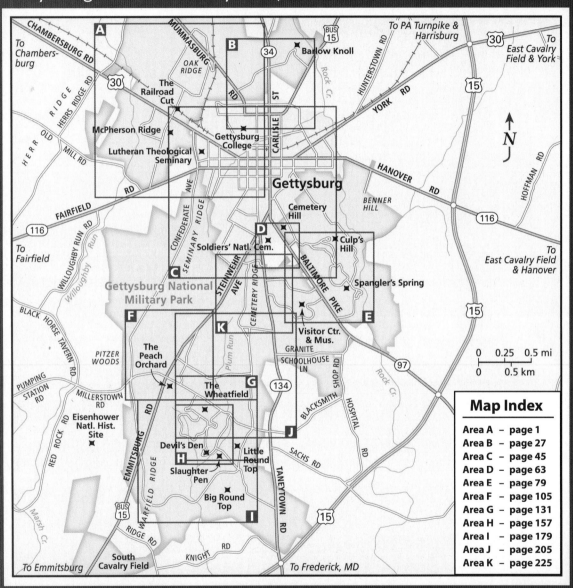

Map Index

Contents

Chapter 7
Area G—Wheatfield, Loop, Plum Run   131

Chapter 8
Area H—Devil's Den, Brooke Avenue   157

Chapter 9
Area I—Round Tops   179

When the Civil War began in 1861, both sides were confident it would be of short duration. President Abraham Lincoln was so certain that his first call for troops was for a commitment of only ninety days. Surely, they wouldn't be needed any longer than that. Sentiment in the South was much the same.

But as we now know, it was not to be. The ninety days dragged into several months, then a year, then two years, and still no end was in sight. By the summer of 1863, thousands of men on both sides had died, yet nothing was settled. The Confederacy still existed, and the Union still resisted the claim that the rebellious states should be allowed to leave.

From July 1 through July 3, 1863, the two sides met on another battlefield. This one was unusual. For the first time, it was in a Northern state. That state was Pennsylvania. The town was Gettysburg. And the nation would never forget.

Those who fought on that battlefield have long since gone on to their reward. Yet we still study what they did, and we visit the field where they did it. And we honor their memories.

Many of those memories are in the form of battlefield monuments. Nearly two million people visit them every year. We pause, we reflect, and we move on. Few of us, however, give much thought to the stories behind those monuments, the stories of the men they represent.

The authors of this book wish to change that. We want visitors to know that each monument has a story. Some are tragic, some triumphant. Some reveal the human spirit, others the darker side of humanity. Whatever the stories, we wish to present them as best we know them: humorous or tragic, unvarnished, warts and all.

In 2010, with that in mind, we wrote *So You Think You Know Gettysburg?* But because thirteen hundred monuments are on the field, we had to decide which ones to include and which to leave out. Some of those decisions were difficult. We would have loved to include them all, but that was not practical. Readers quickly picked up on the fact that we hadn't been able to include everyone's favorite, and we soon began getting requests to do another book. This work is in response to those requests, yet still we can't include each monument. The ones in this volume, combined with those in the first, still represent only a portion.

We encourage readers to visit not only those monuments we have written about, but also those not included. They are no less important. Look at the designs and ask what they represent; search out the stories behind the monuments. They are all interesting in their own right.

As in the first volume, we have divided the battlefield into segments. Each chapter begins with a brief summary of what took place in that area. That description in no way is meant to be a comprehensive study of the area, nor are the battle accounts for the respective regiments meant to be anything but brief summaries. We are merely attempting to provide background that will put the rest of the narration into its proper context.

We have assigned the photos and their accompanying narrations numbers that are shown on the area maps. Those numbers and their accompanying GPS coordinates will allow readers to determine where each photo was taken. For example, photo A-1 is the first photo in Area A, and its story is found in the narration under A-1. The numbers are placed in the logical order in which readers will come upon

the monuments if driving. The Gettysburg battlefield has many one-way roads, and although it may appear that the number placement is inconsistent, it is done deliberately to enable readers to follow the flow as easily as possible. To further aid those also seeking the sites listed in Volume 1, we have included a summary of Volume 1 sites in the general vicinity of those in each area of Volume 2.

We refer throughout the book to Pickett's Charge, rather than the more historically accurate Longstreet's Assault or the more descriptive but unwieldy Pickett-Pettigrew-Trimble Charge. Pickett's Charge is used for simplicity and because it is the name most commonly associated with the famed attack.

From time to time in the narration, we use the word *enemy*. This in no way reflects our feelings toward either side. It merely indicates the opposing side. Whether it refers to Union or Confederate forces depends on the army or regiment being described in that particular narration. We have attempted to avoid any biases, preferring to leave that to readers who are so inclined.

As you traverse the field, remember that this is hallowed ground. Treat it with reverence. Remember also that some of the monuments are now on private property, so please respect the rights of the owners.

We hope you enjoy your visit, and that you will reflect on what the men who fought here experienced. We owe them that.

Acknowledgments

We are deeply indebted to many people for helping bring this book to completion.

Our son, Mike, who accompanied us on many of our visits and took great pride in being the one to locate some of the more hidden treasures on the battlefield, was an invaluable help. He saved us time and effort, and we appreciate it. Thanks, Mike.

Bill Truninger, who did an outstanding job developing the maps, showed a rare talent. Perhaps more importantly, his patience in cheerfully (and repeatedly!) amending what we had thought would be the final product was beyond the call of duty. Thank you again, Bill.

Before the famous Lutheran Seminary cupola was opened to the public, the Adams County Historical Society allowed us access to take photos. We not only appreciated that experience but found it humbling. Standing where some of the main figures in the battle stood to observe troop movements was a rare privilege, and we didn't take it lightly. We hated to leave, thinking at the time that we would never again have the opportunity. Thank you, Wayne Motts (even though you are no longer at the society) and all those who made us feel so welcome. We made sure to keep the door closed so the bats stayed upstairs!

The folks at the National Park Service have always been eager to assist. Without their input, this book would be so much less. We would be remiss if we failed to acknowledge the help of the friendly staff at the visitor center, the licensed battlefield guides, the licensed town guides, and the park rangers. Thanks to all of you.

Some of the stories in this book came from conversations with people from the Civil War Trust, the United States Army Heritage and Education Center (formerly the United States Army Military History Institute), and the Museum and White House of the Confederacy. The staffs there were so helpful, and we want them to know how much it meant to us.

Much of the information about the monuments,

such as the sculptors' names and the dedication dates, came from the Smithsonian Institution Research Information System. This organization is a national treasure. We tend to think of the Smithsonian as a really nice group of museums, but in truth, it is so much more.

The information in Appendix A regarding those who earned the Medal of Honor at Gettysburg would have been much more difficult to obtain without the assistance of the Congressional Medal of Honor Society. The Museum and White House of the Confederacy graciously directed us to a source for the same information about the Confederate soldiers who earned the Southern equivalent, as presented in Appendix B. We owe those organizations a great debt, not only for their help on this book but also for keeping alive the legacy of the men who earned the honors.

To our employers, Carnegie Mellon University and AAA Southern Pennsylvania, thank you for the flexibility that allowed us to travel to Gettysburg to do the research necessary for this work. You made it much easier than it could have been!

Rita Rosenkranz, our agent, has continued to give us valuable hints and guidance. We value her input and friendship. Thank you, Rita, for all you do.

And to the folks at John F. Blair, Publisher, thank you for taking on yet another of our projects. You are a pleasure to work with, and we have enjoyed our relationship. You all work so hard to ensure the success of our books, and we appreciate it.

Thank you to our readers as well. Maybe you've been waiting for this book to come out, or maybe you just saw it on the bookstore shelf. However you happened upon us, we hope you enjoy what we have put together.

And finally, to all our friends and family who continue to be so supportive of our addiction to all things Gettysburg, we give our thanks. We couldn't do it without you! Thanks from the bottom of our hearts.

Introduction

By June 1863, the Civil War was in its third year. The Army of Northern Virginia, under its Confederate commander, General Robert E. Lee, had fought the larger Army of the Potomac to a standstill. A war that most had thought would be over in a matter of months showed no signs of ending. Lee's troops had defeated their opponents at battle after battle, forcing President Abraham Lincoln to shuttle generals into and out of command in his effort to find one who could end the rebellion. Lee defeated them all.

A confident Lee made plans for an invasion of the North, hoping to accomplish three objectives. First, he believed that moving the war northward would allow the states below the Mason-Dixon line to recover from two years of nearly constant fighting on their land. Lee also hoped he could draw the Federal army away from Richmond, as well as Vicksburg, where the ongoing siege was threatening to give full control of the Mississippi to the Union. Losing Vicksburg would divide the Southern states. Lee knew the Confederacy had to hold the city if it was to have any hope of survival. Finally, Lee hoped a victory on Northern soil would force Lincoln to declare an end to the war and give England and France a reason to recognize the fledgling Confederacy as a legitimate government.

Confederate troops looked forward to moving into the North, if for no other reason than their perception that Maryland and Pennsylvania had an abundance of food, something in scarce supply for the Southerners. They also believed those in the North should feel the pain of war that citizens of the South had experienced for two years.

While Lee planned his movement into Maryland and Pennsylvania, Lincoln was becoming increasingly frustrated with his army's leadership. His latest commander, Major General Joseph Hooker, had performed poorly, and relations between the two deteriorated. War Department officials pressured Lincoln to relieve Hooker of command. As Confederate troops advanced into Pennsylvania, Northern governors joined the outcry for Lincoln to do something.

Hooker, seeing the lack of support from both Lincoln and the War Department, made the decision easy by requesting that he be relieved of command.

Lincoln quickly accepted Hooker's offer and ultimately placed Major General George Gordon Meade in command of the Army of the Potomac. A less-than-enthusiastic Meade commented that he had been "tried and condemned."

Within hours, Meade ordered his army to intercept Lee's forces, wherever they may be. That meeting would come on July 1, 1863, in the town of Gettysburg, Pennsylvania.

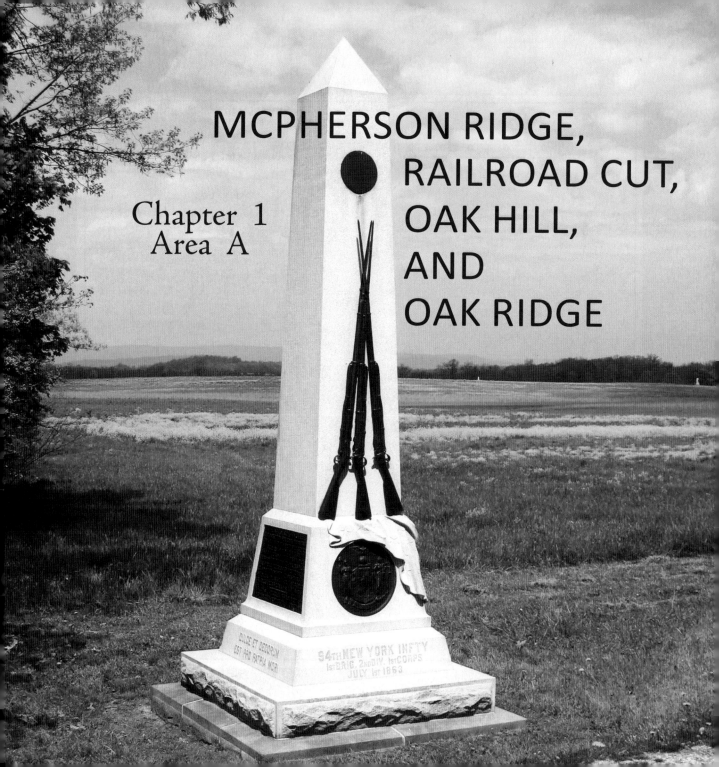

Chapter 1
Area A

MCPHERSON RIDGE,
RAILROAD CUT,
OAK HILL,
AND
OAK RIDGE

Area A

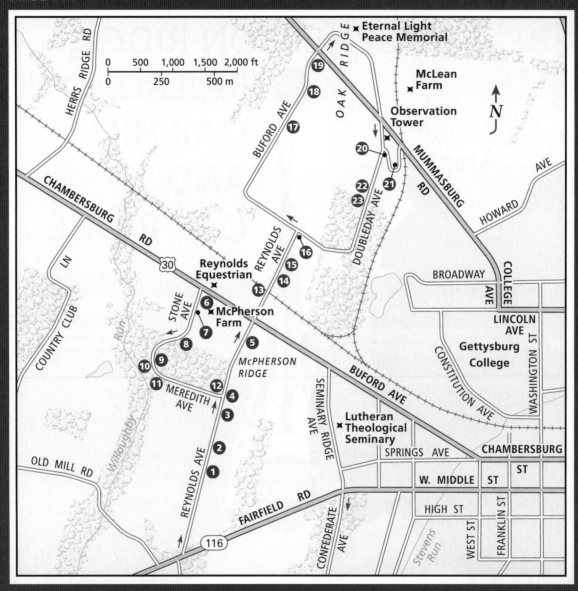

Area A McPherson Ridge, Railroad Cut, Oak Hill, and Oak Ridge

Just as dawn was breaking on July 1, 1863, the brigades of Brigadier General James Archer and Brigadier General Joseph Davis of Major General Henry Heth's division of the Army of Northern Virginia made their way toward Gettysburg. Just outside town, Union pickets saw them approaching and fired on them, then rushed to tell their officers that the Confederates were advancing.

At about eight that morning, the two Confederate brigades rushed across Willoughby Run, a small creek near the McPherson Farm, where they ran into Brigadier General John Buford's division of cavalry. For two hours, Buford's outmanned troops held their ground until reinforcements arrived under the command of Major General John F. Reynolds. A furious counterattack by the new troops temporarily pushed the Confederate line back, but within a short time, Reynolds was killed by a sharpshooter's bullet and Archer was taken captive by the famed Iron Brigade of the Union's Army of the Potomac.

As both sides brought more forces to the field, the battle intensified. The Southern troops began to overwhelm the Federal forces, but here and there, pockets of Union troops started to slowly drive the Confederates back. North of Chambersburg Pike, troops from Mississippi were forced to take cover in an unfinished railroad cut. There, they found themselves trapped. More than two hundred were taken captive.

After a short lull in the fighting around midday, Confederate forces attacked again. Artillery fire struck the flank of the Union army along Oak Ridge. An uncoordinated Confederate attack failed, but another assault was more successful, and Federal troops began to withdraw.

Taking up new defensive positions, the Union troops put up a fierce resistance. They threw back another assault, the fighting resulting in Iverson's Brigade of North Carolinians being nearly wiped out. By midafternoon, however, the Federal line began to dissolve. This area represented the Union's last stand before withdrawing toward the Lutheran Seminary.

Much of Area A in Volume 1 (see sites A-1 through A-20 on pages 3–19) is in the immediate vicinity of this section of Volume 2. The First Shot Markers, along with the interesting story of why two such markers exist and why they are not in the same area, are covered in Volume 1. On the north side of Chambersburg Pike (Route 30) are the markers for Brigadier General John Buford, whose troops put up the first defensive stand against the advancing Confederates, and Major General John Reynolds, the highest-ranking officer on either side to be killed at Gettysburg. Across Route 30 sits the McPherson Farm, where the battle began, and its view toward Seminary Ridge. Proceeding along Stone Avenue, visitors will pass the monument to John Burns and learn the story of how he became a national hero. On the curve between Stone Avenue and Meredith Avenue sits a marker to the Iron Brigade, one of the Union army's most famous units. At the end of Meredith Avenue where it intersects Reynolds Avenue is the Abner Doubleday Monument, where readers will hear the story of why he resigned his commission. Just after the left turn on to Reynolds Avenue, the modest marker commemorating the site of General Reynolds's death sits near the edge of the woods, followed by the monument to the 143rd Pennsylvania, where readers will hear the amazing story of the man depicted on the front.

After crossing the highway and passing a number of monuments described in this volume, visitors will cross the famous Railroad Cut, the scene of ferocious fighting and a large surrender of Confederate troops. At the top of the hill sits the Eternal Light Peace Memorial, designed as a symbol of reconciliation. Back across Mummasburg Pike is the monument to the Ninetieth Pennsylvania Infantry, where visitors will learn the famous story of its bird's nest. Just beyond it is a succession of markers including the monument to the Twelfth Massachusetts, also known as the Webster Regiment; the Eighty-eighth Pennsylvania Infantry Monument, with its many symbols stacked on top; the impressively tiered Eighty-third New York Monument; the Eleventh Pennsylvania Monument and its famous mascot, Sally; and the Sixteenth Maine Monument, where readers will learn how the regiment's men saved their flag. The field behind these monuments is the site of Iverson's Pits, scene of a tragic slaughter of unsuspecting North Carolina troops.

A-1: 121st Pennsylvania Infantry Monument
39° 49.826' N, 77° 15.098' W

When the 121st Pennsylvania arrived at Gettysburg, it had never been in battle. The regiment took a position on the left of the Union line. In heavy fighting, it was flanked by the Fifty-second North Carolina, also fighting its first battle. Despite the danger of being overrun, the 121st resisted the advance of the Tar Heels long enough for the brigade's artillery to withdraw to safety.

During the fighting, the shaft of the company colors was broken in several places by Confederate fire. As the regiment rushed through town in retreat, Color Sergeant William Hardy found a shingle blown off a nearby roof by artillery fire. Hardy picked up the shingle and used it to connect the pieces of the damaged flagstaff. The improvised repair held up for the remainder of the battle.

Ultimately withdrawing to Cemetery Hill, the regiment came under artillery fire on the evening of July 2 but was not otherwise engaged. On July 3, it moved to the left center of the Union line and erected barricades of fence rails in anticipation of another Confederate assault. The artillery barrage that preceded Pickett's Charge, however, destroyed that protection, and the regiment was forced back. The anticipated attack did not materialize in its section of the line.

The two days following the battle saw the men clearing the field and burying the dead.

Lieutenant Colonel Alexander Biddle commanded the regiment, which suffered a casualty rate of 40 percent. Twenty of its men were killed, thirty-eight wounded, and sixty-one either captured or missing.

The monument, designed by Bureau Brothers and fabricated by Heins and Bye, was dedicated July 4, 1888. It is topped by a cap, bedroll, and sword and has a flag draping over the side. A bomb burst is featured on the front. A cartridge box adorned the front of the base at one time but was removed by vandals; the damage is still visible. A musket is shown on the right side of the monument, which sits where the regiment fought on July 1. A second monument to the regiment is along Hancock Avenue (39° 48.655′N, 77° 14.126′ W).

A-2: Eightieth New York Infantry Monument

39° 49.886′ N, 77° 15.077′ W

As the men of the Eightieth New York crossed the state line from Maryland into Pennsylvania, they were greeted by farmers, who offered them bread and fruit from their orchards. Others refused to give anything to the men from New York, saying they were saving it for Pennsylvania troops. Angry at first, the men of the Eightieth quickly learned that the locals could not differentiate one regiment from another. They began telling those along the road they were a Pennsylvania regiment. From that point on, they ate well along the march.

Reaching Gettysburg, the regiment went into action almost immediately, fighting in the area around this monument. It got little rest over the next three days.

The circular disk at the top of the monument represents the First Corps; the raised hand symbolizes the oath the regiment took to help preserve the Union. The monument sits at the approximate location occupied by the regiment in the July 1 fighting. Two days later, the men assisted in the repulse of Pickett's Charge, suffering heavy losses.

The regiment was also known as the Ulster Guard and the Twentieth New York State Militia. A monument under the latter name is located on Cemetery Ridge (see K-1). Commanded by Colonel Theodore Gates, the men of the Eightieth never fully accepted their designation, most of them preferring to call themselves the Twentieth New York, having held that name for several years prior to the change on December 7, 1861.

Lieutenant John Vernou Bouvier of Company E was the great-grandfather of Jacqueline Bouvier Kennedy, wife of President John F. Kennedy.

The regiment suffered 170 casualties out of 375 officers and men engaged. Of those, 35 men were killed, 111 wounded, and 24 declared missing. Casualties mounted among the animals as well. Colonel Gates saw his horse wounded five times on the first day's fighting alone.

Fabricated by Frederick and Field, the Eightieth's monument was dedicated October 4, 1888.

A-3: 142nd Pennsylvania Infantry Monument
39° 49.964' N, 77° 15.051' W

The 142nd Pennsylvania was commanded by Colonel Robert P. Cummins, who was mortally wounded nearby. Its monument is one of the more uniquely shaped on the battlefield.

Shortly after taking a position on the morning of July 1, the regiment came under heavy artillery fire. When Confederate infantry began an assault, the regiment and the rest of its brigade turned to face the oncoming fire. Slowly, the 142nd gave ground and, flanked by the attacking Southerners, began to crumble. Colonel Cummins, whose horse had been shot minutes earlier, suffered his mortal wound at that time. The regiment soon retreated to the seminary,

where its men joined other troops that had also been forced back.

Their position at the seminary was short-lived. Once the batteries along their line were withdrawn, the position became untenable. The regiment joined in the disorganized retreat through town, taking heavy flanking fire the entire way. Reaching Cemetery Hill, the 142nd slowly reorganized, its scattered troops rejoining the ranks over the course of several hours.

After being held in reserve the second day of fighting, the regiment stood on the line along Cemetery Ridge but suffered little when Pickett's Charge

took place to its right on July 3.

Of the regiment's 336 officers and men at Gettysburg, 211 became casualties. Of those, 31 were killed or mortally wounded. Over the course of the war, 935 men served in the 142nd. Of those, 809 became casualties in some fashion. Only 13.5 percent of the regiment's men passed through the war unscathed.

The monument was dedicated September 11, 1889. One of 110 honoring Pennsylvania troops who participated in the Gettysburg Campaign, it sits where the regiment engaged Pettigrew's North Carolina brigade.

A-4: Eighth New York Cavalry Monument
39° 50.012' N, 77° 15.034' W

This monument is not where it was originally placed. It was moved three hundred yards when the Gettysburg Battlefield Memorial Association determined that the Eighth Illinois Cavalry actually occupied the location where the Eighth New York had initially placed its monument. The Eighth New York's flank markers remain at their original sites, near the intersection of Chambersburg Pike and Reynolds Avenue.

The Eighth New York Cavalry was also known as the Rochester Regiment, sharing that nickname with the 108th New York Infantry. The Eighth was one of the first Union regiments to come under fire at Gettysburg. At about six o'clock on the morning of July 1, the regiment's pickets received fire from ad-

vance Confederate skirmishers under Major General Henry Heth. The New Yorkers held their ground for nearly five hours until they were relieved by troops from the First Corps. They then moved to the south end of McPherson Ridge, where they set up a skirmish line.

The Eighth suffered losses of three killed, ten wounded, and twenty-one missing.

The monument was fabricated by Smith and Barry. The relief of a mounted cavalryman was sculpted by F. Muer. Dedication took place June 9, 1889.

A-5: Eighth Illinois Cavalry Monument
39° 50.147' N, 77° 14.968' W

The Eighth Illinois Cavalry Monument sits on the previous location of the Eighth New York Cavalry Monument. The latter unit's monument was relocated in an effort to more accurately depict regi-

memorate that event; that monument is discussed in detail in Volume 1. On the back of the Eighth Illinois Cavalry Monument is the name of Private David Diffenbaugh, the only man in the regiment killed at Gettysburg.

In addition to Private Diffenbaugh, the Eighth had five wounded and one declared missing. Dedication of its monument took place September 3, 1891.

A-6: 149th Pennsylvania Infantry Monument
39° 50.253′ N, 77° 15.083′ W

This monument is one of three for the 149th Pennsylvania. A second is on Hancock Avenue (39° 48.606′ N, 77° 14.146′ W), while a marker for the regiment's Company D sits at the corner of West Confederate Avenue and Fairfield Road (Route 116). That monument is described in detail at C-15.

The 149th Pennsylvania was part of the New Bucktails, formed in July 1862 to augment the original Bucktails. Known as outstanding marksmen, the Bucktails gained their name by wearing deer tails on their kepis (hats).

Gettysburg was the first battle for the 149th. Arriving on the field at approximately eleven in the morning on July 1, the regiment took a position along Chambersburg Pike and quickly was caught in a cross fire from Confederate artillery on Oak Hill and Herr Ridge. The regimental colors were ordered forward to a point fifty yards across the pike, in the general vicinity of the John Buford Monument. Seeing the

mental positions. The Illinois marker is positioned at about the center of the line the men held on the first morning of fighting. Commanded by Major John L. Beveridge, the dismounted Eighth Illinois Cavalry was part of the initial defense against the advancing Confederate army. For nearly two hours, the outnumbered brigade held the Confederates at bay until it was relieved by arriving infantry.

The monument, designed and built by Smith Granite Company, features a cavalry saddle on its top, complete with saddlebags and the cavalry trooper's haversack and blanket roll. Carved into the front is the name of Lieutenant Marcellus Jones, who claimed to have fired the first shot of the battle as a picket early in the morning on July 1. Jones placed his own marker along Chambersburg Pike to com-

colors moved, Confederate artillery officers believed the regiment had relocated and redirected their fire to where they thought the 149th had moved, relieving the regiment from the heavy fire. The monument commemorates this action. The figure gazes in the general direction of the new position for the colors.

When Lieutenant General Richard Ewell's Confederate troops arrived on the field, the 149th found its flank exposed. It and the 143rd Pennsylvania reformed their lines. Anticipating an attack, the 149th moved forward toward the Railroad Cut, from where it conducted its own bayonet charge. Returning from the charge, the men found that a Confederate artil-

lery unit had moved in, forcing the 149th to return to Chambersburg Pike. Not long afterward, the regiment repulsed another attack, its charge employing an unusual front-to-rear maneuver that General Abner Doubleday said was almost impossible to execute under fire.

By midafternoon, the Confederate forces gained the upper hand, and the Federal troops were forced to retreat. The 149th proudly stated that its part of the field never fell into Southern hands until the entire Union line was pulled back. However, in the retreat, the regimental colors could not be brought back and were captured by troops from Mississippi. Color Sergeant Henry Brehm was killed as he fought to keep the colors. When the Union line fell back, Company D, which had been detached as provost guard, held its position along Fairfield Road for twenty minutes to allow the rest of the brigade to reach safety.

The monument to the 149th, fabricated by H. Oursler and Sons, was erected in November 1888. Seeing the finished product, many of the regiment's veterans were unhappy with what they perceived as artistic shortcomings. They demanded changes. Those changes appear in bronze, as opposed to the original granite. On September 11, 1889, the monument was finally dedicated.

The 149th had 66 officers and enlisted men killed or mortally wounded, 159 wounded, and 111 captured or missing. Its 336 total casualties placed it among the highest in losses among all Union regiments at Gettysburg.

A-7: 150th Pennsylvania Infantry Monument
39° 50.212′ N, 77° 15.134′ W

The 150th Pennsylvania was located here on the afternoon of July 1. Assaults from two different directions forced the regiment to re-form its front on several occasions. When the Thirty-second North Carolina Infantry launched an assault, the Pennsylvanians wheeled to the right to stop the advance. However, their success was short-lived. By midafternoon, they were forced back toward the seminary and ultimately to Cemetery Hill.

After the entire color guard was killed or wounded, Corporal Joseph Gutelius of Company D took up the fallen colors. When he was shot in the vicinity of South Washington and West High streets, Lieutenant F. M. Harney of the Fourteenth North Carolina

Infantry captured the flag. Harney was eventually mortally wounded himself. His dying wish was that the flag be presented to Jefferson Davis, the Confederate president. When Davis was captured in 1865, the flag was found in his baggage. It was returned to Pennsylvania in 1869.

Colonel Roy Stone commanded the brigade until he was wounded, at which time Colonel Langhorne Wister took over. When it appeared that the 149th Pennsylvania Infantry and the 143rd Pennsylvania Infantry were in danger of being overrun, Wister split the 150th, Lieutenant Colonel Henry S. Huidekoper taking command of one wing and Major Thomas Chamberlain the other. As Huidekoper's wing advanced, he was severely wounded in the arm. Meanwhile, Chamberlain was wounded in the chest and shoulder. Within minutes, Wister was wounded in the mouth and was unable to continue. Colonel E. L. Dana took command in Wister's place and conducted the regiment's retreat to Cemetery Hill.

Two members of the regiment were awarded the Medal of Honor for their actions at Gettysburg, although it took more than forty years in both cases. Lieutenant Colonel Huidekoper received his medal in 1905 for remaining in command during the battle despite receiving his wound. In 1907, Corporal J. Monroe Reisinger was awarded the Medal of Honor for brave and meritorious conduct in the face of the enemy. His bravery was reflected in the fact that he held the colors and rallied his men while wounded in the foot, knee, and side. His was the only Medal of Honor awarded through an act of Congress for the fighting at Gettysburg.

Ryegate Granite Company fabricated the monument. Dedicated September 11, 1889, it marks the most advanced position the regiment held on the afternoon of July 1. Of the 397 men brought into battle, 53 were killed or mortally wounded, 134 were wounded, and 77 were reported missing.

A-8: Fourteenth Brooklyn Monument
39° 50.148′ N, 77° 15.177′ W

The Fourteenth Brooklyn was a regiment of many names, among them the Brooklyn Phalanx, the Fourteenth State Militia, and it official designation, the Eighty-fourth New York Infantry. A militia unit formed seventeen years before the war, it was more of a social club in its initial years. Early in the war, its men chose to wear a distinctive version of a French uniform, including bright red pants. This was referred to as a Chasseur uniform, which led to another name for the regiment: the Brooklyn Chasseurs. Among the Confederates, however, they were known as those "Red-Legged Devils." The men of the regiment preferred to refer to themselves by their old name, the Fourteenth Brooklyn. They were known as fierce fighters.

Early in the morning on July 1, the regiment opened fire on A. P. Hill's corps, then made a charge to the Railroad Cut. It took several prisoners in this action. Later in the day, the men battled their way to Culp's Hill, where they fought off an advance of Major General Edward "Allegheny" Johnson's division of Lieutenant General Richard Ewell's corps. The regiment lost 13 killed, 105 wounded, and 99 missing at Gettysburg.

This small monument marks the Fourteenth's first position in the battle. Another monument to the regiment is described at A-13, near the Railroad Cut. A third is located on Culp's Hill (39° 49.024′ N, 77° 13.176′ W).

A-9: Twenty-fourth Michigan Infantry Monument
39° 50.094′ N, 77° 15.265′ W

The Twenty-fourth Michigan was part of the famed Iron Brigade. The figure on the monument is shown wearing the brigade's trademark black army dress hat, rather than the kepi of

other brigades. Fierce and determined fighters, the men of the Twenty-fourth paid a heavy price on the first day of fighting, suffering 363 casualties among the 496 soldiers who entered the battle. This casualty rate of 73.1 percent was among the highest of all Union regiment at Gettysburg. As an illustration of the difficulty in ascertaining accurate casualty figures, the regiment's other monument, located on Stevens Knoll (39° 49.174′ N, 77° 13.426′ W), states that only 99 men survived the first morning's fight out of the 496. If that figure is correct, the casualty rate was 80 percent. Still other sources give numbers that vary from these. Whichever figures one wishes to accept, it is generally agreed that every member of the color guard was either killed or wounded, and that five color bearers were killed.

Much of the Twenty-fourth's fighting was against the Twenty-sixth North Carolina, an equally determined regiment. The two nearly annihilated one another in the July 1 fighting (see A-10), shooting from distances of only twenty paces at times.

Colonel Henry Morrow commanded the Twenty-fourth. At one point, so many color bearers had been struck down that Morrow grabbed the colors himself, leading his troops until he, too, was badly wounded as the Twenty-fourth retreated toward Seminary Ridge. Unable to reach a place of safety, he was captured.

Captain Albert Edwards took command when Morrow fell. The regiment took refuge behind a rail barricade near the seminary. There, in a brief lull in the fighting, Edwards found the regimental flag, which was still being held doggedly by one of his mortally wounded men. From its new position, the Twenty-fourth held off two more determined assaults but finally was forced into a retreat through town to Cemetery Hill.

Designed and constructed by Ryegate Granite Company, the monument was dedicated June 12, 1889.

A-10: Twenty-sixth North Carolina Infantry Monument
39° 50.083′ N, 77° 15.277′ W

As the men of the Twenty-sixth North Carolina crossed Willoughby Run early in the afternoon on July 1, they ran headlong into the Union's Iron Brigade, which at that location consisted primarily of the Twenty-fourth Michigan. As they charged, the losses mounted. Four members of the color guard became casualties before they even reached the stream. As others took up the flag, they fell just as quickly. In a span of ten minutes, the Twenty-sixth lost ten different color bearers. All told, fourteen color bearers of the Twenty-sixth became casualties in the first day's fighting.

As the two sides battled each other only a few yards apart, Colonel Harry Burgwyn grabbed the regimental flag after yet another color bearer fell. Rushing toward the Twenty-fourth Michigan's position, Private Frank Honeycutt stepped forward to take the flag from his colonel. Just as Burgwyn turned to hand the banner to Honeycutt, he was mortally wounded. A few seconds later, Honeycutt fell with a fatal head wound. Burgwyn would be awarded the Confederate Medal of Honor for his bravery.

Lieutenant Colonel J. R. Lane, taking command when Burgwyn fell, picked up the flag and led the attack until he was shot in the neck. Captain H. C. Albright was the regiment's final commander at Gettysburg.

Ascending the hill, the Twenty-sixth came under devastating fire that forced it back. Regrouping for one final assault, it successfully drove the Union troops from McPherson Ridge. The assault took a heavy toll, however. The Twenty-sixth started the first day of Gettysburg with an estimated 820 men. At the end of the day, 588 of them were either dead or wounded, a casualty rate of nearly 72 percent. All 90 men in the Twenty-sixth's Company F had fallen. Numerically, no other regiment, Union or Confederate, suffered more losses at Gettysburg.

The Twenty-sixth rested on July 2 but was pressed into service on July 3 as part of Pickett's Charge. Its colors fell eight more times in that assault. A second marker (see K-12) marks its position on the third day.

Designed by Keystone Memorials, the monument was dedicated October 5, 1985. It designates the regiment's battle line on July 1. Colonel Burgwyn suffered his mortal wound not far from the site of the marker.

A-11: Nineteenth Indiana Infantry Monument
39° 50.050′ N, 77° 15.253′ W

The Nineteenth Indiana was part of the Iron Brigade. Its monument sits near the position where

of the Nineteenth by including their names on its sides, along with a listing of the battles in which the regiment participated. It lost 210 men either killed, wounded, missing, or captured at Gettysburg—about two of every three who went into battle. Most of the casualties occurred on the first morning of fighting in the general area around the monument.

The monument was dedicated October 28, 1885, making it the first of the Iron Brigade regimental monuments at Gettysburg.

A-12: 151st Pennsylvania Infantry Monument
39° 50.024′ N, 77° 15.063′ W

Boasting more than a hundred members who had been teachers in civilian life, the 151st Pennsylvania proudly carried the nickname "the Schoolteacher Regiment." Teachers and students from McAllisterville Academy in Juniata County made up nearly the entire Company D.

Recruited for a nine-month regiment, most of the men of the 151st had only a few weeks of service time remaining when they fought at Gettysburg. As they reached the field at noon on the first day, they were just in time to see the sobering sight of the body of General John Reynolds being carried to the rear. Despite this upsetting scene, the regiment hurried into position, coming under fire even as it did so.

The role of the 151st was to provide protection for the withdrawal of the Iron Brigade of the First Corps and the retreat of the three other regiments

the regiment fought in the afternoon on July 1. Of its 308 men, 210 became casualties, a rate of 68 percent. Most of those casualties occurred in the general area around the monument.

As the fighting slowed around noon on July 1, the regiment's colonel, Samuel J. Williams, asked permission to move to better defensive ground on McPherson Ridge. When his request was denied, he told his men that they must hold the colors on this ground or die under them. Prophetically, five color bearers were killed or wounded. Ultimately, the regiment was forced to retreat through town, eventually reaching Culp's Hill.

The monument honors the fallen members

enlistment was nearly completed, they were soon sent back to Harrisburg, where they were mustered out July 27, 1863.

The regiment paid a heavy price at Gettysburg, suffering 15 officers and 322 men either killed, wounded, captured, or missing, a casualty rate of 70 percent.

The monument was dedicated July 1, 1888.

A-13: Fourteenth New York State Militia Monument
39° 50.256′ N, 77° 14.910′ W

The Fourteenth New York State Militia, more commonly known as the Fourteenth Brooklyn, was formed as early as 1844. The unit mustered into the

of Biddle's First Brigade, Third Division, First Corps. The regiment did its duty so well that General Abner Doubleday later credited it with saving not only the First Corps but also the Army of the Potomac. When the 151st's position became untenable, its men slowly retreated across the open fields toward the Lutheran Seminary, where they were soon outflanked. During the disorganized retreat that followed, seventy-five members of the regiment were taken captive.

Those who made it to Cemetery Hill did little fighting during the battle's second day. On July 3, they assisted in throwing back Pickett's Charge. After a three-day rest, the regiment joined in the pursuit of Lee's army. But since the men's nine-month

Commanded by Colonel Edward B. Fowler, the regiment had 13 killed, 105 wounded, and 99 missing, for a total of 217 casualties among the 356 men brought to the battle, a casualty rate of about 61 percent.

The monument sits where the regiment took part in the fight against a brigade of Mississippians under Brigadier General Joseph R. Davis. The Fourteenth took many prisoners at midmorning on the first day of the battle. It remained at this location until forced to retreat, fighting its way back through town.

Designed by Smith Granite Company and sculpted by R. D. Barr, the monument was dedicated October 19, 1887.

Located near the McPherson barn, another monument to the regiment is described in A-8. A third is on Culp's Hill (39° 49.024′ N, 77° 13.176′ W).

Union army during the summer of 1861 and received its official designation as the Eighty-fourth New York Infantry that December. However, the men chose to go by the Fourteenth Brooklyn. The official seal of Brooklyn is displayed on the monument.

The monument shows a member of the regiment in his distinctive uniform, which, if in color, would reveal a red kepi, a blue coat trimmed in red, red trousers, and white gaiters. The uniform had led Confederate soldiers to nickname the Fourteenth "the Red-Legged Devils" after First Manassas. Lieutenant Harry W. Mitchell, wounded at Gettysburg, was the model for the figure. He is shown in the position of "Handle Cartridge," the second of ten steps in loading a musket.

A-14: Brigadier General James Wadsworth Monument
39° 50.297′ N, 77° 14.863′ W

Wadsworth, fifty-three years old when the war began, was a wealthy citizen of New York who personally financed shiploads of supplies to Washington when that city was in danger early in the war. He served as military governor of Washington following First Manassas. At Gettysburg, he commanded the first Union infantry division to see fighting. He is shown in the statue on page 18 directing the positions of his troops in the early fighting.

Wadsworth received a mortal head wound at

land, New York. The town of Wadsworth, Nevada, also carries his name.

The base of the monument was designed by Edward P. Casey and constructed by National Granite Company. The statue was sculpted by R. Hinton Perry, noted for his bas-reliefs on the Library of Congress; it was placed by Gorham Manufacturing Company. The monument was dedicated October 6, 1914.

A-15: Fifty-sixth Pennsylvania Infantry Monument
39° 50.337′ N, 77° 14.837′ W

This interesting monument honors the Fifty-sixth Pennsylvania. Its most conspicuous feature is the eight-foot-high placement of three Springfield rifled muskets identical to those used by the regiment in the battle. They surround a furled and sheathed flag, symbolizing that the fighting was over.

The regiment served as the column's rear guard on the march to Gettysburg and did not arrive in Emmitsburg, Maryland, until one o'clock in the morning the day the battle began. After only a few hours of rest, the regiment took a position that put it second in the brigade column. Any hopes the men had for resting when they got to Gettysburg were quickly dashed.

Commanded by Colonel John W. Hoffman, the Fifty-sixth scurried into position as soon as it reached the field. Confederate troops had already begun advancing. As the Southern army approached, Hoffman gave the order to fire. Immediately, other

the Wilderness less than a year after Gettysburg. While in a field hospital there, he was visited by a local farmer who clandestinely brought him food. The farmer had been imprisoned as a spy in Old Capitol Prison when Wadsworth was military governor. Wadsworth had not only ordered him to be released after hearing his story, he also gave the farmer money to get home to Virginia. The farmer remembered Wadsworth and returned the favor when Wadsworth was hospitalized.

For his gallant conduct at Gettysburg and the Wilderness, Wadsworth would be appointed a brevet major general of United States Volunteers. His name was placed on Fort Wadsworth in South Dakota, as well as on a second Fort Wadsworth on Staten Is-

A-16: Seventy-sixth New York Infantry Monument
39° 50.396′ N, 77° 14.803′ W

Also known as the Cortland Regiment, the Cherry Valley Regiment, the Otsego County Regiment, and the Cromwellian Regiment, the Seventy-sixth New York held this position at midmorning of the first day of fighting. Shortly afterward, it was flanked and forced to retire. It later regained and held its position until the First Corps was forced to retreat.

The monument to the Seventy-sixth was fabricated by Frederick and Field and dedicated July 1, 1888. It sits where the regiment fired its first volley on July 1. The monument is topped by a circle that symbolizes the First Corps. The regiment's number sits within

regiments in the area followed the Fifty-sixth's lead. This would garner the Fifty-sixth the honor of being the first infantry regiment to fire an organized volley at Gettysburg, a fact that was a source of great pride for the men long after the fighting.

The regiment suffered a total of 130 casualties, including 17 killed, out of the 252 who went into the battle.

Designed and built by Bureau Brothers, the monument was dedicated September 11, 1889. It is one of only two Pennsylvania monuments on the battlefield constructed of bronze. The other is the Tenth Pennsylvania Reserves Monument (see I-11) at the foot of Big Round Top.

that circle, indicating its affiliation with the corps. Beneath the circle, the top of the monument is ringed with a series of minie balls.

The regiment lost 32 men killed, 132 wounded, and 70 missing at Gettysburg. Among the dead was Major Andrew J. Grover, a minister who had resigned his charge when the war began. He had been badly wounded at Gainesville, Florida, and was believed to be permanently disabled, resulting in his discharge from the army. When he recovered, he rejoined and was appointed major of the Seventy-sixth. His horse was shot when Confederate troops flanked the regiment near the site of the monument. Grover led his men on foot until he received his mortal wound.

Captain John E. Cook took Grover's place. Cook later was wounded himself at Petersburg.

A-17: Sixth New York Cavalry Monument
39° 50.673′ N, 77° 14.829′ W

This impressive castle-like monument sits on the line occupied by the Sixth New York Cavalry, also known as the Ira Harris Cavalry or the Second Ira Harris Guard, in honor of Senator Ira Harris of New York. A spire tops the monument, which had a turret on each of its four corners; in 2007, one of the turrets was destroyed when the monument was struck by lightning. The relief on the front depicts an officer urging his men into the fight. The back shows a likeness of Major General Thomas Devin, the first colonel of the Sixth. The crossed sabers and horse

heads symbolize the cavalry.

The regiment participated in more than eighty battles and skirmishes during the war; its major battles are listed on the columns on the back of the monument.

On the first day of Gettysburg, the Sixth engaged in a series of skirmishes until it was relieved by the arriving First Corps. It moved to Cemetery Hill and became engaged again the next morning. It then moved southward, contacting Lee's army again on July 8 at Boonsboro, Maryland. The Sixth suffered twenty-two casualties at Gettysburg, including one killed, five wounded, and sixteen missing.

The sculptor of the monument was James Edward Kelly. Fabrication was done by Frederick and Field. The monument was dedicated July 11, 1889.

A-18: Ninth New York Cavalry Monument

39° 50.755′ N, 77° 14.765′ W

Under normal circumstances, a monument as attractive as that of the Ninth New York Cavalry wouldn't be considered controversial. But in fact, it created a major argument when it was installed. The controversy centered on who held the honor of firing the first shot.

Although Lieutenant Marcellus Jones of the Eighth Illinois Cavalry is often credited with firing the first shot of the battle, Corporal Alpheus Hodges of the Ninth New York Cavalry claimed he had fired a shot at the Confederates more than two hours ear-

lier. Although Hodges maintained that position until his death, he stated that he fired his shot in response to shots from the Confederates, which would seem to refute his claim of firing the opening shot of the battle. Moreover, Hodges would not have been where he said he was when he fired his weapon. To confuse the issue further, Private Freeman P. Whitney of the Seventeenth Pennsylvania Cavalry also claimed to have fired the first shot. Over the next several years, numerous additional claims were offered.

Regardless, the Ninth New York Cavalry was one of the first Federal regiments to enter the fighting. Corporal Cyrus W. James became what many believe to be the first Northern soldier killed at Gettysburg when he was shot sometime before nine in the morning on July 1. However, he was not the first Union soldier killed in the Gettysburg Campaign. Corporal William Rihl of the First New York Cavalry had died on June 22 at Greencastle in a skirmish with the Fourteenth Virginia Cavalry, making him the first Union soldier killed in Pennsylvania.

In 1887, the Ninth planned its battlefield marker, including the relief shown on the front. Keeping with the regiment's claim of firing the first shot, the relief is titled *Discovering the Enemy*. A reference to Hodge's claim is inscribed on the back. With the dedication set for July 1, 1888, the New Yorkers were surprised to learn that the Eighth Illinois Cavalry had protested to the Gettysburg Battlefield Memorial Association that the first-shot claim was in dispute. The Ninth was ordered to prove its position, which it did to the GBMA's satisfaction. The inscriptions were allowed to stand. Meanwhile, the dedication had already taken place as planned. The argument was never settled to everyone's satisfaction, and the true claim for first-shot honors has been lost to history.

In the fighting at Gettysburg, the Ninth had two men killed, two wounded, and two missing.

The sculptor of this controversial monument was Caspar Buberl. Fabrication was by Frederick and Field.

A-19: Seventeenth Pennsylvania Cavalry Monument
39° 50.837′ N, 77° 14.728′ W

This is one of the many monuments on the battlefield that is truly a work of art. The monument to the Seventeenth Pennsylvania Cavalry features a life-sized bas-relief of a cavalry vedette, or sentinel, poised to fire a warning shot to his comrades that the enemy has been sighted. George W. Ferree of the regiment's Company L posed for the sculpture, which shows in great detail what a cavalryman and his equipment looked like in 1863. The monument sits in what at one time was the yard of the John Forney farmhouse.

Arriving in Gettysburg on the afternoon of June 30, the Seventeenth Pennsylvania Cavalry, also known as the 162nd Pennsylvania Volunteers, sent out vedettes, as was the procedure for all cavalry units when they encamped. One of the vedettes was positioned in the general area of the monument.

The Seventeenth engaged in heavy fighting until about ten o'clock in the morning on the first day. At that point, low on ammunition and with the enemy rapidly gaining ground, it pulled back into a more defensive position on nearby Oak Ridge. That afternoon, it came under friendly fire from a Union battery on Cemetery Hill, taking a number of casualties.

Colonel Joseph H. Kellogg commanded the Seventeenth. Although the regiment had no men killed or wounded, four of its soldiers were declared missing.

Designed and constructed by Smith Granite Company, the monument was dedicated September 11, 1889.

A-20: Brevet Major General John Cleveland Robinson Monument
39° 50.605′ N, 77° 14.513′ W

A graduate of West Point, John Cleveland Robinson received several brevet promotions for gallantry, including one for his actions at Gettysburg. Brevet promotions were honorary promotions given in recognition of bravery or meritorious service. They held no official authority and included no increase in pay, but recipients were permitted to use the titles. They served to recognize individuals much the way medals are awarded today.

At Gettysburg, Robinson's division held the

right of the First Corps line and participated in heavy fighting. Robinson was credited with skillfully deploying his troops so that, despite fighting against superior numbers, he held his position for several hours. During that time, his men captured a large number of prisoners from Brigadier General Alfred Iverson's North Carolina brigade.

Robinson was seriously wounded at Alsop's Farm on May 8, 1864. The wound necessitated the amputation of his leg, rendering him unfit for further active service in the field. For his gallantry in that battle, during which he led his troops in an assault on an entrenched position, he was awarded the Medal of Honor.

Sculpted by John Massey Rhind, the monument was dedicated September 25, 1917. Among Rhind's other credits are his sculptures at Grant's Tomb and at Macy's department store in New York City.

A-21: Thirteenth Massachusetts Infantry Monument
39° 50.568′ N, 77° 14.47′ W

The Thirteenth Massachusetts was commanded at Gettysburg by Colonel Samuel Haven Leonard. When Leonard was wounded in the first day's fighting, command fell to Lieutenant Colonel Nathaniel W. Batchelder.

The Thirteenth fought in this area on July 1, taking many casualties. Over the course of the three days of Gettysburg, the regiment had seven men killed, 77 wounded, and 101 missing out of 284 brought to the battle. During the fighting, the regiment mounted a

Thirteenth Massachusetts Infantry Monument

125th Pennsylvania Infantry Monument at Antietam

bayonet charge in which it captured 132 prisoners, including seven officers. However, the charge took the men far from their support, and they had to fight their way back to the line. Many of their casualties occurred at that time. When the Union line collapsed, the Thirteenth took part in the retreat through the streets of Gettysburg. Many of its missing were captured during the retreat.

A unique feature of this monument is that it is almost an exact twin of that to the 125th Pennsylvania Infantry at Antietam. The only apparent difference between the two is the face. The likely explanation is that molds were often reused in sculpting monuments in that era. The sculptor for the 125th Pennsylvania Infantry Monument at Antietam was Stanley Edwards, but there is no evidence the same sculptor also worked on the Thirteenth's monument.

The monument depicts the Thirteenth's color bearer, Roland B. Morris, who is said to have been killed at this site. It is located where the regiment fought on July 1. Among the wounded was the brigade commander, Brigadier General Gabriel Paul, who was permanently blinded after being shot through both eyes.

The monument was fabricated by Smith Granite Company and dedicated September 25, 1885.

A-22: 107th Pennsylvania Infantry Monument
39° 50.514' N, 77° 14.563' W

Under the command of Colonel James M. Thomson, the 107th Pennsylvania reached the field

support, again coming under heavy fire.

Over the course of the three days at Gettysburg, the regiment had 16 men killed or mortally wounded, another 43 men and eight officers wounded, and 92 men and six officers missing or taken prisoner. Many of those captured, including an officer, Lieutenant James Carman, would die in prison camps. The total losses were 165 of the 230 men and 25 officers the regiment took into battle.

The monument to the 107th sits on the approximate location where the regiment fought on the afternoon of the first day until it was forced back toward town. It was fabricated by Ryegate Granite Company and dedicated September 11, 1889.

early in the afternoon on the first day of fighting and went into battle almost immediately. The fighting was fierce, and the 107th suffered heavy casualties. One color bearer was killed instantly, and a second was wounded so badly he died the next day. Colonel Thomson was wounded severely and had to retire from the field and turn command over to Captain Emanuel D. Roath.

Eventually outflanked and in danger of being overrun, the regiment retreated through town and took a new position on the left of Cemetery Hill. Immediately, the men began building breastworks near the Bryan House. In 1923, a plaque was placed in Ziegler's Grove (39° 48.948′ N, 77° 14.116′ W) to mark that position, which they held during the second day until early evening, when they moved to a support position near the Round Tops. Returning to Cemetery Hill later that night, they provided battery

A-23: Ninety-fourth New York Infantry Monument
39° 50.477′ N, 77° 14.579′ W

The Ninety-fourth New York had suffered such heavy losses that by March 1863 it had to be consolidated into just five companies. Since it would have limited effectiveness in such a decimated state, it was merged with the 105th New York Infantry, which had suffered similar losses. The combined regiment kept the name of the Ninety-fourth New York, also known as the Bell Jefferson Rifles or the Sackets Harbor Regiment, after Sackets Harbor, New York, where the men had mustered in.

On the morning of July 1, the Ninety-fourth marched with the rest of its division from Emmitsburg, Maryland. As it approached Gettysburg, the

sounds of battle were audible. The division took a position at the Lutheran Seminary. While fighting in this area, it captured several Confederate prisoners and a large number of enemy flags. Post-battle reports noted that eighty-one dead Confederates were found the next day in front of the position held by the Ninety-fourth.

The fighting in this area was intense. General Gabriel Paul was blinded by a bullet that passed through both his eyes. Colonel Samuel Haven Leonard of the Thirteenth Massachusetts took command when General Paul received his wound, but Colonel Leonard himself was wounded almost immediately. At that point, Colonel Adrian R. Root of the Ninety-fourth took command. Root was also soon wounded, and command continued to be passed down the line.

As the fighting raged, the Ninety-fourth was forced back through town, taking a new position on Cemetery Hill. The wounded Root was one of many taken prisoner in the chaotic retreat. The Confederates asked Root to assist in caring for other Union wounded; when the battle was over, he and the rest of the Ninety-fourth prisoners were left behind by Lee's retreating army. The men returned to duty. Root subsequently assumed a position as commandant of Camp Parole in Annapolis, Maryland.

The regiment took 30 officers and 415 men into the battle and lost 12 killed, 58 wounded (many of whom later died of their injuries), and 175 captured or missing, for a total of 245 casualties. Most of the losses occurred on the first day. This was the heaviest loss of any battle in which the regiment fought.

The monument was fabricated by Smith Granite Company and dedicated in 1888. On its face is a Latin inscription, *"Dulce et Decorum est pro Patria Mori,"* a line from the Roman lyrical poet Horace's *Odes*. It translates, "It is sweet and right to die for your country."

HOWARD AVENUE, BARLOW KNOLL

Area B

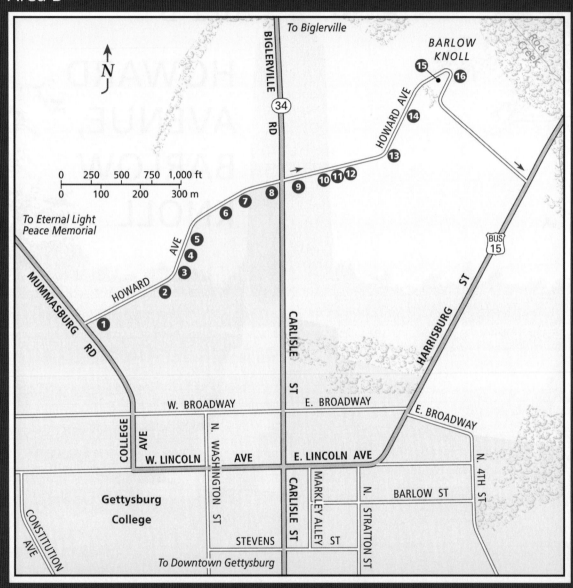

When Major General John Reynolds was killed, Major General Oliver O. Howard took his place. Howard, in turn, was temporarily replaced as commander of the Eleventh Corps by Major General Carl Schurz. Schurz formed his Union line on the right flank of the First Corps in this area.

The First Division of the Eleventh Corps, under the command of Brigadier General Francis Barlow, took a position on a small hill on the right of the line. Soon, fighting broke out along the entire line. Just as General Jubal Early arrived and began a heavy artillery fire on to the Union line, the Fourth and Forty-fourth Georgia infantries began an assault on Barlow's men in the area known today as Barlow Knoll. The combination of heavy fire from Confederate artillery and the onrushing infantry assault by the Georgians was too much for the Federal troops. Their line crumbled. Even though reinforcements arrived to help stem the tide, the position was untenable.

In a short time, the Union troops were forced to fall back. Soon, a chaotic retreat was in full force toward town.

Barlow Knoll itself is discussed in greater detail in Volume 1, as is the monument to Brigadier General Francis Channing Barlow and the unusual and somewhat debatable story of his relationship with Confederate general John Gordon. Also in the Barlow Knoll area is Alms House Cemetery, featured in Volume 1.

B-1: 157th New York Infantry Monument
39° 50.409′ N, 77° 14.191′ W

This monument commemorates the second location of the 157th New York Infantry. Its first location is also marked by a monument (see B-8). A third, smaller marker was placed three hundred yards north of the primary monument to mark the regiment's farthest advance.

Also known as the Madison and Cortland Regiment, after the counties where it was raised, the 157th lost four officers and 23 men killed, eight officers and 158 men wounded, and six officers and 108 men captured or missing out of the 431 brought into the battle, a casualty rate of about 71 percent. Most were suffered on the first day of fighting.

The fabricator of the monument was New England Monument Company. Dedication took place September 8, 1886. The monument was erected by the survivors of the regiment. Features include a crescent moon on the monument's top, symbolizing the Eleventh Corps. On the sides are the battles in which the regiment participated.

The regiment was commanded by Colonel Philip P. Brown, who had been a school principal in civilian life.

B-2: Forty-fifth New York Infantry Monument
39° 50.451' N, 77° 14.084' W

The Forty-fifth New York was often referred to as the Fifth German Rifles because the regiment was made up nearly completely of German immigrants. It was commanded at Gettysburg by Lieutenant Adolphus Dobke, who replaced Colonel George von Amsberg, who had temporarily assumed command of the First Brigade.

As the brigade formed its battle line after arriving on the field, German-born captain Francis Irsch took four companies and moved toward the Moses McClean farm (marked by the large red barn visible from the Oak Ridge observation platform). He immediately came under heavy artillery fire, as well as small-arms fire from sharpshooters hidden in a nearby orchard. As supporting fire arrived, Irsch ordered a charge, during which he and his men took many prisoners.

Irsch's actions marked a high point for the regiment. Fighting along Oak Ridge, the Confederate forces drew closer. Gradually, it became apparent that the Federals could not hold their position. Ordered to fall back through town, the regiment took a new position at Pennsylvania College (now Gettysburg College).

Within minutes, a further retreat was ordered, which the Forty-fifth resisted at first. Finally, however, the regiment realized the Confederate infantry was closing in and moved into town by way of what is

Washington Street today. Confusion reigned in town as panic-stricken Union troops looked for shelter in any available place, while pursuing Confederates pushed closely behind.

Captain Irsch and his four companies formed a rear guard, taking refuge in some of the buildings around the intersection of Chambersburg and Washington streets. This action allowed the rest of the regiment to pass through the alleys and safely reach Cemetery Hill.

Unable to force the small group out, the Confederates met with Irsch under a flag of truce and showed him the positions of the opposing forces. Irsch quickly realized the hopelessness of the situation and ordered his men to destroy their weapons and surrender. Irsch was eventually placed in Libby Prison, from which he escaped through the famous tunnel in 1864, only to be recaptured. He was awarded the Medal of Honor nineteen years after the battle for his "gallantry in flanking the enemy and capturing a number of prisoners and in holding a part of the town against heavy odds while the army was rallying on Cemetery Hill."

The monument marks the approximate position the Forty-fifth held from about noon until late afternoon on July 1, when the regiment was forced to withdraw. The actual position is believed to be farther out in the field. The field was privately owned at the time the monument was erected, so it had to be placed along the road, which was owned by the Battlefield Commission.

The Forty-fifth had 11 killed, 35 wounded, and 178 declared missing.

Fabricated by New England Monument Company, the monument was dedicated October 10, 1888. The sculptor was Caspar Buberl.

B-3: Seventy-fourth Pennsylvania Infantry Monument
39° 50.472′ N, 77° 14.052′ W

Another unit heavily populated by German immigrants, the Seventy-fourth Pennsylvania Infantry quickly acquired the nickname of "the German Regiment." Its monument marks its approximate position on the first day of fighting, until it was forced back with the rest of the Eleventh Corps. The Seventy-fourth was actually in a skirmish line in advance of this line of monuments, but on ground that was in private hands at the time of the monument's placement. As with the Forty-fifth New York's marker, the monument was placed on the only ground owned by the Battlefield Commission, the strip along the roadway. The Seventy-fourth was positioned on Cemetery Ridge the second and third days of the battle.

The regiment brought 381 members to Gettysburg, losing two officers and eight men killed, four officers and 36 men wounded, and two officers and 58 men captured or missing, for a total of eight officers and 102 men listed as casualties.

The Seventy-fourth was commanded by a former Prussian officer, Colonel Adolph von Hartung, until he suffered a leg wound early in the fighting. At that point, Lieutenant Colonel Theobald von Mitzel took command. When von Mitzel was captured in

road has made it vulnerable to vehicles traveling too fast to make the turn. It has been struck and badly damaged on at least two occasions, once in 2003 and again in 2010.

B-4: Sixty-first Ohio Infantry Monument
39° 50.494' N, 77° 14.041' W

Commanded by Colonel Stephen J. McGroarty, the men of the Sixty-first Ohio arrived on the field early in the afternoon on the first day of fighting and were deployed as skirmishers. They later were assigned the duty of supporting Dilger's Battery and were forced back into town with the rest of the Eleventh Corps. In the retreat, the regiment and Dilger's Battery fought their way through town block by block by leapfrogging one another until they reached Cemetery Hill.

The regiment moved to Culp's Hill the next evening and then returned to Cemetery Hill for the remainder of the battle, where once again they supported Dilger's Battery, this time at the gate to Evergreen Cemetery.

The Sixty-first suffered 54 casualties of the 309 men engaged in battle, including six killed, 36 wounded, and 12 missing. Since only 80 men remained for duty, the regiment was consolidated with the Eighty-second Ohio Infantry in March 1865. Before mustering out four months later, the regiment participated in General William Sherman's March to the Sea.

the retreat, command fell to Captain Henry Krauseneck, whose leadership abilities came into question when others in the regiment said he hid between some trees and a brick house during the battle, and later behind a stone wall as the fighting became hand to hand. In January 1864, Krauseneck was brought up on charges of cowardice and found guilty. He was allowed to resign.

The regiment had 10 killed, 40 wounded, and 60 missing or captured out of a force of 381.

The monument depicts a fallen color bearer. Dedicated July 2, 1888, it is located at the approximate position the regiment held on the afternoon of July 1 prior to the retreat of the Eleventh Corps. The sculptor is unknown.

The monument's location at a sharp bend in the

The monument is located in the area where the regiment supported Dilger's Battery. A knapsack is depicted on the top and crossed rifles, cartridge boxes, and other accouterments on the front. The back lists the principal engagements in which the regiment fought. The monument was dedicated September 14, 1887. Fabrication was by M. V. Mitchell and Son.

B-5: Monument to Battery I, First Ohio Light Artillery
39° 50.515′ N, 77° 14.033′ W

Also known as Dilger's Battery, after its commander, Captain Hubert Dilger, Battery I went into battle immediately on arrival on July 1, engaging in an artillery duel with a four-gun Confederate battery at a distance of about fourteen hundred yards. With Wheeler's Battery, Dilger and his men advanced from this location twice. In advancing, Dilger's men had to fill a four-foot-deep ditch while under heavy fire before their guns could be moved. When the Confederate infantry, supported by four batteries, massed on its right flank at a distance of a hundred yards, Dilger's Battery was forced back. In this action, one of Dilger's guns was disabled.

Battery I joined the retreat of the Eleventh Corps but defiantly stopped to engage the advancing Confederate army at least once. Eventually reaching Cemetery Hill, the battery remained there for the rest of the battle. In the first day's action, Battery I lost fourteen men and twenty-four horses, in addition to the disabled gun. Two more men and four more horses were lost over the next two days.

Dilger, known by his men as "Leather Britches" for the leather seat of his trousers, hated to retreat and had gained a reputation for holding his position until he had no other option. Following the lead of its

commander, Battery I was one of the last Union batteries to withdraw from this part of the battlefield. Dilger's refusal to retreat until the last opportunity had earned him the Medal of Honor for his actions at Chancellorsville, where he had delayed his withdrawal until his guns were the last on the field, keeping the onrushing Confederates at bay while he and his men pulled the guns away by hand while covering the Union retreat.

The regiment's motto, *"Fidus et Audax"* ("Faithful and Bold"), appears on the monument, as do the engagements in which Battery I participated. The monument was fabricated by Thomas Fox and dedicated September 14, 1887, chosen by the state of Ohio as the dedication date for all of its monuments at Gettysburg.

B-6: Thirteenth Independent New York Light Battery Monument
39° 50.552' N, 77° 13.977' W

On July 1, the Thirteenth Independent New York Light Battery began its march from Emmitsburg, Maryland. Reaching a point about five miles out of Gettysburg, it was ordered to rush to the battle as quickly as it could. In doing so, the men lost much of their forage when rough road conditions caused some of their wagons to overturn.

The road took a further toll when two caissons broke down just as the battery passed through town. One of those was repaired, but the other was damaged so badly that it had to be abandoned, leaving the battery short of ammunition.

The monument sits where the battery initially took position. It was soon relocated to support Dilger's Battery when that unit moved forward. In that action, one of the Thirteenth's guns was disabled and had to be abandoned. It was recovered on July 5, two days after the battle.

The unit also went by the name of Wheeler's Thirteenth New York Battery, in honor of its commander, Lieutenant William Wheeler. The Thirteenth, along with the rest of the Eleventh Corps, was forced back through town when Confederate troops got so close that the battery was in danger of being taken from the rear. Wheeler's men ultimately took a position on Cemetery Hill. On the third day of the fighting, they assisted in repulsing Pickett's Charge.

Of his 118 men at Gettysburg, Wheeler reported eight wounded and three missing. He also had 12 horses killed. The battery fired 850 rounds of ammunition.

The monument was fabricated by Smith Granite Company and dedicated July 4, 1893.

B-7: Eighty-second Illinois Infantry Monument
39° 50.570′ N, 77° 13.941′ W

Few men in the Eighty-second Illinois were born in the United States. Approximately two-thirds of the regiment's members were German immigrants. Nearly all of the remaining men were immigrants from a variety of countries. Company C was Jewish, while the men of Company I came from the Scandinavian countries.

The monument sits on the regiment's first line of battle prior to its retreat to Cemetery Hill. On the night of July 2, it participated in the bloody fighting near Culp's Hill that resulted in the repulse of General Richard S. Ewell's Second Corps of the Army of Northern Virginia.

Commanded at Gettysburg by Lieutenant Colonel Edward Salomon, a former Chicago attorney, the regiment had 131 killed, wounded, and missing over the three days of fighting. One of those missing, Captain Emil Grey of Company H, had actually been captured. He survived the war and went on to become the first Swiss ambassador to the United States.

After the war, Salomon served as the governor of Washington Territory under President Ulysses Grant.

The Eighty-second was also known as the Second Hecker Regiment, after its first colonel, Friedrich Franz Karl Hecker, who had previously organized the Twenty-fourth Illinois Infantry. After several disagreements among the officers, Hecker resigned and formed the Eighty-second, thus giving rise to the Second Hecker Regiment label.

While the monument's sculptor is unknown, the contractor for building and installing it was Triebel and Sons. Dedication took place September 3, 1891.

B-8: 157th New York Infantry Monument
39° 50.581′ N, 77° 13.879′ W

One of two major monuments to the 157th New York (see also B-1), this one marks the position the regiment held before moving toward the center of the Eleventh Corps line on the first day of the battle.

The 157th arrived at Gettysburg late in the morning on July 1, taking a position behind a battery. Almost immediately, it came under artillery fire. Advancing to the Confederate skirmish line, the regiment captured a hundred prisoners from the Fifth Alabama Infantry.

Also known as the Madison and Cortland Regiment, the 157th saw its fiercest fighting about three hundred yards in front of the monument when it came to the aid of Brigadier General Wlodzimierz Krzyzanowski's brigade, which was coming under heavy attack. The 157th was able to relieve some of the pressure on Krzyzanowski's men but had little support of its own. Soon, it found itself facing Confederate troops on three sides. It was then that the regiment suffered most of its casualties, although it is credited with advancing the farthest of any Eleventh Corps regiment. Forced to retreat, it had to leave behind its wounded, all of whom were taken prisoner.

On July 2, the regiment was deemed too depleted to continue and was placed on duty as provost guard. It remained in that role on July 3, assigned to stop stragglers and force them back to their regiments.

Commanded by Colonel Philip Brown, the 157th lost four officers and 23 men killed, eight officers and 158 men wounded, and six officers and

108 men captured or missing out of the 431 brought into the battle. Several of the wounded died over the coming days and weeks. Following the battle, Captain Charles H. Van Slyke of Company B noted in his report that only 84 men remained in the regiment who could actually carry arms.

The 157th's primary monument was fabricated by New England Monument Company and dedicated September 8, 1886. It was erected by the state of New York.

B-9: 119th New York Infantry Monument
39° 50.588' N, 77° 13.846' W

The 119th New York was commanded at Gettysburg by Colonel John T. Lockman until he was

wounded. Command then fell to Lieutenant Colonel Edward F. Lloyd, who was later killed at the Battle of Resaca on May 14, 1864.

The regiment was heavily engaged on the first two days at Gettysburg, losing nearly half its strength. Of the 16 officers and 284 men taken into the battle, 11 were killed, 70 were wounded, and 59 were declared captured or missing, for a total of 140 casualties. Most of the casualties occurred in this area when the men fought against the Fourth, Twelfth, Thirteenth, Twenty-first, and Forty-fourth Georgia infantries of General Richard Ewell's Second (Confederate) Corps. The New Yorkers came under especially heavy attack when the Twenty-sixth Wisconsin Infantry, positioned on the right, was overrun. When that happened, the 119th's flank was left unprotected. After the flag bearer was killed, the regiment's flag was captured by the Thirteenth Georgia Infantry. The Georgians returned the flag at an 1885 reunion.

The action on July 2 on Cemetery Hill was with fixed bayonets. Hand-to-hand fighting was necessary to drive the Confederates off the hill. Most of the fighting was after dark. Soldiers used the flashes from gun muzzles to identify where enemy troops were located.

The 119th's monument was erected by the state of New York. The dedication on the rear states that the men were patriotic citizens who obeyed the summons of their country and offered their lives for the causes of union and liberty. Dedication took place July 3, 1888. The monument was fabricated by Smith Granite Company.

B-10: Eighty-second Ohio Infantry Monument
39° 50.596′ N, 77° 13.802′ W

Commanded by Colonel James S. Robinson, the Eighty-second Ohio arrived on the field around noon on the first day of fighting, moving immediately to provide support for Dilger's Battery. At about three that afternoon, it advanced to a position about 125 yards in front of the site of the monument until it was outflanked. Robinson was wounded, at which time command was taken over by Lieutenant Colonel David Thomson. Overpowered, the regiment was forced to fall back through town, where it would reassemble on Cemetery Hill.

Of its 22 officers, only two got through the battle unscathed. Four were killed, 14 were wounded, and two were declared missing. The enlisted men didn't fare much better, as 161 of the 236 who fought were lost. Of those, 14 were killed or mortally wounded, 71 were wounded, and 76 were missing. Many of those declared missing were taken prisoner, but several were never accounted for.

From the time the Eighty-second mustered in until it mustered out, it lost more officers than any other Ohio regiment, including its original colonel, James Cantwell, who was killed at Second Manassas when he was thrown from his horse as he directed his men in a charge.

At the close of Gettysburg, the Eighty-second engaged in a hot dispute with the Seventy-fifth Pennsylvania over which was the last Union regiment to leave its position. The disagreement never was settled to everyone's satisfaction.

The Eighty-second's monument marks the approximate location the regiment occupied while in support of Dilger's Ohio Battery I. The monument was fabricated by Thomas Fox and dedicated September 14, 1887.

B-11: Seventy-fifth Pennsylvania Infantry Monument
39° 50.601′ N, 77° 13.776′ W

The Seventy-fifth Pennsylvania was another Union regiment made up primarily of German immigrants. It fought as part of Włodzimierz Krzyzanowski's brigade. Battling in close quarters, the regi-

leave their position, an argument hotly disputed by the Eighty-second Ohio, which made a similar claim. In truth, there really was no way to know which regiment stayed in position the longest, considering the chaos and the poor visibility from the smoke of the battle.

The commander of the Seventy-fifth, Colonel Francis Mahler, was wounded twice. The first time, his horse was also wounded and fell on him, causing more injury. Mahler remained on the field, however, until receiving his second wound, which proved mortal. He succumbed on July 4. When Mahler was wounded the second time, command of the regiment fell to Major August Ledig.

Two monuments to the Seventy-fifth are on the battlefield. This is the main monument, erected by the commonwealth of Pennsylvania. The second, in the National Cemetery (39° 49.285′ N, 77° 13.828′ W), marks the approximate position the regiment held on July 2. That monument was erected by the Seventy-fifth's survivors. The regiment took part in hand-to-hand fighting at that location during the evening on July 2.

The Seventy-fifth's main monument was dedicated October 6, 1888.

ment lost 111 men and officers in fifteen minutes. When the Union line collapsed, the regiment was forced to retreat.

While artillery raked their ranks from one side and infantry poured a fierce wall of fire from the other side and from the front, the men of the Seventy-fifth served as a rear guard, enabling many to reach Cemetery Hill who would otherwise have been captured or killed. All five regimental commanders in Krzyzanowski's Brigade were either killed or wounded, and Krzyzanowski himself was injured when his horse fell on him. After the battle, the men of the Seventy-fifth claimed they were the last Union regiment to

B-12: Twenty-sixth Wisconsin Infantry Monument
39° 50.603′ N, 77° 13.758′ W

Made up mostly of German immigrants, the Twenty-sixth Wisconsin was recruited primarily

men killed and 129 wounded. Forced to withdraw, it fought its way back to Cemetery Hill, where it remained for the rest of the battle. In a classic understatement, Major Frederick Winkler of the regiment later wrote that the retreat was "not as orderly as it might have been."

The Twenty-sixth was commanded by Lieutenant Colonel Hans Boebel, who was wounded badly enough on July 1 that he had to have his leg amputated. Boebel would gain a measure of fame after the war as an actor and an official in Milwaukee city government. Captain John W. Fuchs took command when Boebel was wounded. Of the 516 officers and men the regiment brought into the battle, 46 were killed, 134 were wounded, and 37 were declared missing.

In late 1864, the regiment took part in General William Sherman's March to the Sea.

The monument, fabricated by Ryegate Granite Company, was dedicated June 30, 1888. It marks the approximate position of the Twenty-sixth on the first day of fighting.

from the Milwaukee area. Also known as the Sigel Regiment, after General Franz Sigel, the Twenty-sixth had lost nearly two hundred men at Chancellorsville just two months prior to Gettysburg.

At Gettysburg, the regiment was positioned on the right of Krzyzanowski's Brigade, exposing it to heavy Confederate fire from the Thirty-first and Sixtieth Georgia infantries. Union troops on Barlow Knoll had just been overwhelmed and were in a panicked retreat when the Twenty-sixth encountered General John Brown Gordon's brigade of Georgians. In a matter of minutes, the Twenty-sixth lost 26

B-13: Fifty-eighth New York Infantry Monument
39° 50.624′ N, 77° 13.683′ W

The Fifty-eighth New York was another unit comprised mostly of immigrants. A portion of the regiment was raised directly by Colonel Wlodzimierz Krzyzanowski. The regiment was also known as the Morgan Rifles, the United States Rifles, the

Polish Legion, and the Gallatin Rifles. The first two names arose from the regiment's formation as a consolidation of the Morgan Rifles and the United States Rifles, both of which were incomplete when the need for a new regiment arose. Recruited mostly in New York City, the regiment was made up of immigrants from Poland, Russia, Denmark, France, Italy, and Germany. "Morgan Rifles" was the nickname also given to the Ninety-third New York Infantry, which occasionally caused confusion.

The monument sits at the approximate location where two companies of the Fifty-eighth were positioned during the first day's fighting. When they retired to Cemetery Hill, they were joined by the rest of the regiment. The men fought there on July 2 and 3.

On the morning of July 4, a patrol of ten men went into town to determine if the Confederates had retreated. With the help of some local citizens, the patrol located a house occupied by Southern sharpshooters, who were captured as they slept. Shortly afterward, a second patrol arrived in the area and also captured a number of Confederates. The two patrols captured a combined two hundred prisoners.

The Fifty-eighth was commanded on the first day and part of the second by Lieutenant Colonel August Otto, a native of Holstein, Germany. On July 2, Otto was assigned to General Carl Schurz's staff, at which time Captain Emil Koenig took command of the regiment.

At Gettysburg, the regiment suffered two killed, 16 wounded, and three missing of the 222 men brought to the field.

Dedicated July 2, 1888, the monument was fabricated by New England Monument Company. In June 1939, it was hit by lightning. In May 2004, it suffered extensive damage when it was struck by a car.

B-14: 107th Ohio Infantry Monument
39° 50.677' N, 77° 13.651' W

The 107th Ohio lost 220 officers and men at Chancellorsville. Its experience at Gettysburg was just as bad. The regiment lost 211 of the 400 who

then rushed toward the flag. Adjutant P. F. Young attempted to wrest the flag from the badly wounded flag bearer, but the Louisianan pulled out a revolver and shot him in the shoulder. Young then killed the flag bearer with a thrust of his saber, capturing the flag. A later examination of the flag bearer's body revealed that he had been shot seven times.

The next day, the regiment's men served as skirmishers in front of the artillery. On July 4, with barely enough men to fill out a company, the 107th joined in the pursuit of the Army of Northern Virginia as it made its way back across the Potomac.

Remembering their comrades, the surviving members of the regiment erected this monument and dedicated it to those who had fallen. The monument contains a list of the principal engagements in which the regiment participated. It was constructed by Smith Granite Company and dedicated September 14, 1887.

entered the fray. Of those, 23 were killed, 111 were wounded, and 77 were declared missing.

The regiment, under the command of Colonel Seraphim Meyer, arrived at Gettysburg early in the afternoon on July 1. It engaged the Confederates within an hour and fought until about four o'clock. Exposed to heavy artillery fire, the regiment suffered many casualties, including Colonel Meyer. Unable to sustain the fight, it was forced to fall back to Cemetery Hill. There, it re-formed in support of Wiedrich's Battery, remaining until the evening of July 2. Following Meyer's injury, command of the regiment fell to Captain John M. Lutz.

In the evening on July 2, the men participated in repulsing the attack of Brigadier General Harry T. Hays's Louisiana brigade. Again suffering heavy losses, the 107th fell back, gathering behind Wiedrich's Battery. When the flag of the Eighth Louisiana suddenly appeared through the smoke, it became apparent that the defensive line had been breached. Several men from the 107th fired at the color guard at once,

B-15: Twenty-fifth and Seventy-fifth Ohio Infantries Monument
39° 50.719′ N, 77° 13.601′ W

The Twenty-fifth and Seventy-fifth Ohio infantries arrived from Emmitsburg, Maryland, on July 1 and fought side by side at Gettysburg, setting up their positions in this area in support of Battery G of the Fourth United States Artillery, all while under heavy artillery fire.

Forced into retreat with the rest of the Eleventh Corps, they set up their new position at the base of

by Colonel Andrew L. Harris. When Harris took charge of the brigade on July 1, Captain George B. Fox assumed command of the regiment. After the war, Harris became a member of the Ohio legislature before being elected governor.

Having fought together, the two regiments agreed to erect a common monument honoring both. The monument is said to sit near where the two joined in the first day's fighting. Thomas Fox sculpted the monument, which was dedicated September 14, 1887.

Cemetery Hill, marked by a second monument (39° 49.391′ N, 77° 13.712′ W). They held their position slightly beyond that monument for the next two days, fighting hand to hand against the famed Louisiana Tigers on the night of July 2. On July 4, the Twenty-fifth and Seventy-fifth jointly led the advance back into town.

The ferocity of the fighting at Gettysburg is illustrated by the unofficial casualty rate for the two regiments. They began the battle with 469 men, of whom 54 were killed, 158 wounded, and 157 declared missing.

The Twenty-fifth had four different commanders at Gettysburg, beginning with Lieutenant Colonel Jeremiah Williams. When Williams was captured on July 1, Captain Nathaniel J. Manning took over until he was wounded. Then Second Lieutenant William Maloney briefly commanded the regiment until Lieutenant Israel White took over. White was in command for the remainder of the battle.

The Seventy-fifth was initially commanded

B-16: Seventeenth Connecticut Infantry Monument
39° 50.725′ N, 77° 13.572′ W

When the Eleventh Corps moved into position around midday on July 1, the Seventeenth Connecticut

took this elevated position, believing it offered the best field of fire. Its commander, Lieutenant Colonel Douglas Fowler, braved the incoming artillery as he encouraged his men from atop his white horse. As they watched, however, Fowler was decapitated by a shell fragment. His body was never identified, and he was likely buried as an unknown soldier in the National Cemetery.

Facing the Confederacy's Second Corps, its old foe from Chancellorsville, the Seventeenth and the rest of the unprotected right flank of the Union line were quickly overrun. The men undertook a fighting retreat, the regiment working its way back through town to Cemetery Hill.

The next night, the men fought in the hand-to-hand combat that accompanied the Confederates' night assault on Cemetery Hill. A monument (39° 49.356′ N, 77° 13.687′ W) marks the Seventeenth's position there.

Of the regiment's 369 men who entered the battle, 206 became casualties.

The regiment's survivors erected the monument and dedicated it to those members who fell at Gettysburg. Their names are listed on the back and sides. The sculptor was W. H. Curtis of Stratford, Connecticut. The monument was installed June 24, 1884, and dedicated a week later, on July 1. The next year, the survivors placed the nearby flagpole to mark the location where Lieutenant Colonel Fowler was killed.

Chapter 3
Area C

IN TOWN, SEMINARY RIDGE NORTH

Area C

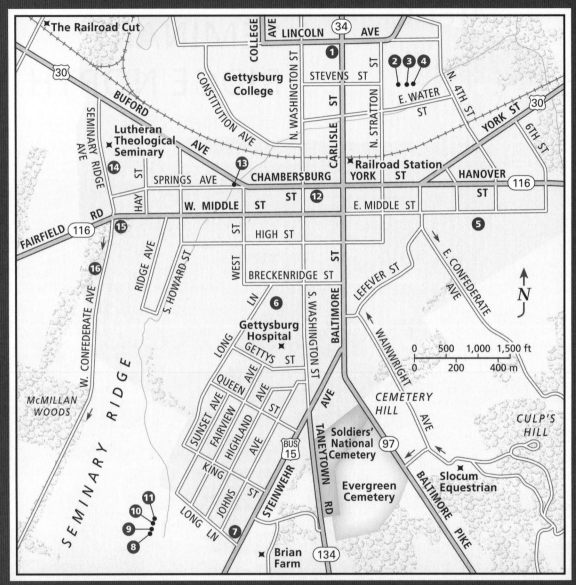

The Railroad Cut

LINCOLN AVE
COLLEGE AVE
34
STEVENS ST
Gettysburg College
N. WASHINGTON ST
CARLISLE ST
N. STRATTON ST
N. 4TH ST
E. WATER ST
1
2 3 4

30
BUFORD AVE
CONSTITUTION AVE

SEMINARY RIDGE AVE
Lutheran Theological Seminary
14

YORK ST
30
6TH ST

SPRINGS AVE
CHAMBERSBURG
Railroad Station
YORK ST
HANOVER ST
116
13
HAY ST
W. MIDDLE ST
ST
12
E. MIDDLE ST

FAIRFIELD RD
116
15
RIDGE AVE
S. HOWARD ST
HIGH ST
WEST ST
BALTIMORE ST
LEFEVER ST
E. CONFEDERATE AVE
5

16
BRECKENRIDGE ST
N

W. CONFEDERATE AVE

6
Gettysburg Hospital
LONG LN
GETTYS ST
S. WASHINGTON ST
WAINWRIGHT AVE

0   500   1,000 1,500 ft
0   200   400 m

McMILLAN WOODS

SEMINARY RIDGE

QUEEN AVE
FAIRVIEW AVE
HIGHLAND AVE
SUNSET AVE
ST
CEMETERY HILL
CULP'S HILL

Soldiers' National Cemetery
97
Slocum Equestrian

KING ST
JOHNS ST
STEINWEHR AVE
BUS 15
TANEYTOWN RD
Evergreen Cemetery
BALTIMORE PIKE

11
10
9
8
LONG LN
7

Brian Farm
134

CHAPTER 3

Area C In Town, Seminary Ridge North

When the Union line collapsed on Barlow Knoll and Oak Ridge, the retreat into town became an every-man-for-himself free-for-all. In the chaos, regiments were separated, men became lost, and officers found themselves with no troops to command. The Confederate army fell in right behind the Union soldiers, capturing many in the process. Brigadier General Alexander Schimmelfennig lost his entire Union command and was forced to hide in a pig shed for two days while Confederate troops moved all around him.

The line collapsed like dominoes. First the troops on Oak Ridge and then those on McPherson Ridge fell back to the seminary. When the men were unable to hold their positions there, the retreat resumed, Federal troops rushing toward Cemetery Hill.

Before reaching town, Union forces under Colonel Charles Coster met Confederate troops led by General Harry Hays and Colonel Isaac Avery in a small brickyard. A brief but fierce skirmish broke out in which the Federals were quickly overrun. Those who could joined the retreat. Those left behind were captured or killed in what has become known as the Battle of the Brickyard.

Union troops rushed through town with Confederates close behind. The streets were littered with discarded weapons and equipment as the panicked Union troops lightened their loads so they could run faster. Unfamiliar with the town, many headed into blind alleys or tried to take refuge in houses, only to find they had no escape. Those unfortunates almost invariably became prisoners.

The exhausted survivors of the debacle formed on Cemetery Hill, while Southern troops took up positions in houses and businesses in town. Sharpshooters moved to upper floors and plied their deadly skills on any Union soldier unfortunate enough to come into their line of sight.

As the day drew to a close, Union troops regrouped. General Robert E, Lee ordered General Richard S. Ewell, who had lost a leg at Second Manassas, to push the Confederate attack before the enemy could set up a strong defense. Ewell made the fateful decision to wait until General Edward Johnson's division arrived. That never happened, as Johnson stopped at Culp's Hill. Lee lost his advantage, and both sides dug in and prepared for whatever was to come the next day.

Numerous features of the town are discussed in Volume 1, including historic buildings such as Pennsylvania Hall on the Gettysburg College campus; the Wills House, where President Abraham Lincoln completed writing what would come to be known as the Gettysburg Address; and the train station where he arrived, which had served as a hospital for wounded soldiers. The unusual mural at the site of Kuhn's Brickyard provides context for the Union retreat into town and sets the stage for the discussion of the monument to Amos Humiston, the only enlisted soldier to have his own marker at Gettysburg. His poignant story illustrates the pain families felt when loved ones were lost. Volume 1 covers a building with an artillery shell still embedded in its front, as well as a cannon barrel partially implanted in a sidewalk. The story of how that came to be never fails to surprise and amuse visitors. Also covered are a Confederate sharpshooter stronghold, as well as a building with dozens of bullet holes in its side that give mute testimony to Union troops' efforts to bring an end to the sharpshooters within. Finally comes the story of Jennie Wade, the only civilian killed in the battle, and the house where she was hit by a stray bullet. Most of these sites sit along Baltimore Street and are easily reached on foot.

C-1: Monument to Battery K, First Ohio Light Artillery
39° 50.211' N, 77° 13.879' W

Captain Lewis Heckman had been in command only three weeks when Battery K went into position as a reserve unit at this location at noon on July 1. When the Eleventh Corps was forced back, the battery was activated. Its mission: slow the Confederate

attackers enough to buy time for the retreating and demoralized Eleventh Corps to pass safely through town in its rush to Cemetery Hill.

Under the best of conditions, this would have been difficult, and these were hardly ideal conditions. Since the panic-stricken Union troops were so closely pursued by Confederate attackers, Heckman's men could not fire immediately without wiping out large segments of retreating Federals. Finally, seeing mostly enemy troops in front, the battery was able to fire. Primarily using canister, Battery K fired 113 rounds in the fighting around what had been John Kuhn's brickyard. Badly outnumbered, the battery could only slow the Confederate advance. Within thirty minutes, it was about to be overrun. Heckman reluctantly gave the order to withdraw, which came too late for some of his men. Two of the battery's guns, along with their gunners, were captured by the Sixth North Carolina Infantry. Two other guns that were saved were so badly damaged that they were useless in the next day's fight.

The First Ohio Light Artillery consisted of twelve batteries, each of which served independently of the others, fighting on separate battlefields. Battery K took fifteen casualties at Gettysburg, with two killed, eleven wounded, and two declared missing.

Battery K was transferred to the Army of the Cumberland in late September 1863. It subsequently fought in the West at such places as Chattanooga, Lookout Mountain, and Mission Ridge.

Frederick and Field fabricated the monument, which was dedicated September 14, 1887.

C-2: Twenty-seventh Pennsylvania Infantry Monument
39° 50.106′ N, 77° 13.681′ W

The Twenty-seventh Pennsylvania gained a measure of fame shortly after leaving home for the first time. With the Sixth Massachusetts Infantry, the regiment proceeded by rail to Baltimore in April 1861. On arrival, the first five cars of the train, containing seven companies of the Sixth Massachusetts, were drawn by horses through the city. After the cars passed, an angry pro-secession mob blocked the tracks. The remainder of the Massachusetts companies had to force their way through the crowd. The mob then turned its attention to the Pennsylvanians, who had not yet received their weapons. Defenseless, the Twenty-seventh was forced to fall back. Several of its number were killed or wounded by the secessionists in the process.

Upon returning to Philadelphia, the regiment was reorganized with Max Einstein as colonel. About half of its men were German.

The Twenty-seventh arrived in Gettysburg at midday on July 1 and was assigned the task of defending the entrance to town from the north. With the retreat from Oak Ridge already under way, the Twenty-seventh and the 134th New York were then rushed to a position near a brickyard, where they were ordered to support the retreating troops. As the Confederates advanced, the Union forces, including the men of the Twenty-seventh, found themselves flanked. Fighting desperately, the regiment tried to retreat with the rest of the Union army toward Cemetery Hill, but many of the men were surrounded and taken prisoner.

Those who made it back to Cemetery Hill took a position along the small stone wall on the north side of the hill. A second monument marks that position (see D-1). There, they participated in the brutal fighting on the evening of July 2.

On July 3, they maintained their position, although they came under heavy artillery fire when they moved temporarily to assist other troops in danger of being overrun. They were among the first Union troops to re-enter town on July 4. Over the next few days, they were part of the army following Robert E. Lee's troops back into Virginia.

This monument to the Twenty-seventh was one of the earliest on the battlefield. It marks the regiment's position in the late afternoon on July 1. Sculpted by A. Donnelly and fabricated by J. C. Moore, it was originally installed on East Cemetery Hill in 1884 and dedicated at that time. It was moved to its current location in 1889.

Commanded by Lieutenant Colonel Lorenz Cantador, the regiment suffered six men killed, 29 wounded, and 76 missing of the 324 brought to the field.

C-3: 154th New York Infantry Monument
39° 50.108′ N, 77° 13.654′ W

On June 30, a detachment of fifty men from the 154th New York Infantry joined fifty from the Seventy-third Pennsylvania Infantry to make a reconnaissance to Strykersville. They were commanded by Major L. D. Warner of the 154th. This left the regiment short-handed.

Upon arriving in Gettysburg at about four in the afternoon on July 1, the main body of the 154th rested in the cemetery, cleaning their guns. Almost immediately, the men were ordered into action, as events on Oak Ridge were not going well for the Union army.

While the battle raged on Oak Ridge, Colonel Charles Coster's brigade, which included the 154th, encountered a brigade of North Carolinians under Colonel Isaac Avery and Brigadier General Harry Hays's Louisiana brigade in a small brickyard. The Confederate troops and Coster's men, who had taken a position behind a small split-rail fence, saw each other at about the same time. Both sides fired almost simultaneously. After a brief fight, the 154th was overrun, the New Yorkers joining in the panicked retreat through town.

The 154th was also known as the Hardtack Regiment. In the fighting, one man was killed. Another 20 men and one officer were wounded. However, the bulk of the casualties were those classified as captured or missing. Nine officers and 169 men were categorized in that manner. Most of those were taken captive as they tried to retreat. Sadly, 42 members of the regiment, many of them captured at Gettysburg, would die in Southern prisons.

The few men of the regiment who made it to Cemetery Hill joined their detachment, which had been ordered back to Gettysburg. The entire group then joined the 134th New York and aided in repelling the assault by the Louisiana Tigers against Wiedrich's Battery on July 2.

The mural behind the monument is discussed in detail in Volume 1. It depicts the fighting in this area, which was farmland at the time.

The monument was fabricated by Frederick and Field and dedicated July 1, 1890. It is located at the position taken by the regiment in the brickyard fight on the afternoon of July 1.

C-4: 134th New York Infantry Monument
39° 50.110′ N, 77° 13.629′ W

Commanded by Lieutenant Colonel A. H. Jackson, the 134th New York moved into this area to assist in protecting retreating Union troops as they moved from Oak Ridge. In 1863, this area was an open field, John Kuhn's small brickyard being the only structure in the immediate vicinity. From here, the men of the 134th could see the Union line collapsing on Barlow Knoll.

With the Eleventh Corps in full retreat and the Confederates in close pursuit, it was not long until the regiment found itself facing overwhelming odds. Occupying the extreme right, it was quickly outflanked and forced to join the retreat to Cemetery Hill.

The marker indicates the approximate position the regiment occupied on the afternoon of the first day of fighting. Its actual position is believed to have been west of the marker. A second monument (see D-2) on Cemetery Hill locates the position the 134th held on July 2 and 3.

The tablet here, while far less impressive than the regiment's monument on Cemetery Hill, held greater meaning for the survivors because it marked the position where the 134th suffered more casualties than in any other battle in which it engaged. Combined with losses on the second and third days of fighting, the regiment had 42 killed, 151 wounded, and 59

missing, for a total of 252 casualties out of 400 men engaged.

The bronze tablet was erected in 1905.

C-5: Culp Farm
39° 49.758' N, 77° 13.411' W

Henry Culp's farm sat within the battle lines of the Confederate army. This position brought it under heavy fire from Union artillery. It also made it an ideal site for a Confederate field hospital. The Army of Northern Virginia's Second Corps used it for that purpose.

Colonel Isaac Avery of the Sixth North Carolina Infantry was brought to the farm after receiving what proved to be a mortal wound to the neck. He lived only a day before succumbing. Before arriving at the Culp Farm, Avery wrote a short but now famous note to a friend, Major Samuel Tate: "Tell my father I died with my face to the enemy."

The house and barn served as a temporary field hospital during the fighting on Culp's Hill. After the battle, both served as medical aid stations. The orchard and the area around the house and barn were utilized as a Confederate cemetery.

C-6: Lincoln Cemetery
39° 49.560' N, 77° 14.092' W

In the segregated society that existed in 1863, African-American veterans were not permitted to be buried in the National Cemetery. In 1867, the Lincoln Cemetery was created to provide for "the proper burial of Gettysburg's African American citizens and Civil War veterans." The cemetery is now the final resting place of about thirty members of the United States Colored Troops. Over the years, many non-veterans were also laid to rest here. A large number of reinterments took place in 1906, when the town's "colored cemetery" was razed for home construction.

While attitudes did not change appreciably in the twenty years following the war, they relaxed enough that the first African-American veteran was buried in Soldiers' National Cemetery in November 1884, when Henry Gooden of the 127th United States Colored Troops was reinterred from the Alms House Cemetery. It took fifty-two more years for the second African-American burial, when the remains of Charles H. Parker of the Third United States Colored Troops were relocated from Yellow Hill Cemetery north of Gettysburg.

C-7: Eighth Ohio Infantry Monument

39° 48.964' N, 77° 14.223' W

The Eighth Ohio was commanded at Gettysburg by Lieutenant Colonel Franklin Sawyer. The regiment's monument was placed at its approximate position on the afternoon of July 2 through the next day, when the men served as skirmishers and fought along Emmitsburg Road. In the fighting on July 3, the regiment attacked the flank of Pickett's Charge and was able to take several prisoners, along with three flags.

Two men of the Eighth received the Medal of Honor, both for capturing those flags. Private James Richmond of Company F captured one, and German-born sergeant John Miller captured the other two, those of the Thirty-fourth North Carolina and the Thirty-eighth Virginia.

In the three days of fighting, the regiment lost 18 killed, 83 wounded, and one missing, for a total of 102 of the 209 men brought into battle.

The monument was sculpted by R. R. King, fabricated by New England Granite Works, and dedicated September 14, 1887. It consists of a granite shaft topped by a bronze sculpture of a soldier's cap, canteen, knapsack, and blanket roll, all resting on top of a drum. These accouterments were not part of the original monument, which at one time had a soldier standing on top where the drum and the other components now sit. Stars surround the top of the shaft. Each side shows a column topped by a trefoil, the symbol of the Second Corps.

C-8: Fourteenth Connecticut Infantry Monument

39° 48.985′ N, 77° 14.523′ W

The Fourteenth Connecticut arrived in Gettysburg on the evening of July 1. It held the position around the site of the monument for the next three days. The regiment was particularly busy on the morning of the third day, when it captured and burned the barn and house of William Bliss. The mound behind the monument is all that remains of the ramp that led into the Bliss barn at the time of the battle. The monument, erected in 1884, marks the location of that action, which was taken to remove the Confederate sharpshooters whose fire was so devastating to nearby Union troops.

A few hours later, the regiment took part in the repulse of Pickett's Charge, performing heroically

once again. In that assault, the regiment took more than 200 prisoners and captured five battle flags. Of its 160 men, 62 were either killed or wounded.

Three men from the Fourteenth Connecticut received the Medal of Honor for what they did at Gettysburg. During Pickett's Charge, Sergeant Major William Hinks rushed forward of his line a distance of fifty yards under heavy fire and captured the flag of the Fourteenth Tennessee. Two companions started out with him, but one was immediately shot, and Hinks outran the other. Private Elijah Bacon of Company F and Corporal Christopher Flynn of Company K received the Medal of Honor for capturing flags on the same day. Bacon captured the flag of the Sixteenth North Carolina, while Flynn captured that of the Fifty-second North Carolina.

A second monument to the regiment sits on Hancock Avenue (39° 48.828′ N, 77° 14.126′ W).

C-9: Twelfth New Jersey Infantry Monument

39° 48.994′ N, 77° 14.518′ W

The Twelfth New Jersey rushed to the area of the hotly contested Bliss Farm on July 2 with orders to drive off the Confederate sharpshooters who had taken positions in the barn. That assault was successful, as the regiment returned with seven officers and eighty-five men as prisoners. The next morning, the Twelfth mounted another assault on the farm, this time helping burn it to the ground to prevent reoccupation by the Confederate army.

On the afternoon of July 3, the men of the Twelfth took part in the fight against Pickett's Charge.

This monument honors the regiment for its efforts at the Bliss Farm. Another monument to the Twelfth (39° 48.908′ N, 77° 14.126′ W) along Hancock Avenue recognizes the buck-and-ball charges used by the regiment. That marker is topped with a large musket ball and three buckshot. It also contains a plaque showing the regiment's charge on the Bliss barn.

The Twelfth lost six officers and one hundred men at Gettysburg.

The monument was carved by M. Reilly and fabricated by Beattie and Brooks. It was dedicated May 26, 1886. The bronze relief plaque was cast in 1892.

C-10: Site of the Bliss House
39° 49.013′ N, 77° 14.513′ W

The sixty-acre farm of William and Adelina Bliss occupied this location when the battle began. By its end, their home lay in ashes.

The family members hurriedly vacated their home early in the battle, leaving the doors open and the table set for a meal in their haste to get away. By July 2, the fighting on their farm was in full force, both sides pushing back and forth through their wheat field. The intensity of the battle drove many combatants into the Bliss home and outbuildings, the only substantial shelters in the immediate area. Confederate sharpshooters quickly moved into vantage points on the second floor of the barn, from which they were able to fire effectively with little resistance. Three companies of the 126th New York were ordered to push the sharpshooters from their positions. Led by Captain Charles Wheeler, the New Yorkers were successful in capturing the barn and taking several prisoners. Wheeler would die the next day on a skirmish line. The 126th New York was relieved in the afternoon by the First Delaware and one company of the Twelfth New Jersey.

When troops from the Nineteenth and Forty-eighth Mississippi forged forward in late afternoon, the Union forces were driven back, a retreat that saw Lieutenant Colonel Edward Harris arrested for abandoning his position (see C-11). Once again, Confederate troops controlled the Bliss Farm. An hour after the retreat, four companies of the Twelfth New Jersey were ordered to retake their former position. Crossing nearly a quarter-mile of open field, the New Jersey troops took heavy fire from the sharpshooters in the barn and artillery along Seminary Ridge. Despite their casualties, the Union troops recaptured the barn, taking fifty prisoners in the process. However, Confederate sharpshooters still controlled the Bliss House. The New Jersey men turned their attention to the house, successfully capturing it and taking more prisoners, including a number of officers.

Early in the evening, Confederate troops began moving toward the gap in the Union line created when General Dan Sickles moved his Federals into John Sherfy's peach orchard. The fighting intensified, and Confederate sharpshooters once again moved into the Bliss buildings. In the morning, five companies from the Twelfth New Jersey rushed to the barn and house again, forcing the Southerners out but losing five of their own men killed and twenty-five wounded in the action. A strong counterattack pushed the New Jersey troops back again. Four com-

panies of the Fourteenth Connecticut were ordered to support the New Jersey men and to stay in position once they got to the farm. Meeting strong resistance, they were successful but saw that their position was not tenable. After they discussed the situation with their officers, the decision was made to burn the buildings so they would no longer provide cover for Southern sharpshooters. The Federals set fires and burned the buildings to the ground.

The monument marks what was once the center of the Bliss House. The mound of dirt covers the foundation. The house was erected in 1884. Nothing remains of the farm today.

C-11: First Delaware Infantry Skirmish Line

39° 49.016′ N, 77° 14.511′ W

On July 2, the First Delaware sent skirmishers forward to the Bliss Farm to observe Confederate lines on Seminary Ridge. Several other regiments did the same. The fighting around the farm grew more intense. Finally, Lieutenant Colonel Edward Harris ordered a withdrawal. The retreat, anything but orderly, left a gap in the Union line. The men of the First Delaware rushed back to the relative safety of Cemetery Ridge, where Harris was immediately placed under arrest by Major General Winfield Scott Hancock for failing to hold his position.

The men from Delaware acquitted themselves well the next day. Their monument is positioned at the point from which the regiment launched a charge across the stone wall on July 3, capturing several Confederate flags and taking scores of prisoners. In fierce fighting, the regiment lost seventy-seven men. By the time the battle was over, it had lost nearly all its officers and was commanded by a lieutenant.

Three members of the regiment received the Medal of Honor for their actions at Gettysburg. Private John B. Mayberry of Company F and Private Bernard McCarren of Company C earned the honor for capturing enemy flags, while Captain James Park Postles of Company A was honored for volunteering to deliver an order a distance of six hundred yards through heavy enemy fire.

The monument sits in the area of the advance skirmish line. It was erected in 1886. A second monument is on Hancock Avenue at the site from which the regiment launched its July 3 charge (39° 48.874′ N, 77° 14.127′ W).

C-12: Reverend Horatio S. Howell Monument

39° 49.849′ N, 77° 13.953′ W

The Reverend Horatio S. Howell, chaplain of the Ninetieth Pennsylvania Infantry, attended to wounded Union soldiers inside Christ Lutheran Church. This marker notes the approximate location where he was shot and killed.

Different versions of Howell's death have circulated. The most likely was offered by Sergeant Archibald Snow, who had just had his wounds treated and was immediately behind Howell as the minister exited the church. Snow described Howell leaving the church by way of the center door at the top of the steps, wearing his dress sword as part of the regulation uniform for chaplains. A Confederate soldier standing at the approximate location denoted by the small marker demanded Howell's sword. Howell reportedly started to explain that he was a noncombatant and was not required to surrender it. At that point, the Confederate fired his weapon. The forty-two-year-old chaplain died almost instantly, falling at the landing on the top of the steps.

The monument was erected in 1889 in Howell's memory by his friends in the regiment.

The church is often referred to as "the College Church" for hosting numerous graduation ceremonies for both Gettysburg College and the Lutheran Seminary. The structure served as a hospital during and after the battle. At its peak, it accommodated approximately 150 wounded soldiers.

C-13: Twenty-sixth Pennsylvania Emergency Militia Monument
39° 49.857′ N, 77° 14.218′ W

Formed just a few weeks before the battle, the Twenty-sixth Pennsylvania Emergency Militia had never before faced the enemy. Commanded by Colonel William W. Jennings, the militia consisted mostly of men from the surrounding area, with only a few exceptions. One company was made up of students from Pennsylvania College, now Gettysburg College. The regiment's inexperience would prove costly.

pany were left behind to guard the militia's gear. The rest marched out Chambersburg Pike on June 26, only four days after being formed and a week before the main battle.

At the Samuel Lohr farm, the men encountered Lieutenant Colonel Elijah V. White's Confederate cavalry, making the militia the first Union regiment to engage the Confederates at Gettysburg. In the ensuing action, in which the militia pickets retreated without firing a shot, dozens of men from the Twenty-sixth were captured. The main body rushed back toward town, offering minimal resistance to White's experienced troopers. More of the militia's men were captured a short time later in a surprise attack by Colonel William French's Seventeenth Virginia Cavalry.

The monument was dedicated September 1, 1892. Sculpted by Edward Ludwig Albert Pausch, it depicts an infantryman as he enters battle, musket ready to fire.

As an emergency militia, the regiment served only from June 22 until July 30. Of its 743 members, 176 were captured at Gettysburg.

The militia consisted of eight infantry regiments, two batteries, six companies of cavalry, and four independent infantry companies. Joined with the local Adams County Cavalry Company, also a new unit, the two inexperienced forces were ordered to move westward into the nearby mountains and seek out any advancing Southern troops. One company of militia and part of the Adams County Cavalry Com-

C-14: View from the Cupola
39° 49.907' N, 77° 14.649' W

Schmucker Hall on the campus of the Lutheran Theological Seminary served several important functions during the battle. Both sides used its cupola as an observation post. The scene on page 60 shows what they might have seen. The view is toward

the John Herbst farm in the general direction from which Brigadier General James J. Archer's brigade crossed Willoughby Run and smashed into the Iron Brigade on the morning of July 1.

Schmucker Hall was thirty-one years old when the battle began. Named for the seminary's founder, Samuel Simon Schmucker, a staunch abolitionist, it had served as a stop on the Underground Railroad. Union troops destroyed antislavery materials in the basement to prevent them from being seen by oncoming Confederates.

Following the fighting, the building served as a hospital. It is now the home of the Adams County Historical Society.

C-15: Monument to Company D, 149th Pennsylvania Infantry
39° 49.771' N, 77° 14.641' W

This monument illustrates perfectly the strength of brotherly love. It was erected and presented to Company D of the 149th Pennsylvania Infantry by George W. Baldwin in memory of his brother, Joseph H. Baldwin, and Alex M. Stuart. Joseph Baldwin was killed at this approximate location on July 1. Wounded on the same date, Stuart died five days later.

Known as the Headquarters Guards, the company occupied this ground for only twenty minutes on the evening of July 1 before being overrun by

Brigadier General Alfred M. Scales's brigade. Scales would later become the forty-fifth governor of North Carolina.

The 149th arrived on the field July 1, taking up a position at the nearby Lutheran Theological Seminary. Unable to hold its position, the regiment moved to this location near the Schultz House. By midafternoon, it was outflanked, along with the entire First Corps. Moving back again, the regiment became separated from the rest of the corps. Soon, Company D, two pieces of artillery, and a small cadre of cavalrymen were the only Union troops left. A full-scale retreat began. Joseph Baldwin was killed in the final action before the retreat.

The monument was erected in 1886. Monuments to the entire regiment sit adjacent to the McPherson barn along Chambersburg Pike (see A-6) and along Hancock Avenue on Cemetery Ridge (39° 48.606′ N, 77° 14.146′ W).

C-16: Army of Northern Virginia Itinerary Tablets
39° 49.643′ N, 77° 14.684′ W

This row of ten tablets was placed in 1901 and 1902 by the War Department. Each tablet represents a period of time between June 29 and July 5, 1863, describing the activities of the Army of Northern Virginia during that particular time. Altogether, they cover the actions of Robert E. Lee's army just prior to, during, and just after the battle. As such, they are an invaluable resource for those wanting a concise but informative summary of the movements of the various corps and divisions.

After being removed for visitor safety and improved traffic flow, the tablets were refurbished and repositioned in the summer of 2006. Similar tablets for the Union's Army of the Potomac sit along Baltimore Street on Cemetery Hill (see D-5).

The tablets were designed by Colonel Emmor Bradley Cope and made by Albert Russell & Sons of Newburyport, Massachusetts. An architect, Cope was instrumental in helping develop early battlefield maps, surveying the field on horseback. He also designed the camp layout for the 1913 veterans' reunion and served as the first superintendent of Gettysburg National Military Park.

NATIONAL CEMETERY, EAST CEMETERY HILL

Area D

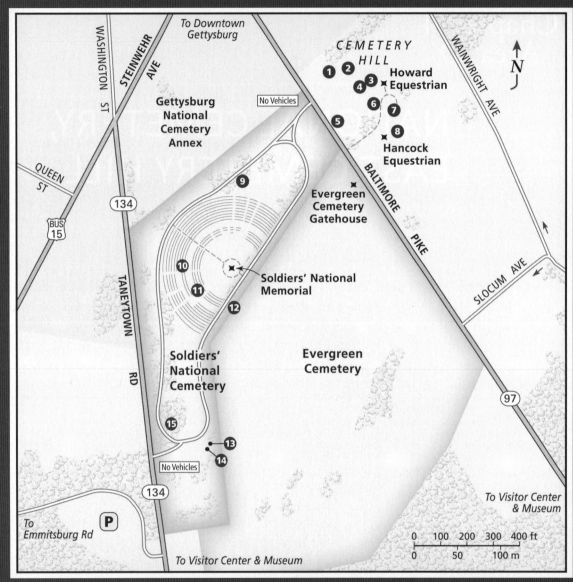

Gettysburg National Cemetery Annex

To Downtown Gettysburg

No Vehicles

CEMETERY HILL

Howard Equestrian

Hancock Equestrian

Evergreen Cemetery Gatehouse

Soldiers' National Memorial

Soldiers' National Cemetery

Evergreen Cemetery

No Vehicles

To Emmitsburg Rd

P

To Visitor Center & Museum

To Visitor Center & Museum

WASHINGTON ST

STEINWEHR AVE

WAINWRIGHT AVE

QUEEN ST

BUS 15

134

TANEYTOWN RD

BALTIMORE PIKE

SLOCUM AVE

97

134

N

0 100 200 300 400 ft
0   50   100 m

The day had been a disaster for the Union army. As darkness fell on July 1, 1863, the dispirited men straggled onto Cemetery Hill. The Union army established defensive positions and dug in by morning.

At dusk on July 2, General Harry Hays and Colonel Isaac Avery sent their Confederate brigades across the Henry Culp farm and up the eastern slope of Cemetery Hill. Union troops could hear the sounds of the approaching Southerners. Then, with little warning, the Confederates charged up the hill and clashed with the waiting Union defenders.

The charge brought the two armies nearly face to face. It wasn't long before the blue and the gray were intermingled in desperate hand-to-hand struggle. Rocks were used as weapons, and with no time to reload, muskets became clubs. Again, many Union troops found themselves in a panicked retreat, despite the best efforts of their officers to hold them in their positions.

The Louisiana Tigers pushed their way forward to the Union batteries lining the top of the hill. Artillerists used their ramrods, their bayonets, and even their fists in a desperate attempt to save their guns. The Sixth North Carolina Infantry and the Ninth Louisiana Infantry briefly were able to place their flags on the guns, but Union reinforcements soon arrived to drive them back.

The fight continued until nearly midnight, when the last Confederate was finally pushed off the hill and the Union could lay claim to the bloody ground. Both sides had suffered terribly. The hillside was strewn with the dead and dying. Among those wounded was Colonel Avery, who suffered a mortal neck wound.

Both armies stubbornly refused to quit, plans were drawn up for the next day, and the Battle of Gettysburg continued.

Volume 1 describes numerous sites and monuments in this area. On East Cemetery Hill, it honors the generals, reveals their stories, and describes the scene of the bloody hand-to-hand fighting. Readers will learn the story of the Fourth Ohio Infantry Monument and why its unusual construction material created a major headache for the Gettysburg Battlefield Memorial Association and helped set the standard for future monuments.

In Evergreen Cemetery, visitors will see battle-damaged headstones and the graves of several soldiers, including some Confederates, who were buried where they fell. Volume 1 reveals the unusual story of Elizabeth Thorn, who dug more than a hundred graves by hand in extreme heat despite being six months pregnant. Her monument is one of the first seen upon entry into the cemetery; it also serves as a tribute to all Civil War women. Not far into the cemetery, visitors will reach the graves of Jennie Wade, the only civilian killed in the battle, and John Burns, the elderly citizen who took his musket, entered the battle on the first day, and received several wounds in the process.

In the National Cemetery sits a monument to Lincoln's famous Gettysburg Address. A walkway takes visitors along the graves of those who paid the ultimate price; the text discusses how the graves were laid out, how the remains were identified, and what became of unidentifiable remains. Volume 1 tells why Kentucky has a memorial in the cemetery, despite having no troops fight at Gettysburg. It also discusses the impressive figures on the Soldiers National Monument. Visitors will see the tallest monument in the cemetery and learn the symbolism of the many scenes shown on the column. At the Baltimore Street entrance sits the portrait statue of General John Reynolds, the highest-ranking officer killed at Gettysburg; it is one of three monuments honoring Reynolds. In the annex just outside the main portion of the cemetery sits one of the newer markers at Gettysburg, the Friend to Friend Masonic Memorial. It depicts a dramatic moment in the battle and symbolizes the brotherhood of the Freemasons.

D-1: Twenty-seventh Pennsylvania Infantry Monument
39° 49.324' N, 77° 13.783' W

On July 1, the Twenty-seventh Pennsylvania Infantry, also known as the Washington Brigade, offered support to the retreat of the Eleventh Corps until the regiment was also forced back. Several of its number were taken prisoner in the process. Those who escaped made their way to Cemetery Hill, where they reorganized.

On the evening of July 2, the Confederates launched their evening attack, at which time an officer in a Union uniform ordered the Twenty-seventh to fall back. Several of the men refused, believing they were in no danger of being overrun. Seeing the refusal of the men to obey his order, the officer quickly rode away. He is believed to have been a Confederate wearing a Federal uniform.

The Twenty-seventh's troops soon found themselves in hand-to-hand combat. Not having sufficient time to reload, the men used their weapons as clubs and eventually helped force the Southern troops back. The regiment's adjutant, Walter S. Briggs, was killed during this action. When the fighting subsided, the regiment relocated to the cemetery, where it remained for the rest of the battle.

At Gettysburg, the regiment, commanded by Lieutenant Colonel Lorenz Cantador, lost six men killed, 29 wounded, and 76 missing of the 324 brought to the field.

Following the battle, the Twenty-seventh participated in the pursuit of the Confederate army as it retreated southward. In that action, it engaged Southern troops at Hagerstown and Funkstown, Maryland.

The monument, dedicated September 12, 1889, replaced the original when it was relocated to its present position on Coster Avenue (see C-2). The sculptor is unknown.

D-2: 134th New York Infantry Monument
39° 49.325' N, 77° 13.765' W

The primary monument to the 134th New York Infantry sits where the regiment was positioned on the second and third days of the battle. Earlier, the 134th was posted in the area now occupied by the National Cemetery. When a Confederate assault on

Cemetery Hill began on the evening of the second day, the regiment moved to this location. A small bronze tablet sits at the regiment's first position on Coster Avenue (see C-4).

The 134th was commanded by a Harvard Law School graduate, Lieutenant Colonel Allan H. Jackson, who would be wounded at Peachtree Creek a year later.

The regiment suffered 252 casualties at Gettysburg, including 42 killed, 151 wounded, and 59 missing.

The monument includes several symbols. A minie ball tops the entire structure. Also part of the monument are a bronze knapsack, a cartridge box, and the crescent insignia of the Eleventh Corps. Fabricated by Frederick and Field, the monument was dedicated July 2, 1888.

D-3: Monument to Battery I, First New York Light Artillery

39° 49.315′ N, 77° 13.744′ W

As Battery I was coming into Gettysburg, its men could see the Eleventh Corps already in the process of retreating. Most of the battery assumed a position on Cemetery Hill and remained there throughout the battle. One portion under Lieutenant Christopher Schmidt moved to a position west of the cemetery. From there, Schmidt's men took part in the artillery duel that preceded Pickett's Charge.

While the main body was on Cemetery Hill, it reported an incident similar to that experienced by the Twenty-seventh Pennsylvania (see D-1), in which an unknown officer appeared and gave an or-

der to cease its actions because the battery was firing into Union troops. After the officer disappeared, the suspicious men of the battery resumed their fire, knowing their targets were Confederates. The officer was believed to have been a Confederate in a Union uniform, although he was never captured.

Three of the battery's members were killed and ten wounded over the three-day battle. Several of the wounded were shot by sharpshooters who had taken a position in a church steeple in town; they also killed several of the battery's horses. One of the battery's gunners, despite orders to the contrary, fired a shell into the steeple and silenced the sharpshooters.

The unit was also known as Wiedrich's Battery, after its commander, Captain Michael Wiedrich. The monument, sculpted by William Lautz and fabricated by Lautz and Company, marks the position the battery held during the battle. It was dedicated May 20, 1889. The relief depicts a battery loading a cannon.

D-4: Seventy-third Pennsylvania Infantry Monument

39° 49.312′ N, 77° 13.753′ W

On July 1, the Seventy-third Pennsylvania arrived on the field, taking a position on Cemetery Hill. Within an hour, the men were sent to the center of town to provide support for the chaotic retreat of the Eleventh Corps. They then returned to Cemetery Hill, serving as a reserve unit positioned in Evergreen Cemetery.

The next day, still in reserve, they were called to assist in defending Ricketts's and Wiedrich's batteries. Within a short time, they found themselves going from the relative safety of standing in reserve to vicious hand-to-hand fighting.

Their actions that day on East Cemetery Hill are re-created in the plaque on the front of their monument. The crescent on top of the marker reflects their affiliation with the Eleventh Corps. The inscription on the left side of the monument lists regimental losses, while a similar inscription on the right side lists the engagements in which the regiment participated.

Under the command of Captain Daniel F. Kelly, the regiment suffered losses of seven killed and twenty-seven wounded at Gettysburg.

Sculpted by Alexander Milne Calder and fab-

ricated by Giles, Michael and Company, the monument was dedicated September 12, 1889.

D-5: Army of the Potomac Itinerary Tablets
39° 49.291′ N, 77° 13.777′ W

These nine bronze tablets are the Union counterpart of the itinerary tablets for the Army of Northern Virginia (see C-16). Installed by the War Department in the early 1900s, the tablets represent the activities of the Union army on each day from June 29 through July 7, 1863.

The tablets originally sat near the top of the hill, across from Evergreen Cemetery and facing Baltimore Pike. They were eventually removed. When replaced in 2008, they were moved a short distance and turned away from traffic to eliminate the possibility of vehicles slowing down to allow their occupants to read the markers, thus creating traffic congestion.

Reading the tablets for both armies will provide

visitors a deeper understanding of the battle and the days just before and after the fighting.

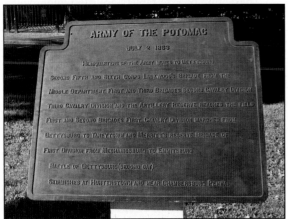

D-6: Seventh West Virginia Infantry Monument
39° 49.299' N, 77° 13.739' W

Rushed into battle at this location, the Seventh West Virginia immediately engaged with General Harry Hays's Louisiana brigade, which was close to capturing Wiedrich's Battery of the First New York Light Artillery. In the ensuing fight, the Seventh successfully drove the Louisiana troops back in a charge down the hill, saving the battery.

When it came time to design their monument, the survivors of the regiment insisted the figure be placed so it faced in the direction in which they fought, even though the front of the monument faced in the other direction. Thus, to the casual eye, the monument appears to be facing the wrong way.

West Virginia had been a state for only two weeks, having gained admission to the Union on June 20, 1863. Thus, the mountaineers were entering their first battle with their new name. They had been called the Seventh Virginia Infantry prior to West Virginia's statehood.

The Seventh West Virginia was commanded at Gettysburg by Lieutenant Colonel Jonathan H. Lockwood. It brought 319 men to the field, of whom five were killed, 41 wounded, and one declared missing. Lockwood was among the wounded. He also had his horse shot from under him.

The monument shows a soldier in his winter coat, holding his rifle in front of him. On the front of the base is the slogan "Sons of the Mountains." The monument was fabricated by W. E. Spragg Granite and Marble Works. It was dedicated September 28, 1898, and rededicated October 3, 1998.

D-7: Ricketts's Battery Monument
39° 49.295′ N, 77° 13.723′ W

Officially designated the First Pennsylvania Light Artillery, Batteries F and G, the unit carried the name of its commander, Captain R. Bruce Ricketts. The two undermanned batteries were joined just weeks before the battle to make one complete battery.

It moved onto East Cemetery Hill the afternoon of July 2 and engaged the Army of Northern Virginia that evening. In the gathering darkness, the men of the Fifty-fourth and Sixty-eighth New York infantries retreated in a panic, unknowingly rushing in front of the battery's guns. The cannoneers of Ricketts's Battery continued firing, inadvertently killing several of the New Yorkers with friendly canister fire. The battle became so fierce that the battery soon depleted its ammunition, forcing the men to use rammers and handspikes to defend their guns in deadly hand-to-hand combat.

Ricketts's Battery consisted of three officers and 141 men. Of those, seven men were killed, one officer and 13 men were wounded, and three men were captured or missing.

The monument features a bas-relief of two cannoneers manning their positions at their gun. The designer and contractor was Smith Granite Company. The monument was dedicated July 2, 1894, thirty-one years to the day after the unit's brutal fight.

D-8: Monument to Battery B, First Pennsylvania Light Artillery
39° 49.282' N, 77° 13.721' W

Commanded by Captain James H. Cooper, this unit was often referred to as Cooper's Battery B. It had 114 officers and men at Gettysburg and suffered three killed and nine wounded. Post-battle reports proudly mentioned that many others members were also wounded but that Captain Cooper never reported any man as such as long as he was still able to fight.

The battery arrived at Gettysburg at noon on the first day of the battle, taking a position near Willoughby Run. It then moved to its right so the men could fire at Oak Hill, after which they relocated to the area of the seminary, where they fought until Captain Cooper received word that the infantry on his left had moved out and that he should relocate his guns or be captured. The message came just in time for Cooper to move his men to this position on Cemetery Hill, where they remained until the next

Original marker

day, when they were relieved at about seven in the evening by Ricketts's Battery after Cooper's men ran out of ammunition. Just before being relieved, the men were using ammunition borrowed from an adjoining battery.

Many of the battery's casualties resulted from a single incident on July 2, when a Confederate shell exploded under one of the guns, killing two and wounding three. Not long afterward, the axle of the battery's number 2 gun was struck by a shell and broken. The crew continued firing until the carriage collapsed.

On July 3, the battery moved under fire to the front line of Cemetery Ridge, where it participated in the artillery duel. When Pickett's Charge drew nearer, the battery used double charges of canister against General Cadmus Wilcox's Alabama brigade, opening up huge gaps in the Confederate line.

The battery's four guns fired 1,050 rounds of ammunition during the battle.

A small marker, now illegible, is the original monument to the battery. It was placed in 1879.

The large monument to Cooper's Battery was fabricated by Sholl and Robinson and dedicated September 11, 1889.

D-9: Unknown Remains from Railroad Cut

39° 49.248' N, 77° 13.863' W

In March 1996, human bones were observed on the embankment of the Railroad Cut in the vicinity of the flank markers for the Ninety-fifth New York and Sixth Wisconsin infantries, following a heavy rain that washed out the surrounding fill. Portions of a left humerus and ulna, a left femur, a right tibia, a portion of a jaw, pieces of a skull, and other, smaller bone pieces were found. The size of the femur indicated a male, and the maturity of the bones and the progress of cranial sutures placed the age at between twenty and forty. The remains were the first unearthed at Gettysburg since 1939, when the bones of a soldier from General Cadmus Wilcox's Confederate brigade were found on the Klingel Farm along Emmitsburg Road.

Despite efforts to determine the identity of the more recent remains and which regiment the man fought for, he remains an unknown soldier. Material

D-10: Remembrance Day Flags and Luminaries
39° 49.189′ N, 77° 13.919′ W

Every year on the weekend closest to the dedication date of the National Cemetery, Remembrance Weekend honors those who fought at Gettysburg.

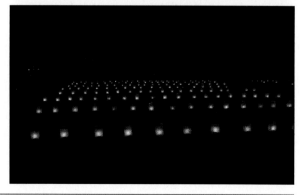

found with the bones indicated he was more likely a Confederate, possibly from the Second Mississippi Infantry, although that is not definite.

Over the years, partial remains of nine other soldiers had been collected from various parts of the battlefield. Never identified but believed to be both Confederate and Union troops, they were buried collectively in a vault in 1991. Those remains were subsequently placed in the same casket with the remains found in 1996.

On July 1, 1997, all the remains were given a proper burial. The Third United States Infantry Honor Guard from Arlington National Cemetery carried the casket while a crowd of more than fifteen hundred watched in a drizzle. Present in the crowd were two honored guests, Daisy Anderson of Denver, Colorado, and Alberta Martin of Elba, Alabama. The two were widows of Civil War veterans. Each placed a long-stemmed red rose on the casket.

The arrow indicates the location of the grave in the small row of markers.

Marked by parades, ceremonies, and the authentic Civil War Ball with its reenactors in period uniforms and dresses, the event draws thousands to the town.

Among the events held in the National Cemetery is the placement of flags and luminaries on every Civil War soldier's grave. Many state flags are also placed, usually by reenacting groups representing regiments from those particular states. Remembrance Day is one of the most popular events on the Gettysburg calendar.

D-11: First Minnesota Infantry Monument
39° 49.169′ N, 77° 13.916′ W

This marble urn sits at the head of the Minnesota section of the National Cemetery. The First Minnesota was the only regiment from the state to fight at Gettysburg, and it represented its state well. After a heroic charge during the second day of fighting, its men found their ranks decimated but continued to fight. They then gave another good account of themselves the next day in helping repel Pickett's Charge.

The regiment was first commanded at Gettysburg by Colonel William Colville, who had been wounded a year earlier at Frazier's Farm in Virginia. He was wounded again at Gettysburg on the second day of fighting. When Colville fell, he was replaced by Captain Nathan S. Messick, who was killed the next day. Captain Henry C. Coates took command of the regiment after that.

Placed in 1867 by the surviving members of the

regiment and dedicated to their fallen comrades, the urn was the first regimental monument anywhere on the battlefield. The inscription on the urn, "All time is the millennium of their glory," was taken from Edward Everett's speech at the dedication of the National Cemetery in 1863.

This is one of three Gettysburg monuments to the First Minnesota. The best known among them (39° 48.396′ N, 77° 14.102′ W) is discussed in Volume 1. The remaining monument shows the regiment's location during the July 3 fighting (see K-3).

D-12: Monument to Battery H, First United States Artillery
39° 49.162′ N, 77° 13.874′ W

Commanded by Lieutenant Chandler P. Eaken, Battery H of the First United States Artillery held a position at this approximate location on July 2 and 3. When Eaken was severely wounded in the fighting, command fell to Lieutenant Philip D. Mason. Eaken

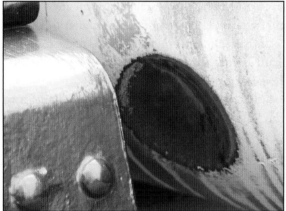

the gun sometime during the battle. Also note that the marking on the tube indicates that it was made at Revere Copper Company, started by none other than Paul Revere following the Revolutionary War.

The monument was manufactured by Van Armitage Granite Company and dedicated September 14, 1907.

D-13: Witness Tree and Sickles Fence
39° 49.067′ N, 77° 13.893′ W

Witness trees are so named because they were already growing at the time of the battle, and thus "witnessed" the fighting. Several still dot the landscape of Gettysburg. This particular witness tree, a honey locust, sits in the National Cemetery. Although it suffered storm damage in 2008, it stands tall and appears to be recovering. Most of the damage was to the upper part of the tree, where an estimated 70 percent of the growth was blown off.

Many of the witness trees at Gettysburg can be identified by their small brass tags. Others have grounding cables running down the trunks to provide lightning protection.

The iron fence behind this witness tree separates the National Cemetery from Evergreen Cemetery. It originally stood in Lafayette Square in Washington, D.C. While it may appear to be "just a fence," it has an interesting history.

Philip Barton Key was the son of Francis Scott Key, who wrote "The Star-Spangled Banner." In 1859,

had also been wounded at Williamsburg.

Also known as Randol's Battery, Battery H suffered one man killed, one officer (Eaken) and seven men wounded, and one man missing.

An interesting feature of the gun sitting on the site is the dent in the cannon tube, or barrel, indicated in the photo by the arrow. The dent is shown in close-up in the second photo. It is believed to have been made by a Confederate artillery shell that struck

the younger Key was having an affair with Teresa Sickles, the wife of Congressman Dan Sickles. When he learned of the affair, Sickles confronted Key. The furious Sickles, who could claim his own share of lurid affairs, shot Key several times, mortally wounding him. Key fell against the fence that now sits behind the witness tree.

When Sickles went to trial for murder, his defense team insisted he had been temporarily insane. That defense, common today, had never been offered before, and it served Sickles well. He was declared innocent.

During the Civil War, Sickles, by then a Union general, gained further notoriety for his decision to move his Third Corps into the Peach Orchard at Gettysburg, despite his orders to position his troops about a mile farther back, at the south end of Cemetery Ridge. The result was a large gap in the Union line that the Confederates exploited.

In 1888, it was determined that the fence surrounding Lafayette Square was no longer needed. Sickles urged Congress to give it to the town of Gettysburg rather than scrap it. A joint resolution of Congress approved the request. As a result, many even today refer to it as the "Sickles Fence."

D-14: First Massachusetts Light Battery Monument
39° 49.065′ N, 77° 13.895′ W

The First Massachusetts Light Battery occupied this position on July 3. The unit was assigned to the area at about four o'clock that afternoon, by which time the fighting had nearly concluded. As a result, the men fired only four shots at Gettysburg. They suffered no casualties, except for several horses lost on the march.

After the Battle of Cedar Creek on October 19, 1864, the battery was absorbed by the Fifth United

States Artillery for a short period, then transferred to the Ninth Massachusetts Battery, in which the men completed their term of service.

On the back of the monument is the Greek cross, symbol of the Sixth Corps. Above it is an artillery symbol. Palm fronds form a wreath around both. Fabricated by William Van Armitage for Smith Granite Company at a cost of $550, the monument was dedicated October 8, 1885. Its carvers were Dan Kelleher and John Carney, its letter cutter was Frank McNelly, and its stonecutters were George H. Sweeney and Sam Slocum.

D-15: First New Hampshire Battery Monument
39° 49.081′ N, 77° 13.929′ W

This unit was the only light battery furnished by the state of New Hampshire in the Civil War.

Under Captain Frederick M. Edgell, the First New Hampshire Battery occupied this ground on July 2, arriving on the field in midmorning and moving here in late afternoon. Edgell's Battery replaced Captain James A. Hall's Second Maine Battery, which had been posted here on the evening of July 1 but had been disabled.

The First immediately came under heavy fire, but not from its front. The incoming fire was from its left, and the guns had to be turned to redirect their fire. In about forty minutes, the opposing battery was silenced.

That evening, the battery relocated just south of Evergreen Cemetery when Confederate assaults threatened that area. Its orders were to cover a possible Union retreat. When no retreat became necessary, the battery remained in position without firing a round.

At about two-thirty the next afternoon, the battery returned to its original position, from which it participated in the repulse of Pickett's Charge.

Despite the heavy fire, the battery had only four men wounded, two of whom suffered minor injuries. Three of the battery's horses were killed, and a wheel and axle on one of its guns were broken. The wheel and axle were repaired on the field the next day. In the two days the battery was on the field, it fired 353 rounds of ammunition.

The monument was dedicated July 3, 1912.

CULP'S HILL

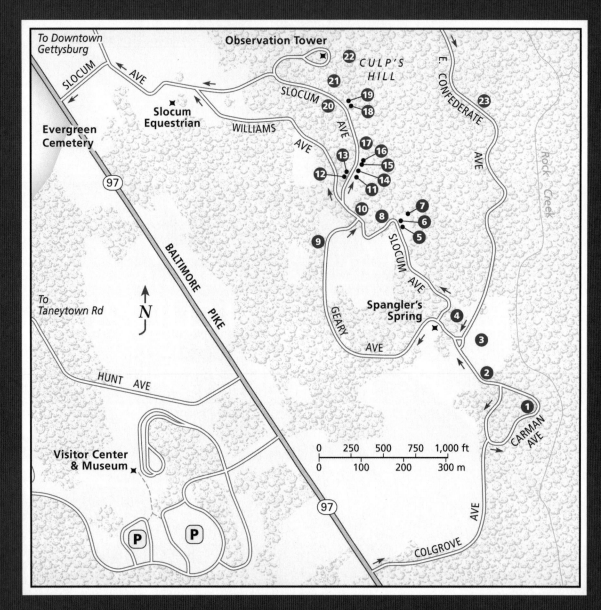

To Downtown Gettysburg

Observation Tower

CULP'S HILL

SLOCUM AVE

Evergreen Cemetery

Slocum Equestrian

WILLIAMS AVE

E. CONFEDERATE AVE

Rock Creek

97

To Taneytown Rd

N

BALTIMORE PIKE

GEARY AVE

Spangler's Spring

SLOCUM AVE

CARMAN AVE

HUNT AVE

Visitor Center & Museum

P   P

97

COLGROVE AVE

0	250	500	750	1,000 ft
0	100	200	300 m	

As the first day's fighting drew to a close, Union troops took defensive positions immediately upon their arrival on the battlefield. Soon, a long line extended along Cemetery Ridge from Cemetery Hill to Little Round Top, a distance of nearly three miles, the line taking the form of a fishhook. On a small rise that ran roughly parallel to Cemetery Ridge a mile to the west, Confederate troops were setting up their own position along Seminary Ridge and into town, forming a six-mile-long arc.

Lee's plan of attack for the second day called for General Richard Ewell to strike the Union right at Culp's Hill, the point of the fishhook, while General James Longstreet attacked the Union left. At approximately four in the afternoon on July 2, Ewell began by launching a cannonade. However, Union artillery quickly responded with a barrage of its own, and many of the Confederate batteries were soon forced to retire.

At dusk, Major General Edward Johnson's division began to move onto Culp's Hill. Unbeknownst to Johnson, many of the Union troops had been moved off Culp's Hill to reinforce the left of the Union line as Longstreet's assault unfolded. As a result, the hill was only weakly defended.

Brigadier General George Greene extended his Union line to provide as much defense as possible. In the darkness, his men released a deadly fire into the ranks of the unsuspecting Confederates. Soon, the battle was in full swing. Johnson had no idea he was facing a small force. Believing he was outnumbered, he opted to wait until morning to continue his attack.

To his left, in the Spangler's Spring area, Confederate forces under Brigadier General George "Maryland" Steuart were more successful, overrunning Union breastworks and capturing many prisoners and their colors. By midnight, the fight for Culp's Hill drew to a close.

As Union troops returned to the positions they had held before being sent to defend their left, they found their breastworks now occupied by Confederates. At four in the morning on July 3, the battle resumed, the returning troops attacking the now-entrenched Southerners. The fighting raged for several hours, the two armies coming within a few yards of one another. Finally, the Sixty-sixth Ohio left its trenches and swept down the face of the hill in a courageous move that drove the Confederates back. Other Southern troops, seeing their companions in retreat, followed suit.

By late morning, the fight for Culp's Hill drew to a close. The hill was still in Union hands. The exhausted Confederates withdrew, setting the stage for what would become the deciding assault of the battle.

In this same area sit several monuments discussed in Volume 1. Across the road from the Twenty-seventh Indiana Infantry Monument is the monument to the Second Massachusetts Infantry. The two regiments charged together on July 3, each suffering extensive casualties. The state of Indiana erected a memorial in Spangler Meadow, where the advance marker of the Twenty-seventh shows how far that regiment got before being forced to retreat. The famous Spangler's Spring, provider of water to both sides, is just to the left of the intersection. To the right a short walk down East Confederate Avenue, visitors can look for a boulder with the name of Augustus Coble of the First North Carolina carved in it, marking the spot where Private Coble fought that day.

Above Spangler's Spring, visitors can take the road to the left to see Pardee Field, the scene of ferocious fighting. The road to the right leads to the Twenty-ninth Pennsylvania Monument, which sits across from the Second Maryland Infantry (Confederate) Monument. At the intersection where the road splits again is a monument featuring the figure of General John Geary. The monument wasn't dedicated until ninety-two years after it was erected. The interesting monument honoring the Seventy-eighth and 102nd New York infantries sits on the right side of Slocum Avenue. Children will enjoy looking for the animal on the monument, disguised among the rocks that protect the soldier.

At the top of Culp's Hill, sitting below the observation tower, is the monument to General George Greene. Although his story is not well known, even Confederate general James Longstreet complimented Greene, who many believed saved Culp's Hill for the Union. Proceeding down the hill, visitors will reach Stevens Knoll and the equestrian statue honoring General Henry Slocum. Volume 1 reveals Slocum's nickname and how he got it. Also on Stevens Knoll is the small marker for the Twenty-fourth Michigan Infantry. Its inscription tells the story of Gettysburg all too vividly.

E-1: Thirteenth New Jersey Infantry Monument
39° 48.778′ N, 77° 12.883′ W

Featuring a bas-relief of an infantryman in battle, the monument to the Thirteenth New Jersey is located where the regimental colors stood on July 3. Although it arrived on the field late in the afternoon on July 1 and occupied positions at Wolf Hill, Culp's Hill, and Little Round Top over the course of the three days of battle, the regiment opted to position its monument where it supported the effort to drive Confederate troops off Culp's Hill the morning of the third day.

Colonel Ezra Carmen, commander of the regiment, became active with the Antietam Battlefield Board after the war. He is credited with being the driving force behind getting the many descriptive War Department tablets placed on that battlefield. He was also instrumental in setting up markers at Shiloh and Chickamauga.

At Gettysburg, the regiment lost two men killed and nineteen wounded.

A unique feature of the Thirteenth's monument is that it was designed entirely by members of the regiment. Built by Smith Granite Company, it was dedicated July 1, 1887, the twenty-fifth anniversary of the opening of the battle.

Sixteen-year-old lieutenant Franklin Murphy of Company A, who told the enlistment officer he was eighteen so he could join the army, survived the war and went on to serve as governor of New Jersey.

E-2: Twenty-seventh Indiana Infantry Monument
39° 48.811' N, 77° 12.957' W

On the final day of fighting, an order was given for an ill-fated charge across what is known today as Spangler Meadow. With the Second Massachusetts, the Twenty-seventh Indiana made that charge despite knowing it was suicidal. Confederate troops oc-

cupied the hillside to the left of the meadow, as well as the ground at the far end. Within minutes, nearly one-third of the Twenty-seventh was cut down. One hundred ten men were killed or wounded and another was declared missing out of 339 who entered the advance. Eight color bearers were among the casualties.

Under Colonel Silas Colgrove, the brigade commander, the regiment was forced back. Its monument marks the area over which its left wing made the attack. The boulder on which the monument stands provided cover for many of the wounded.

Nearby Colgrove Avenue was named for Colonel Colgrove.

The monument was erected in 1885 at a cost of five hundred dollars. It was dedicated October 28 of

that year. The bronze plaque on the back of the monument summarizing the unit's casualties was added later.

E-3: Twenty-seventh Indiana Infantry Advance
39° 48.856' N, 77° 12.961' W

The Twenty-seventh Indiana began its farthest advance in the attack across Spangler Meadow at the location of the monument indicated by the arrow on the right of the photo. It fought its way to the site of the small marker pointed out by the arrow on the left. Confederates belonging to the brigades of Brigadier General George "Maryland" Steuart and Brigadier General James Walker were positioned behind the small stone wall at the end of the meadow and among the boulders of Culp's Hill, giving the Hoosiers little chance for success.

In a poorly coordinated attack with the Second Massachusetts Infantry, the men of the Twenty-seventh reluctantly pushed forward, only to be struck by musket fire from three sides. The regiment stood in this open field, exchanging fire with the well-entrenched Confederates. Within minutes, the regiment was pushed back, suffering heavy losses. Four color bearers were among the dead.

The Forty-ninth and Fifty-second Virginia infantries unwisely launched a counterattack into the open field as the two Union regiments retreated. Second Lieutenant David C. Van Buskirk of the Twenty-seventh Indiana's Company F, believed at nearly seven feet to be the tallest soldier in the Union army, was captured at this location. However, the Confederates could not hold their positions. They, too, were forced back.

When the action in this area ended, both sides occupied the same ground they had when the fight began.

E-4: First Maryland (Union) Monument
39° 48.884' N, 77° 13.003' W

Under the command of Colonel William P. Maulsby, the First Maryland arrived late in the afternoon on the second day of fighting and quickly made a name for itself, launching a charge and recapturing three artillery pieces. In an amazing display of compassion, Assistant Surgeon James Willard was said to have remained on the field throughout the night, ignoring his own safety and treating the wounded where they lay until they could be removed to field hospitals.

This monument is positioned where the First Maryland, also known as the First Potomac Home Brigade, Maryland Infantry, fought in the predawn hours of July 3. In late morning, the regiment moved to assist the Second Division of the Twelfth Corps, fighting steadily for four more hours.

The First Maryland lost 104 men at Gettysburg. Of those, 23 were killed, 80 wounded, and one declared missing.

The monument was damaged in 1894 and repaired in 1902. The slogan "Maryland's Tribute to Her Loyal Sons" appears on all the state's Union monuments, referring to those who remained loyal to Maryland and the Union.

The monument's sculptor and fabricator are unknown. The monument was dedicated October 25, 1888.

E-5: 123rd New York Infantry Monument
39° 48.993' N, 77° 13.092' W

The monument to the 123rd New York is unusual in that it does not depict an event of the battle or a member of the regiment. Instead, it features a female figure representing Clio, the muse of history from Greek mythology. Clio is shown recording the events of the battle. Titled *History Recording*, the monument was designed by Smith Granite Company and sculpted by J. G. Hamilton. It was dedicated September 4, 1888.

Under Lieutenant Colonel James C. Rogers while Colonel Archibald McDougall was in command of the brigade, the regiment arrived at Wolf Hill on July 1 and moved to this area the next day. The monument sits where the regiment built heavy breastworks of logs and dirt on the second day of the battle. That evening, it moved to support the Union left near Little Round Top. When the men returned, they found that Confederate troops had moved into the fortifications. Late the next morning, the New Yorkers charged and recovered their breastworks. The remains of the breastworks are still visible behind the monument. A small marker about a hundred yards below the monument marks the position of the regiment's skirmish line ahead of the charge.

The 123rd spent little time in the cover of the protection it had constructed, however. After only a few hours, it was ordered to Cemetery Ridge, where it assisted in the repulse of Pickett's Charge.

The 123rd New York, also known as the Washington County Regiment, spent the next day, July 4, on reconnaissance duty. It lost three killed, ten wounded, and one missing at Gettysburg.

During the fighting, Private Thomas J. Wrangham of Company C was on the picket line. As the pickets fell back and Wrangham attempted to climb over the breastworks, a bullet struck the brass plate on his cartridge box. It passed through the brass plate, the thick leather flap, the box itself, and his cartridges, then lodged in the leather cover next to his hip. Wrangham escaped the bullet without a scratch but was no doubt a bit shaken.

The regiment absorbed a portion of the 145th New York Infantry in December 1863.

E-6: Second Maryland Infantry (Confederate) Monument
39° 49.002' N, 77° 13.098' W

Originally known as the First Maryland Battalion (Confederate), this unit served in General Richard Ewell's Second Corps. Its monument stands at the approximate location where it broke through the Union line on July 2. It captured and held the position until repulsed with the rest of the Confederate line late in the morning on July 3.

In October 1884, the regiment's survivors sought and received permission from the Gettysburg Battlefield Memorial Association to erect a monument to show their position during the battle. Union veterans immediately protested, one of their arguments being that it would create confusion because two Union regiments with similar names—the First Maryland, Eastern Shore (see E-19), and the First Maryland, Potomac Home Brigade—fought nearby. A compromise was reached in which the Confederate regiment, seeing no other way to get its monument, reluctantly agreed to change its name to the Second Maryland Infantry, CSA. That change is noted on the base of the monument.

On all four sides of the monument is the Baltimore cross, included because most of the regiment's members were recruited from the Baltimore area.

The monument was fabricated from Richmond

granite by Flaharty and Rummel. Dedication took place November 19, 1886. The first Confederate marker placed at Gettysburg, this is the only monument on the battlefield built by a Confederate veterans' organization. A small marker about 120 yards in front of the monument (39° 48.988′ N, 77° 13.170′ W) marks the battalion's farthest advance into Pardee Field.

The battalion was commanded by Lieutenant Colonel James Herbert until he was wounded on July 2. Command then fell to Major William Goldsborough, who was also shortly wounded. Captain John W. Torsch then led the battalion until relieved by Captain James P. Crane. It brought 400 men to the field in eight companies, losing 56 killed, 118 wounded, and 15 missing. Many of the casualties occurred in an ill-advised bayonet charge against a strong Union position late in the morning on July 3.

Among those killed was the battalion's mascot, a small dog named Grace. Ordering his men to bury Grace, war-weary Union brigadier general Thomas Kane remarked that she was "the only Christian-minded being on either side."

In a cruel twist of fate, the First Maryland Battalion (CSA) met the First Maryland, Eastern Shore (Union), at this general location. Nothing better illustrates how this was truly a brothers' war. The opposing color sergeants, Robert Ross and P. M. Moore, were cousins. Moore, the Confederate color sergeant, was wounded and captured by his former neighbors.

E-7: Confederate Grave
39° 49.010′ N, 77° 13.083′ W

Directly behind the Second Maryland Infantry (Confederate) Monument (see E-6) lie the remains of what are believed to be a Confederate soldier.

Based on the location, he was likely a member of the Second Maryland. His name has been lost to history. The site is lovingly maintained in excellent condition by visitors.

While not an official cemetery, the entire battlefield may contain many similar resting places still to be found. Visitors are asked to respect not only this burial site but all areas of the battlefield.

Because of the heavy fire, it moved one man at a time in changing locations, using an average of 160 rounds of ammunition for each man.

Of the 259 officers and men brought into the battle, six were killed and one officer and 16 men wounded.

On July 4, the regiment assisted in burying the dead, at which time the men found a large number of Confederate soldiers lying just in front of the breastworks.

In March 1865, the regiment was merged with the 109th Pennsylvania Infantry.

Ryegate Granite Company fabricated this monument. The engagements in which the regiment participated are listed on the back. The monument was dedicated September 11, 1889.

E-8: 111th Pennsylvania Infantry Monument
39° 49.006′ N, 77° 13.126′ W

Having enlisted just six months before the battle, the 111th Pennsylvania Infantry arrived on the field on July 1 and took a position on the left of Baltimore Pike. Commanded by Lieutenant Colonel Thomas M. Walker, the regiment moved to Culp's Hill the next morning. Like the rest of the Twelfth Corps, the men of the 111th built breastworks in this area, only to find them occupied by Confederate troops when they returned after being withdrawn to assist on the left of the line. A fight of nearly eight hours resulted in the regiment's regaining its works the next morning.

E-9: Fifth Ohio Infantry Monument
39° 48.972′ N, 77° 13.221′ W

The Fifth Ohio Infantry was positioned in a wood lot near the site of its monument early in the morning on July 2 when artillery fire erupted. The regiment moved a short distance and was relatively unharmed until late in the afternoon, when several men were wounded as they lay on the ground. At sunset, the regiment moved to the right, where it served on picket duty until about midnight, when it returned to its original position in the woods.

The next morning, the regiment engaged in fighting in the area now marked by the monument. Late in the afternoon, however, it came under heavy

artillery fire. Although in the direct line of fire, the regiment again emerged relatively unscathed. Over the entire battle, it suffered losses of only two men killed and six wounded out of 315 present for duty. The regiment took part in the pursuit of Lee's army as it retreated southward.

The monument to the Fifth Ohio Infantry sits where the regiment fought on the morning of the third day of the battle. It contains a relief of a Union flag crossed with a musket. A star, the insignia of the Twelfth Corps, appears on each face of the monument's cap. Displayed on the top of the monument are two knapsacks leaning against one another. An owl, the regiment's mascot, appears beneath the apex formed by the knapsacks. The back of the monument lists the major engagements in which the regiment fought.

The boulder behind the monument contains a plaque symbolizing the regimental badge. It features an owl and the regiment's motto: "Boys, Keep the Colors Up." Visitors who look closely may be able to discern the remains of the old Spangler Farm lane in front of the boulder. Union troops used the lane to get from Baltimore Pike to their positions on Culp's Hill.

Because the recruiting station for the Fifth Ohio was at the public landing in Cincinnati, the regiment was also known as the Cincinnati Regiment. Reflecting the steamboat activity in the area, most of those who mustered in were steamboat workers such as cabin boys, stevedores, and cooks.

The Fifth was reactivated in 1898 and served in the Spanish-American War. The regiment was placed in the Seventh Army Corps, which ironically was commanded by Major General Fitzhugh Lee, the former Confederate general.

The artist and fabricator of the monument was J. McElwaine. Dedication took place September 14, 1887.

E-10: 109th Pennsylvania Infantry Monument

39° 49.016' N, 77° 13.158' W

The 109th Pennsylvania was also known as the Curtin Guards, after Governor Andrew Curtin. On July 2, it built the breastworks seen around the monument. Withdrawn with the rest of their brigade that evening, the men found their works occupied by Confederate troops when they returned later that night. Fighting took place throughout the night. The next morning, after a brutal fight, they recaptured their works and remained there for the rest of the battle.

In a report afterward, the regiment noted that the ground in front of Company A was steeply sloped, making it difficult to see the enemy. The men of the company were forced to take turns running forward to a large tree, firing their shots, and rushing back so the next man could have his turn. This constant fire, interrupted only by the time needed for the next man to take his position, made the tree an obvious target for the Confederates. The side of the tree facing the Southerners was said to have been completely stripped of its bark by their bullets.

The regiment took 149 officers and men into the battle, losing one color sergeant and two men killed, one color sergeant and five men wounded, and one man missing.

After the Gettysburg Campaign, the regiment was detached and sent to the Western theater to relieve Major General William S. Rosecrans's army at Chattanooga. In March 1865, it was merged with the 111th Pennsylvania Infantry.

The monument was fabricated by P. F. Eisenbrown and Sons. Dedication took place September 11, 1889.

E-11: 137th New York Infantry Monument

39° 49.054' N, 77° 13.170' W

By the time the 137th New York arrived at Gettysburg, it had lost nearly 50 percent of the men who had joined when it was formed just eight months earlier. Those losses came from deaths, illnesses, desertions, details on detached service, and the resignations of several officers.

Nicknamed "the Ironclads," the 137th was

known Twentieth Maine on the left flank (see I-8).

The 137th's casualties—40 killed, 187 wounded, and 10 missing—exceeded those of every other regiment in the Twelfth Corps. Although unscathed at Gettysburg, Colonel Ireland would die of dysentery a year after the battle.

The right side of the monument reflects the regiment's pride in what it accomplished throughout the war, stating that the 137th "holds a proud position in the history of the Great Rebellion."

Fabricated by Frederick and Field, the monument was dedicated in 1888.

E-12: Twenty-third Pennsylvania Infantry Monument
39° 49.054' N, 77° 13.186' W

Also known as Birney's Zouaves, after the regiment's first commander, General David Birney, the Twenty-third Pennsylvania was part of the retaking of Culp's Hill on July 3. Their nickname notwithstanding, the men wore the Zouave uniform only a short time, taking on the standard Union uniform early in the regiment's existence.

The regiment lost two officers and twenty-nine enlisted men killed and wounded. It had already suffered significantly on the march to Gettysburg in intense heat. Just two weeks before the battle, the division saw twenty-two of its men suffer sunstroke, six of whom died.

The men of the Twenty-third continued skirmishing on July 4. When they weren't fighting, they

commanded by Colonel David Ireland at Gettysburg. Its monument sits in the approximate location it held from July 2 until the close of the battle.

The 137th arrived at Two Taverns, Pennsylvania, on the morning of July 1 and received orders to move to the sound of the cannonade, to the left of the Union line, around three that afternoon. By the next morning, however, it had moved to the right of the line in the general area of the monument. The men immediately began building breastworks, which they completed by late afternoon. That evening, the regiment bore the brunt of an attack on that part of the line, mounting a bayonet charge at one point in a desperate effort to protect the right flank of the army. Its actions were eerily similar to those of the better-

retrieved their wounded and buried the dead. On July 5, the regiment was ordered in pursuit of Lee's army, engaging in a small skirmish on Chambersburg Pike five miles outside Gettysburg. That night while on picket duty, the regiment captured eighty-three Confederate troops.

Captain John Fassett of Company F was awarded the Medal of Honor in 1894 for his actions at Gettysburg, where he volunteered to lead a regiment on a mission to recapture a battery that had been taken by the Confederates.

When the time came for the regiment's survivors to erect their monument, there was considerable debate as to its location. One option was on Little Round Top, where the men had arrived on the field. Another was behind General George Meade's headquarters, where they were positioned during Pickett's Charge. The prevailing thought, however, was that the monument should sit where the men did their heaviest fighting, even though it was on a less prominent part of the battlefield. This Culp's Hill location was finally chosen, although some evidence exists that the monument originally sat near where the 137th New York's is now positioned.

The cross on the monument is the symbol of the Sixth Corps, while the blue color denotes the Third Division. The crossed flags on the front represent the national and state flags. The regiment had already erected its monument when the Pennsylvania legislature appropriated funds for the various state regiments to put their markers on the field. The original monument contained a stack of cannonballs where the figure of the soldier now stands. The regiment's Veteran's Association decided to use the money to replace those cannonballs with the soldier, rather than construct a new monument. The regiment's survivors chose to honor their secretary, William J. Wray, by using his likeness for the soldier. Wray, however, asked that he not be depicted because his face had been scarred after he was shot in the eye at Fredericksburg. As a compromise, another member of the regiment, Matthew Spence, posed for the head portion of the monument, while Wray's torso was used as the model for the rest. Spence's youthful appearance reflects the average age of the regiment, which at the time of their enlistment was only nineteen. The monument was designed by a member of the regiment.

The contractor for the statue was John Ferguson Marble and Granite Works. The base, constructed by

Bing and Cunningham, contains a small box holding some mementos contributed by members of the regiment. The monument enjoyed two dedication dates as a result of the change from the cannonballs to the statue. It was dedicated August 6, 1886. The altered monument was rededicated June 12, 1888.

E-13: Sixty-seventh New York Infantry Monument
39° 49.063' N, 77° 13.184' W

The monument to the Sixty-seventh New York sits in the area the regiment occupied on the morning of July 3. Better known as the First Long Island Volunteers or the Brooklyn Phalanx, the regiment was one of those charged with driving the Confederates off Culp's Hill that day. It was commanded by Colonel Nelson Cross, brother of Edward Cross, who was killed on the second day of fighting, and for whom Cross Avenue is named.

Titled *It Is Over*, the bronze plaque on the front of the monument depicts a soldier standing at parade rest in honor of the fallen. His position is known as "reverse arms." Around his feet can be seen the equipment of war, broken and no longer needed.

Casualties for the regiment were amazingly light. Only a single man was declared missing out of 356 who entered the battle.

Dedicated June 13, 1888, the monument was designed by Frederick and Field and sculpted by S. J. O'Kelley. The dedication address was given by the Reverend Thomas K. Beecher, who had officiated

at his friend Mark Twain's wedding in 1870. Beecher was the half-brother of Harriet Beecher Stowe, author of *Uncle Tom's Cabin*. Beecher also founded the American Bible Society.

The regiment consolidated with the Sixty-fifth New York Infantry in September 1864.

E-14: Twenty-ninth Ohio Infantry Monument
39° 49.063' N, 77° 13.164' W

The Twenty-ninth Ohio Infantry occupied several positions on Culp's Hill on July 2 and 3. Its monument is not representative of any particular location.

A bas-relief on the front depicts a camp tent with various weapons and other military symbols, including a drum, a knapsack, muskets with bayonets, a cartridge box, and a canteen. The cartridge box con-

tains an interesting and unexplained feature: the *S* on the front is carved backwards.

Another interesting feature is the inscription on the monument, which states that Captain Edward Hayes commanded the regiment, although Captain Wilbur F. Stevens was actually in charge until he was wounded on the third day of fighting. This discrepancy may have been politically motivated, as it is believed that Adjutant J. B. Storer and Stevens did not get along. Stevens had been wounded in 1862 at Cedar Mountain, Virginia, and left the field. Storer and others believed his wound to be minor. Storer may have used this as a reason to omit Stevens's name when the monument was designed.

The Twenty-ninth gained a level of fame by reenlisting more veterans than any other Ohio unit. Of its 332 men engaged in the fighting at Gettysburg, nine were killed or mortally wounded and 29 wounded. The regiment captured five Confederates as the fighting on Culp's Hill slowed down.

The Twenty-ninth was also known as the Giddings

Regiment, after Congressman Joshua Reed Giddings, who organized the unit. Some also referred to it as the Abolition Regiment because Giddings was a vocal abolitionist. Those who served in the regiment were screened to ensure that they held the same antislavery beliefs.

Sculpted by Patrick McGinn and fabricated by Ryegate Granite Company, the monument was dedicated September 14, 1887.

E-15: 122nd New York Infantry Monument
39° 49.071' N, 77° 13.160' W

The 122nd New York Infantry served in this location on July 3 and aided in the repulse of a Confederate assault that morning. The regiment was also known as the Third Onondaga, having been recruited in Onondaga County, New York. Commanded by Colonel Silas Titus, it suffered 15 killed or mortally wounded and two officers and 25 men less seriously

wounded, among the 456 men brought to the battle. Those numbers were taken from battle reports and the regimental history and do not agree with the inscription on the monument. The regiment captured 75 Confederates.

The monument was one of the earliest on the battlefield, having been placed just after Slocum Avenue was constructed and before most of the national park was designed.

Francis and Company fabricated the monument, which was dedicated June 13, 1888.

E-16: 149th New York Infantry Monument
39° 49.076' N, 77° 13.157' W

Although a monument to the 149th New York would probably have been erected eventually, its actual construction came about almost as an afterthought. Several years after the war, two former officers of the regiment, Captain George K. Collins and Major Orson Colville, visited Gettysburg and were disappointed to learn that few markers existed on Culp's Hill, and none to the 149th. They formed a monument committee to correct this oversight.

A design was decided on and a contract for the monument drawn up, only to be canceled when the regiment's men thought the contractor was deviating from the design. A second contract was awarded to Francis and Company.

Design suggestions from the 149th included one that would show the breastworks used by the regi-

ment. Another suggested that a statue of Sergeant William C. Lilly, the regiment's color bearer, be included. Both became part of the final design of the relief now seen on the front of the monument. The desired sketch was formalized in the design of Edwin Forbes, and the relief was sculpted by Ralph Cook, based on Forbes's drawing.

The relief depicts an event that occurred during the July 3 fighting. The regiment's flag received more than eighty bullet holes, and its shaft was shot into two pieces. In a brave attempt to capture the flag, a Confederate sergeant was shot five times and fell within two feet of reaching his goal. Sergeant Lilly, while under fire, repaired the damaged shaft with slats from a nearby cracker box and straps from his knapsack. He was slightly wounded when he replaced the flag on the breastworks. The plaque, appropriately titled *Mending the Flag under Fire*, depicts Lilly's actions.

Six men of the regiment were killed, 46 wounded, and three declared missing in the fight for Culp's Hill. Six members eventually received the Medal of Honor, although no medals were awarded for actions at Gettysburg.

Francis and Company did the fabrication. The formal dedication was conducted September 18, 1892. Miss Helen Collins, a Daughter of the Regiment, did the unveiling. Her father, Captain George K. Collins of Company I, was one of those who had proposed the monument.

E-17: Breastworks
39° 49.096′ N, 77° 13.160′ W

Culp's Hill was the point of the well-known fishhook defensive line established by the Union. The hill was heavily wooded at the time of the battle, as it is now, although much of the undergrowth had been

E-18: 150th New York Infantry Monument
39° 49.145' N, 77° 13.175' W

While not apparent at first glance, the 150th New York Infantry Monument has significant symbolism. It is built of thirteen layers of stone, commemorating the original colonies that formed the Union. The stones are stacked in such a way that each holds the next layer in place. This construction is said to symbolize the unity and mutual respect between the regiment's officers and men. The structure itself represents what the regiment called a "tower of invincible strength." Intertwined laurel and oak leaves on the back of the monument represent the crowning of the citizen soldier. A plaque lists the names of those from the regiment who died at Gettysburg. A history of the regiment is on the front.

Colonel John Ketcham was commander of the 150th, also known as the Dutchess County Regiment, in honor of the county that was home to many of the men. Gettysburg was their first battle. The regiment gave a good account of itself. At one point, it made a bayonet charge past the base of Little Round Top and through the Wheatfield, capturing more than two hundred Confederates and three pieces of artillery. On another occasion, it joined the Thirty-ninth New York Infantry in a charge that resulted in the recapture of the guns of the Ninth Massachusetts Battery near the Trostle Farm.

Of the regiment's 609 men who entered the battle, seven were killed, 23 wounded, and 15 declared missing.

removed to allow the larger trees more room to grow to a harvestable size for lumber. The Union's First Corps spent much of the evening of July 1 building a line of log and earth breastworks, which were added to when the Twelfth Corps joined in. Earthen breastworks such as those shown in the photo are still visible in many places on Culp's Hill.

When the Union army relocated to support the left of the line during the evening of July 2, Confederate troops moved in. A fierce fight ensued, culminating with the Union retaking the breastworks. The breastworks in this photo were occupied by both sides.

As part of the National Park Service's plan to return the battlefield to its 1863 appearance, the breastworks have been repaired and restored. Visitors are asked to refrain from walking on them, to preserve their fragile state.

The sculptor of the monument was George Edwin Bissell. Fabrication was done by Van Wyck and Collins. The monument was dedicated September 17, 1889. The flag used to drape the monument was the one raised over Atlanta by General William Sherman's men after the capture of that Southern city in 1864. The unveiling of the monument was done by Colonel Ketcham's daughter.

E-19: Monument to First Maryland Infantry, Eastern Shore
39° 49.149' N, 77° 13.182' W

The quotation on the front of the monument to the First Maryland, Eastern Shore—"Maryland's Tribute to her Loyal Sons"—tells the sad story of a state divided. Maryland had troops on both sides of the battle line at Gettysburg. The monument is to one of five Northern regiments from the state. The reference to loyal sons appears on all of Maryland's Union monuments on all Civil War battlefields and refers only to those who served in the Union army.

The monument to the First Maryland, Eastern Shore, sits where the regiment fought on the morning of July 3. The breastworks behind the monument provided it protection. The bas-relief on the front shows a soldier in prone position, defending the breastworks. The monument is one of many on the battlefield that can truly be called a work of art.

Ironically, much of the regiment's fighting was against its counterparts from the First Maryland Battalion (Confederate), giving true meaning to the expression "brother against brother." Robert Ross, the color sergeant of the First Maryland, Eastern Shore, and Color Sergeant P. M. Moore of the Confederate battalion were cousins; Moore was wounded and captured by his former neighbors.

The First Maryland Infantry (Confederate)

changed its name to the Second Maryland Infantry, CSA (see E-6).

The commander of the First Maryland, Eastern Shore, was Colonel James Wallace, a lawyer, state legislator, and slave owner who resigned his commission in December 1863 over his disagreement with the enlistment of blacks to fight for the Union.

The regiment brought 583 men into the battle, of whom five were killed, 18 wounded, and two declared missing.

The monument, designed and built by Frederick and Field, was dedicated October 25, 1888.

E-20: Twenty-eighth Pennsylvania Infantry Monument
39° 49.150′ N, 77° 13.210′ W

Under the command of Captain John Flynn, the Twenty-eighth Pennsylvania Infantry arrived on the field in the middle of the afternoon on July 1. The next day, it moved to the Rock Creek area before returning to its original position early in the morning on July 3 after skirmishing throughout the day.

Smith Granite Company fabricated the monument, which was dedicated October 13, 1885, and rededicated September 11, 1889. The monument has been modified. The original had a kepi, or cap, resting on the top, where the star now stands. At some point, the kepi was relocated to the front portion of the monument base and the star was added. The star, the insignia of the Twelfth Corps, also appears on top of the kepi.

Also known as the Goldstream Regiment, the Twenty-eighth had 13 officers and 290 men at Gettysburg. Its casualties included six men killed or mortally wounded, one officer and 19 men wounded, and two men captured or missing. The breastworks erected by the regiment were credited with keeping the casualty rate low.

After the battle, the regiment assisted in burying the enemy's dead and gathered up five hundred Confederate muskets in front of the breastworks. The next day, the men of the Twenty-eighth, many without shoes, joined the pursuit of Lee's army, marching seventy-five miles before ending their chase.

A second monument is located along Rock Creek off East Confederate Avenue (39° 48.986′ N, 77° 12.876′ W) between the Twenty-seventh Indiana and the Forty-third North Carolina monuments, where the regiment skirmished the morning of July 2.

Another monument on Hancock Avenue (39° 48.868′ N, 77° 14.113′ W) honors Lieutenant John

Page Nicholson. Nicholson was active in veterans' affairs after the war and became chairman of the Gettysburg National Park Commission, serving from 1893 until 1922.

E-21: Sixtieth New York Infantry Monument

39° 49.175′ N, 77° 13.205′ W

On the afternoon of July 2, while resting behind the breastworks they had built, the men of the Sixtieth New York observed Southern troops moving into position. Five guns from a nearby battery swung into position and began firing, driving the Confederates back. In the brief fight, several cannoneers were wounded. Short-handed, the batteries were in danger of falling silent until several men from the Sixtieth who had some knowledge of artillery took their place.

That evening, both sides became active once more, and the Sixtieth received the order to advance. Almost immediately, the regiment captured fifty-six enemy troops, including two officers, along with a

Company I position marker

regimental flag and a brigade battle flag. The bodies of seven Confederate officers were found in front of the regiment's works. At one point, the men ran out of ammunition and fixed their bayonets, prepared to do whatever was necessary to hold their position.

The regiment, under the command of Colonel Abel Godard, had 11 men killed and 41 wounded, of whom one officer and six enlisted men subsequently died. The Sixtieth brought 273 men into the fight.

Frederick and Field fabricated the monument, which was dedicated July 2, 1888. The monument was relocated about thirty feet in October 1902 to better reflect the regiment's actual position.

A position marker for the regiment's Company I sits a short distance away (39° 49.170′ N, 77° 13.201′ W), marking the location where two members of the company were killed.

E-22: Sixty-sixth Ohio Infantry Monument

39° 49.205′ N, 77° 13.178′ W

Early in the morning on July 3, a furious fight took place on Culp's Hill as Union troops struggled to retake positions they had held just a few hours earlier. Near the summit, Louisiana men under Brigadier General Francis Nicholls advanced under heavy fire, getting within thirty feet of the Union line. The Sixty-sixth Ohio rushed down the slope, pushing the Confederates from the face of the hill. The regiment occupied this position just prior to advancing toward the Confederates on the slope.

The Sixty-sixth was commanded at Gettysburg by Colonel Eugene Powell. A machinist in civilian life, Powell had been wounded at Antietam.

The regiment had only one man killed and 17 wounded of the 316 engaged. The man killed was Major Joshua G. Palmer. The site of his death is marked by its own stone just a short distance away (39° 49.206′ N, 77° 13.167′ W). Major Palmer, thirty-four years old, was a dentist in civilian life in his hometown of Urbana, Ohio, and had been instrumental in raising the regiment's Company B.

Fabricated by J. McElwaine, the monument was supposed to have been dedicated September 14, 1887. However, it arrived too late, and the dedication took place several days later. The monument to the Sixty-sixth has suffered from the elements over the years, having been toppled by heavy winds on two occasions. In September 1896, the shaft was recut and the pieces replaced; the work took until July 1899. In 1987, repairs were again needed when another windstorm knocked the shaft from its base.

E-23: Forty-third North Carolina Infantry Monument
39° 49.114' N, 77° 12.830' W

Under the command of Colonel Thomas Stephen Kenan, the Forty-third North Carolina Infantry arrived at Gettysburg on the morning of July 1. By early afternoon, it was positioned on open ground,

where it had little protection against the heavy fire it encountered. As a result, the Forty-third suffered heavily in the first day's fighting and spent the late afternoon and evening regrouping and preparing for the next day.

On July 2, the regiment was positioned just north of the Lutheran Seminary, where it supported a battery. It took more casualties as it came under fire from nearby Union artillery. Early in the evening, the Forty-third moved to the southern edge of town. The next morning, it relocated to the left and took part in the assault on Culp's Hill, where it temporarily took possession of abandoned earthworks.

As the men pushed forward, they received severe fire in the form of canister, shrapnel, and shell at short range. Colonel Kenan was wounded, after which Lieutenant Colonel William G. Lewis took command for the remainder of the battle. Pushed from Culp's Hill, the regiment returned to the area around the marker, remaining in the low area behind

the site of the monument for the rest of the afternoon. Early that evening, it recrossed Rock Creek in the retreat to Virginia.

The regiment brought 572 officers and men to the battle and lost 149 killed, wounded, and missing. The slogan on its monument reads, "All that men could do, was done nobly."

This is one of the newer monuments on the field, having been erected by the state of North Carolina and dedicated in 1988.

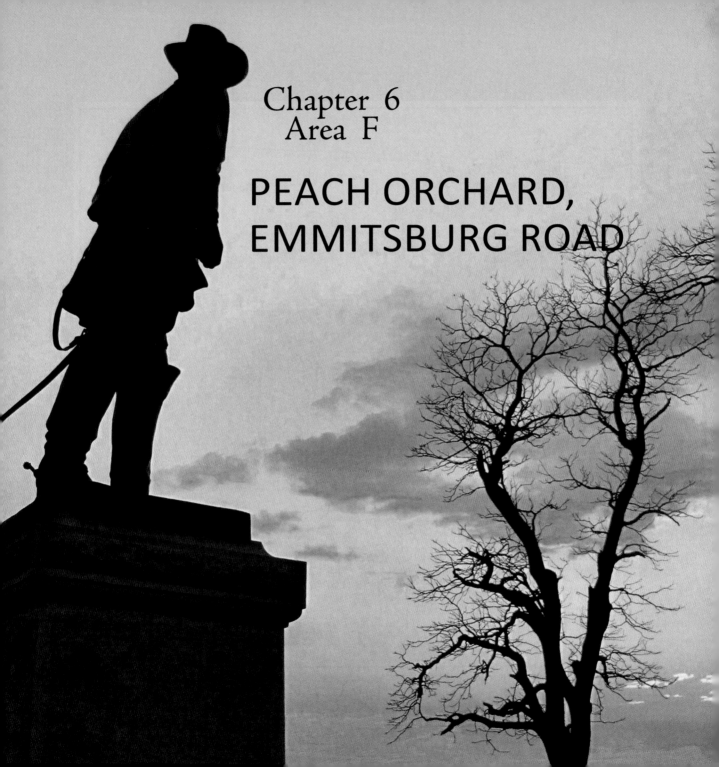

Chapter 6
Area F

PEACH ORCHARD, EMMITSBURG ROAD

Area F

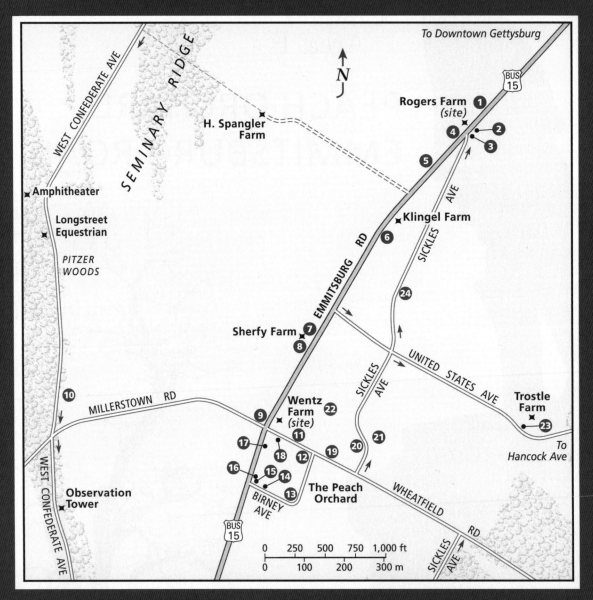

To Downtown Gettysburg

BUS 15

WEST CONFEDERATE AVE

SEMINARY RIDGE

H. Spangler Farm

Rogers Farm *(site)* 1
4 2
3

Amphitheater

Longstreet Equestrian

PITZER WOODS

5

Klingel Farm 6

SICKLES AVE

24

EMMITSBURG RD

Sherfy Farm 7
8

UNITED STATES AVE

10

MILLERSTOWN RD

Wentz Farm *(site)* 22

SICKLES AVE

Trostle Farm 23

To Hancock Ave

9

11

17

18

19 20 21

12

WEST CONFEDERATE AVE

16 15 14

Observation Tower

13

BIRNEY AVE

The Peach Orchard

WHEATFIELD RD

SICKLES AVE

BUS 15

0   250   500   750   1,000 ft
0   100   200   300 m

CHAPTER 6

Area F Peach Orchard, Emmitsburg Road

On the second day of the fighting, General George Meade formed his Union defensive position in the famed fishhook line that extended from Cemetery Hill to Little Round Top. His position was strong, and he chose to go on the defensive. Meanwhile, Robert E. Lee ordered General A. P. Hill to hold the center of his line while General James Longstreet attacked the Union left and General Richard Ewell assaulted the right.

At about the same time, General Daniel Sickles determined from a brief skirmish in Pitzer's Woods that the Confederates were gathering in a position that threatened his left flank. Against orders, he moved his troops forward to Joseph Sherfy's peach orchard, believing he was gaining an advantage. In truth, he left a huge gap in the Union line, which the Confederates would soon exploit. When Meade came to inspect the line, he realized what Sickles had done, but it was too late. The Confederate assault was about to get under way.

Longstreet had begun his march, doubling back when he believed his troops would be seen by Union signalmen on Little Round Top. Arriving at Seminary Ridge in midafternoon, his men had little time to rest from their eighteen-mile march before they were called to launch their attack. The vulnerable position established by Sickles would be a tempting target.

At six o'clock, Brigadier General William Barksdale's Mississippi brigade launched an attack directly toward Sickles's line. Joined on his left by Brigadier General Cadmus Wilcox's Alabama brigade, the Southerners soon overwhelmed Sickles, whose line began to crumble. Pushed back to the Trostle Farm, Sickles received a wound that resulted in the amputation of his leg.

Joseph Sherfy's house was riddled with bullets. His barn, occupied by several wounded men who had tried to find shelter from the hail of bullets and artillery shells, caught fire. Those inside burned alive.

Union general Charles Graham was thrown from his horse and taken captive. Barksdale was mortally wounded. Colonel George Willard, who commanded the Union Second Corps' Third Brigade of the Third Division, was also killed. Rank bought no man immunity from the effects of the brutal fighting.

As Confederate forces converged on the Peach Orchard from three directions, it was inevitable that the Union forces could not hold their position. Sickles's gamble had failed. Confederate artillery now had a good location from which to fire on Union troops along Cemetery Ridge. Despite his error, Sickles would be awarded the Medal of Honor in 1897 for his gallantry.

The next day, the Washington Artillery, positioned in the Peach Orchard, would fire the guns signaling the beginning of the artillery barrage that led to Pickett's Charge.

Few monuments in Volume 1 sit in the immediate area surrounding the Peach Orchard and Emmitsburg Road. One famous farm, however, is along the road. The Sherfy Farm was owned by the Reverend Joseph Sherfy. The Peach Orchard is part of that farm. The prominent monument on the right side of Wheatfield Road, accessed by the left turn off Emmitsburg Road, is that to Hampton's Battery F. One member of the battery earned the Medal of Honor at Gettysburg. His actions are described in Volume 1.

The next left turn takes visitors on to Sickles Avenue, where the monument to the Excelsior Brigade sits. One of the most ironic stories from Gettysburg is associated with that monument; it is told in detail in Volume 1. General Daniel Sickles, one of the great characters of the war, was directly involved. The site of his wounding is marked on the Trostle Farm along United States Avenue. His show of bravado and his unusual decision of what to do with his amputated leg will leave visitors shaking their heads.

West Confederate Avenue is visible on the left side of the map for this area. Markers for the various Confederate states represented at Gettysburg sit along the road, along with individual markers for General James Longstreet, the Eleventh Mississippi, the First United States Sharpshooters (who found themselves in the midst of the Confederate line), and the location where Robert E. Lee waited for his troops as they returned from Pickett's Charge. One of the most popular monuments on the battlefield,

the Virginia Memorial, is located along West Confederate Avenue. The statue of General Lee on top depicts the Confederate leader looking across the field of Pickett's Charge at his opponent, General George Meade.

F-1: First Massachusetts Infantry Monument
39° 48.523' N, 77° 14.622' W

The monument to the First Massachusetts sits where the regiment was positioned from late morning until evening on July 2. Its skirmish line (represented by a small marker at 39° 48.623' N, 77° 14.712' W) was about eight hundred feet in front of the monument.

Corporal Nathaniel M. Allen of Company B was carrying the national flag as the regiment fell back. Seeing the color bearer who was carrying the regi-

both the monument and the actual landscape. This unusual positioning allows visitors the illusion of being part of the action of July 2, 1863.

F-2: Brigadier General Andrew Atkinson Humphreys Monument
39° 48.490′ N, 77° 14.633′ W

An 1827 graduate of the United States Military Academy, Andrew Humphreys was fifty-three years old at the time of the battle. Tall and slender, with a reputation for being a strict disciplinarian, Humphreys was known as "Old Goggle Eyes" by his troops, after the glasses he wore for reading. Depending on who was talking, Humphreys was either a real gentleman, a description offered by Theodore Lyman of General George Meade's staff, or the loudest swearer ever known, a man of "distinguished and brilliant profanity," according to Assistant Secretary of War Charles Dana.

On July 2, Humphreys found himself shorthanded, his reserve brigade having been sent to assist Major General David Birney. The disgusted Humphreys, with only two brigades, was forced to face a Confederate attack, which prompted him to later issue a scathing report condemning the practice of moving reserve units away from one division to help another when they were needed where they had been originally positioned.

During the Confederate assault, Humphreys was thrown from his horse when it suffered its seventh wound of the day. He mounted an aide's horse

mental colors fall, Allen ran back under heavy fire and retrieved the flag from under the color bearer's body. He was able to bring both flags safely off the field. Corporal Allen was awarded the Medal of Honor for his actions.

Commanded by Lieutenant Colonel Clark B. Baldwin, the regiment had twenty-one men killed or mortally wounded, eighty with lesser wounds, and fifteen taken prisoner.

The monument was installed June 30, 1886, by Smith Granite Company. Dedication came two days later, on July 2.

The relief depicts a skirmisher stepping through a fence line similar to the one behind the monument today. Seminary Ridge is visible in the background of

The sculptor of this statue was J. Otto Schweitzer. The commonwealth of Pennsylvania erected the monument in 1914.

F-3: Eleventh Massachusetts Infantry Monument
39° 48.483′ N, 77° 14.642′ W

Lieutenant Colonel Porter D. Tripp commanded the Eleventh Massachusetts Infantry, which arrived at Gettysburg at two in the morning on July 2. Six hours later, the men were ordered to the front to support a line of skirmishers. They remained there until the middle of the afternoon. At that time, they

and continued fighting, moving back and forth and keeping his troops together as they were forced back. Although his fighting retreat left fifteen hundred men dead or wounded over a half-mile of ground, he was able to successfully withdraw his division.

Five days later, Humphreys was rewarded for his coolness under fire by being promoted to major general, replacing Dan Butterfield as chief of staff for General George Meade. When General Winfield Scott Hancock stepped down in November 1864 because of continued complications from his Gettysburg wound (see J-14), Humphreys assumed command of the Second Corps.

A native of Philadelphia, Humphreys died December 27, 1883, in Washington, D.C.

moved into a line of battle in response to Barksdale's advance (see F-10). They subsequently made two charges of their own in helping to repel Barksdale.

The Eleventh suffered twenty-three killed, ninety-six wounded, and ten missing.

Fabricated by Smith Granite Company, the monument was dedicated in 1886. In 1896, it was

moved from the intersection of Emmitsburg Road and Sickles Avenue to its present site, which marks the approximate location where the regiment stood on July 2 in support of the skirmish line west of the monument. The inscription notes, "All's well that ends well."

The monument was topped by an arm holding a saber until it was destroyed by vandals in 2006. It took seven years and a painstaking effort, but the arm and saber were accurately restored by the National Park Service and repositioned atop the base in April 2013. The reconstruction of the missing part was accomplished by consulting photos and fitting together the small pieces of the arm and saber that were found. Many of the photos were submitted by the public, angered at the actions of the vandals. Photos showing the monument with and without the vandalized arm are shown here.

F-4: Monument to Company G, First Regiment Wisconsin Sharpshooters
39° 48.482' N, 77° 14.663' W

On July 2, the men of Company G were deployed as skirmishers about two hundred yards west of Emmitsburg Road. They kept up a continuous fire from eight in the morning until midafternoon, when the advance of Barksdale's and Wilcox's Confederate brigades forced them to retire.

Part of the famed Berdan Sharpshooters, the men from Wisconsin were commanded at

no Company J, as a *J* too often looked like an *I*, causing confusion. The Berdan Sharpshooters wore green uniforms, rather than the Union blue. The green was an early version of camouflage.

The monument, fabricated by Ryegate Granite Company, was dedicated July 2, 1888. A small position marker west of the monument denotes the company's advanced position.

F-5: Fifth New Jersey Volunteers Monument
39° 48.446′ N, 77° 14.711′ W

Dedicated June 30, 1888, this monument marks the second position held by the Fifth New Jersey on the second day of the battle. The sculptor is unknown.

The regiment originally held a position four hundred yards to the front and left of the monument. After calling in the skirmish line, the Fifth took this position near the Klingel House, supporting Lieutenant Francis Seeley's Battery K, Fourth United States Artillery. The Fifth was ultimately forced back by the advance of Barksdale's and Wilcox's Confederate brigades.

Commanded by Colonel William J. Sewell, the regiment suffered badly that day, losing thirteen killed, sixty-five wounded, and sixteen missing, numbers representing about half the regiment. One of the wounded was Colonel Sewell, who would receive the Medal of Honor for his actions at Chancellorsville. He also served as both a state and United States senator. When Sewell was wounded, Captain

Gettysburg by Captain Frank E. Marble. Each company within the Berdan Sharpshooters was made up of men from a single state. Company G was recruited in Wisconsin. Together, the various companies made up two regiments, which were officially considered United States Army regiments. After the war, each state erected a monument to the company representing it.

The First Regiment, including the Wisconsin Sharpshooters, Company G, was commanded by Colonel Hiram Berdan, organizer of both sharpshooter regiments. When Berdan was appointed brigade commander, Lieutenant Colonel Casper Trepp took his place. Of the 371 men engaged from the First Regiment, six were killed, 37 wounded, and six declared missing.

Also in the First Regiment were Companies A, B, D, and H from New York; Companies C, I, and K from Michigan; Company E from New Hampshire; and Company F from Vermont. Typically, there was

The regiment came under such ferocious artillery and infantry fire at this location at the Klingel Farm that nearly 60 percent of its men, including every officer above the rank of lieutenant, were killed or disabled. Of the regiment's 275 men on July 2, at least 18 were known to be killed, 130 wounded, and six missing.

The Eleventh was commanded by Colonel Robert McAllister. When McAllister was wounded during the second day's fighting, Captain Luther Martin assumed command. Martin was soon wounded himself. While making his way to an aid station, he was wounded again, this time mortally. Captain William Lloyd replaced Martin until he was also wounded, at which time Lieutenant John Schoonover took command. Unbelievably, Schoonover was wounded late

Thomas C. Godfrey took command, followed by Captain Henry Woolsey. Woolsey, slightly wounded at Gettysburg, would be mortally wounded at Petersburg in June 1864.

Over the course of the war, the Fifth New Jersey fought in thirty-two battles.

F-6: Eleventh New Jersey Infantry Monument
39° 48.354′ N, 77° 14.799′ W

This unusual monument marks the position the Eleventh New Jersey's right flank reached on July 2.

in the afternoon. Captain Samuel Sleeper took over, becoming the regiment's fifth commander of the day.

The Eleventh fought in twenty-eight battles in addition to Gettysburg.

The monument takes the form of an upright book with the spine facing the road. A flag drapes the book, which is topped by a small cap called a kepi. Fabricated by Smith Granite Company, the monument was dedicated June 20, 1888.

F-7: Fifty-seventh Pennsylvania Infantry Monument
39° 48.221′ N, 77° 14.918′ W

The Fifty-seventh Pennsylvania arrived at Gettysburg after dark on July 1, thus missing the first day's fighting. The men bivouacked in the open field to the right of Emmitsburg Road, moving to the front early the next morning.

On July 2, the regiment mounted a charge with the 114th Pennsylvania Infantry against Mississippi troops under General William Barksdale. The regiment held its position in the vicinity of the monument for two hours before advancing to a point near Joseph Sherfy's house, where it engaged the Confederate army until the left flank collapsed, forcing the regiment to fall back. In the noise of the battle, however, several men failed to hear the order to retreat and were taken prisoner.

The regiment was commanded by Colonel Peter Sides. When Sides was wounded on July 2, Captain Alanson H. Nelson took command. The regiment's

losses at Gettysburg were twelve killed, forty-five wounded, and forty-seven missing or captured. Among those captured was the brigade's commander, Brigadier General Charles Graham, who was wounded in the hip and shoulders. Graham was exchanged for Major General James L. Kemper on September 19, 1863. A civil engineer, Graham would later serve as surveyor of the port of New York.

Carved by an artist named McMenamin, the monument was dedicated July 2, 1888. It marks the first position taken by the regiment prior to advancing.

F-8: 114th Pennsylvania Infantry Monument

39° 48.209′ N, 77° 14.926′ W

This monument to the 114th Pennsylvania was placed by the surviving members of the regiment in memory of their fallen comrades. It marks the position the regiment held on the second day of the fighting. That afternoon, the regiment took this position to cover the withdrawal of a Federal battery. At about that time, General William Barksdale began his Confederate advance (see F-10). Within a short time, the 114th found itself face to face with the Thirteenth and Seventeenth Mississippi infantries. Joined by the Fifty-seventh and 105th Pennsylvania infantries, the Union troops temporarily delayed the Mississippians' advance. Before being pushed back, the 114th was replaced by the Seventy-third New York Infantry.

Officers from the regiment reported after the battle that men from the Mississippi units humanely removed many of the 114th's wounded from Emmitsburg Road before moving their artillery across. However, other wounded troops from the 114th took refuge in the nearby Joseph Sherfy barn, only to be trapped and burned to death when artillery fire ignited the structure.

Also known as the Collis Zouaves or the Zouaves D'Afrique, the regiment suffered nine killed, eighty-six wounded, and sixty missing or captured. Most of those captured were cut off from the regiment as it retired. One of them was Lieutenant Colonel Frederick Cavada, who was in command. Following

Cavada's capture, Captain Edward R. Bowen took command. Bowen moved the regiment to a line connecting Cemetery Hill with Little Round Top, where it remained until the end of the battle.

The name Collis Zouaves came from the colonel of the regiment, Charles H. T. Collis, who was absent from Gettysburg, still recovering from wounds suffered at Chancellorsville in May. A monument to Colonel Collis has been erected in the National Cemetery (39° 49.196′ N, 77° 13.919′ W). Collis would later build a summer home in Gettysburg, naming it Red Patch. The home still stands on Seminary Ridge near the Schultz Woods.

The monument's sculptor was E. A. Kretschman. Dedication of the base took place July 2, 1886; the sculpture was dedicated November 11, 1888. On February 16, 2006, the monument was vandalized when it was pulled from its pedestal and thrown to the ground.

F-9: Sixty-third Pennsylvania Infantry Monument
39° 48.108' N, 77° 15.006' W

The Sixty-third Pennsylvania, under the command of Major John A. Danks, arrived on the field as part of the Third Corps. When the corps bivouacked along Emmitsburg Road, the Sixty-third was ordered to spend the night on picket duty. The next morning, it was placed on a skirmish line in the rear of Joseph Sherfy's house.

When the men took fire early in the morning, a company of sharpshooters was dispatched to determine the whereabouts of the Rebels. It didn't take long to find them. Skirmishing took place until about three in the afternoon, when Confederate troops opened a heavy cannonade. After a period of heavy fighting, the Union troops were forced to retreat. They moved to the rear to replenish their ammunition and to gain some much-needed rest. That evening, they once again found themselves on the picket line.

The next morning, the men moved to support a battery directly in front of General George Meade's headquarters, where they remained for the rest of the battle. As they nervously lay in wait during the cannonade that initiated Pickett's Charge, the men were ordered by Brigadier General Alexander Hays to gather all the discarded weapons they could find, clean them, and get them loaded and ready to fire. This served to keep them busy and to take their minds off what was to come. By the time the infantry assault began, some of the men of the Sixty-third had as many as six loaded weapons at their side.

Of the regiment's 296 officers and men at Gettysburg, only one man was killed. Another 26 men and three officers received wounds, and four men were declared captured or missing.

The monument was fabricated by Van Gunden, Young, and Drumm and dedicated September 11, 1889. It marks the general position the regiment's skirmishers held on July 2.

F-10: Marker for Barksdale's Advance
39° 48.143′ N, 77° 15.346′ W

This marker notes the point from which Brigadier General William Barksdale's Mississippi brigade began its July 2 charge toward the Sherfy and Trostle farms. Longstreet's First Corps was fighting in a line that extended from Little Round Top to Sherfy's Peach Orchard. Barksdale had waited impatiently for orders to advance. At six o'clock that afternoon, those orders came.

Barksdale himself led the charge across the open ground in front of the marker shown in the photo, overwhelming the Union troops and forcing them back toward the Trostle Farm. Union reinforcements arrived and stemmed the attack, pushing Barksdale's men back across the same ground they had just crossed. As his men retreated, Barksdale was mortally wounded. In the confusion, he could not be re-moved from the field. It was later that night before men from the Fourteenth Vermont Infantry found him. He was taken to a Union field hospital at the Jacob Hummelbaugh farm, where he died a few hours later.

Several Union soldiers helped themselves to buttons and gold trim from Barksdale's uniform before he was buried in the farmhouse's yard. After the war, his body was removed for reburial in Jackson, Mississippi. Shortly after his reburial, many of the items taken from his uniform were returned to his family.

Proving that war plays no favorites, Barksdale's counterpart on the Union side, Colonel George Willard, who commanded the Second Corps' Third Brigade of the Third Division, received a mortal wound in the same fighting.

F-11: Sixty-eighth Pennsylvania Infantry Monument
39° 48.083′ N, 77° 14.950′ W

The Sixty-eighth Pennsylvania was initially commanded by Colonel Andrew H. Tippin. Captain Milton S. Davis took over when Tippin was placed in command of Brigadier General Charles Graham's brigade after Graham was wounded in the hip and shoulders. Tippin survived the battle unscathed, though his horse was shot from under him. Graham, however, did not fare as well. Near the close of the action, he returned to the field and resumed command. Weak from loss of blood and in pain from his wounds, he was quickly captured. He was held

This monument to the Sixty-eighth was fabricated by W. C. Gallagher and dedicated July 2, 1888.

F-12: 141st Pennsylvania Infantry Monument
39° 48.064′ N, 77° 14.928′ W

With Colonel Henry J. Madill commanding, the 141st Pennsylvania took a position facing southward along Wheatfield Road at dawn on the morning of July 2. The regiment's position on the angle in Major General Daniel Sickles's line was the most exposed on the whole field. The 141st was raked with converging artillery fire.

captive until being exchanged for Confederate general James Kemper in September 1863.

Also known as Scott's Legion, the regiment held a line here along Wheatfield Road on July 2. When Brigadier General Joseph Brevard Kershaw's Confederate brigade drove back the skirmishers near the Rose Farm, the Sixty-eighth was moved into the Peach Orchard, where a second monument (see F-16) notes its position in that part of the fighting.

The regiment brought 383 men to the battle, suffering 13 killed, 126 wounded, and 13 missing. Although it was held in reserve the third day, it was exposed to heavy artillery fire. Some of its losses took place at that time.

After holding its position for several hours, the 141st moved into the Peach Orchard when South Carolina troops advanced. For two hours in late afternoon, it repulsed efforts by the South Carolinians to take the guns of the Fifteenth New York Light Artillery, allowing them to be retrieved from the field by hand after all the battery's horses were killed. Not long afterward, the 141st was outflanked. Forced to retire, the regiment did so in an orderly fashion, firing as it retreated.

Present at Gettysburg were nine officers and two hundred men. At the end of the fighting on July 2, only three officers and fifty-seven men were available for action. One officer and forty-one men had been killed, five officers and eighty-one men wounded, and twenty-one men declared captured or missing, a casualty rate of more than 71 percent, exceeded at Gettysburg only by the First Minnesota's 82 percent among Union regiments. Over the entire war, only the First Minnesota, the First Texas (82.3 percent at Antietam), and the Twenty-first Georgia (76 percent at Second Manassas) had higher casualty rates in one battle.

As the regiment retreated, Major General Sickles shouted to Colonel Madill over the din of battle, "Colonel! For God's sake, can't you hold on?" Fighting back tears, Madill looked around, saw the dead and wounded, and is said to have replied, "Where are my men, General?"

The monument was dedicated September 11, 1889. The sculptor is unknown.

F-13: Third Michigan Infantry Monument
39° 48.009′ N, 77° 14.956′ W

Initially, the Third Michigan Infantry was assigned a position along Fairfield-Gettysburg Road, where it faced the task of protecting the supply trains moving toward Gettysburg. At midafternoon on July 1, the regiment was ordered to set up camp on the grounds of St. Joseph's Academy in Emmitsburg, Maryland, where it spent most of the night. Breaking camp at about three in the morning, the regiment moved to Gettysburg, arriving around dawn.

At midafternoon on July 2, the Third extended a skirmish line 150 yards south of the Peach Orchard,

covering the ground from the orchard eastward toward the Rose Farm. Intense fighting ultimately drove the men back around seven that night.

On July 3, the regiment again came under fire during Pickett's Charge but held its position. Throughout the evening and into the night, the Third carried in the wounded and cared for captured prisoners. The men spent the days after the battle burying the dead.

The regiment was commanded by Colonel Byron Root Pierce until he was wounded, at which time his brother, Lieutenant Colonel Edwin S. Pierce, took over. The Third went into action with 19 officers and 267 men. Of those, seven men were killed, three officers and 28 men were wounded, and seven men were declared missing.

The fabricator of this work was Mitchell Granite Company. Dedication took place June 12, 1889. The monument was placed at the position the regiment held on the evening of July 2.

The regiment served through the entire war, beginning with First Manassas and ending with the Confederate surrender at Appomattox.

F-14: Third Maine Infantry Monument

39° 48.023′ N, 77° 15.004′ W

On the morning of July 2, the Third Maine, accompanied by a hundred Berdan Sharpshooters, engaged in a skirmish in Pitzer's Woods. Several men of the regiment were killed or wounded. Later

in the day, the Third took a position in an exposed line of battle near the Peach Orchard. When General James Longstreet's corps attacked, the men of the Third were nearly surrounded and were forced to give ground.

In that fighting, every member of the entire color guard company, Company K, was killed, wounded, or captured, including the company's captain and its only lieutenant. With none of the color company left and darkness closing in, the loss of the colors was not noticed until the following morning. Colonel Moses Lakeman, commanding the regiment, reported the loss of his colors.

The regiment entered the day's fighting with 210 officers and men. By evening, only 88 had made it through without becoming casualties. The day was a bloody one for the regiment, which had one officer and 17 men killed, two officers and 57 men wounded, and 45 men missing. The regiment, or what remained of it, moved the next day to support the center of the Union line.

The monument marks the position the regiment held in the afternoon on July 2. It was installed in 1888 but was not dedicated until October 3, 1889. The name of the sculptor is unknown.

Two other monuments to the Third Maine are on the battlefield. One at West Confederate Avenue and Berdan Avenue (39° 48.476′ N, 77° 15.436′ W) marks the location where the regiment fought in the morning on July 2. The other sits on Hancock Avenue (39° 48.766′ N, 77° 14.117′ W) and notes the regiment's position on the third day of fighting.

F-15: Second New Hampshire Infantry Monument
39° 48.031′ N, 77° 15.021′ W

At three in the afternoon on July 2, the Second New Hampshire, which had been recruited for three months' service, arrived at Gettysburg and was ordered to support Battery G of the First New York Artillery. A quick roll call revealed that eight men had already fallen from the ranks due to sunstroke and heat exhaustion.

By four-thirty, the Confederate attackers had ap-proached close enough that Colonel Edward L. Bailey, in command of the regiment, ordered his men to charge. Their effort pushed the Confederates back to a small ravine about 250 yards in front of the monument. A heavy return fire from artillery, however, forced the men from New Hampshire to retire. In the charge, the flagstaff of the regimental colors was shot out of the color bearer's hands and was broken into three pieces. Several members of the color guard were wounded.

The regiment continued to suffer heavy losses over the next several hours. Official casualties for the Second were 20 killed, 137 wounded, and 36 missing out of 354 engaged. Visitors may notice that this

differs slightly from the unofficial numbers on the monument.

Of those killed, Corporal Thomas Bignall undoubtedly suffered the most. A Confederate shell struck Bignall's cartridge box, driving the cartridges into his body, where they proceeded to explode individually over a period as long as thirty seconds. Major Samuel P. Sayles was badly wounded in the thigh. Nearby comrades wrote that "there was never a more complete and comprehensive gospel of damnation laid down than that he recited to the rebel who, while he lay crippled and helpless, pulled the boot from his wounded leg."

Colonel Bailey had served as a clerk in the Manchester, New Hampshire, post office in civilian life. Wounded at Williamsburg a year earlier, he was wounded again in the fighting on July 2. He would continue as an officer in the regular army after the war until his dismissal by court-martial in March 1893 for conduct unbecoming an officer and a gentleman. Charges against him included entering a house while in uniform and beckoning the owner's wife to come with him, conversing with a prostitute while in uniform, and borrowing money from another officer without repaying the loan. In an odd contradiction, Bailey also received four brevet promotions for gallantry during the Civil War.

The monument marks the advanced position the Second took on the afternoon of July 2. Sculpted by Thomas Nahn, it was dedicated July 2, 1886.

Interestingly, the men of the Second wore gray with dress coats trimmed in red cord, despite the danger that their uniforms might be confused with those of the Confederates. They wore the uniforms not just at Gettysburg but for the entire war, refusing to switch to the standard blue of the Union.

F-16: Sixty-eighth Pennsylvania Infantry Monument
39° 48.035′ N, 77° 15.026′ W

The Sixty-eighth Pennsylvania arrived on the field after dark on July 1, missing the first day's fighting. It was posted here, near the John Wentz house.

Also known as Scott's Legion, the regiment

was commanded at Gettysburg by Colonel Andrew H. Tippin, who had his horse shot from under him during the fighting. Tippin was elevated to replace Brigadier General Charles Graham when Graham was wounded. Captain Milton S. Davis took Tippin's position.

The Sixty-eighth advanced through the Peach Orchard in the afternoon on July 2, then turned to face west. As Brigadier General Joseph Brevard Kershaw's Confederate brigade advanced, the Sixty-eighth squared off against the Twenty-first Mississippi. Soon, however, the Seventeenth Mississippi moved on the Pennsylvanians' right, placing the regiment's flanks in danger and forcing it into a fighting retreat back through the Peach Orchard.

Regimental records indicate that 383 soldiers entered the battle, contrary to the number listed on the monument. Of those, 13 were killed, 126 wounded, and 13 declared missing.

The sculptor of the monument is unknown. Installed in 1886, the monument was placed at the regiment's advanced position on the afternoon of July 2. It is one of two erected to the Sixty-eighth (see F-11).

F-17: Monument to Battery G, First New York Light Artillery
39° 48.077' N, 77° 15.007' W

In late afternoon on July 2, General Daniel Sickles ordered Battery G of the First New York Light Artillery into the Peach Orchard, where it remained until early evening. When its ammunition became

dangerously low, the battery fought desperately to save its guns. It not only succeeded in doing so but also was able to remove its wounded with the rest of the regiment when forced to retire.

Also known as Ames's Battery, the regiment occupied this position in the afternoon on July 2. Captain Nelson Ames was one of the organizers of the battery and served as its commander at Gettysburg.

The battery's ammunition was replenished that night. The next day, Battery G took part in the artillery duel that preceded Pickett's Charge. A marker along Hancock Avenue (39° 48.165′ N, 77° 14.067′ W) marks the position it held during that time.

The post-battle report noted that, despite the heavy fighting, the battery suffered only eight casualties, all of them wounded. One of those eventually succumbed to his wounds. Fourteen horses were also killed.

The next summer, the battery gained admiration in the fierce fighting at Spotsylvania Court House, where it fired all six of its guns, plus nine guns that were captured from the Confederates, along with the Southerners' ammunition. Having insufficient numbers of men to fire the nine captured guns, battery officers convinced General Winfield Scott Hancock to supply infantry troops. Hancock complied, and the guns, manned by infantry under the direction of the battery's officers, took a heavy toll on the Confederates, who mounted several unsuccessful charges to recapture their guns. Several of the infantry troops were killed or wounded as they manned the guns.

Frederick and Field fabricated the monument, which was dedicated July 3, 1893. The dedication was far less formal than most, with no speeches. The thirteen survivors who attended preferred to conduct the dedication in relative silence, remembering their lost comrades.

F-18: Pennsylvania Independent Battery C Monument
39° 48.086′ N, 77° 14.981′ W

Commonly known as Thompson's Battery C for Captain James Thompson, the battery occupied this position late in the afternoon on July 2. Two of its guns faced west, and four faced south. For an hour, the battery engaged in a fight with not only the Confederate artillery but also the infantry. When the Rebel infantry advanced, the Union infantry fell back, leaving the battery unsupported. One of its west-facing guns was captured.

A Union counterattack recaptured the gun, but in the back-and-forth fighting, it was lost a second time. Captain Thompson had his horse killed under him. The battery lost one killed, nine wounded, and four missing in a short span. Eighteen of its horses were killed or wounded.

The next day, after its horses were replaced, the battery took a position on the right of the First Volunteer Brigade Reserve Artillery and participated in the artillery duel that preceded Pickett's Charge. Its losses that day were fourteen wounded, including Captain Thompson.

A month before arriving at Gettysburg, the battery had consolidated with Battery F. The two served as one battery in the battle. They were separated again in 1864 for the remainder of the war. Each battery has its own monument at Gettysburg. Battery F's is located adjacent to this one in the Peach Orchard. The two have a combined monument on Hancock Avenue (39° 48.086′ N, 77° 14.981′ W).

The monument to Battery C was fabricated by Ryegate Granite Company and erected in 1893.

F-19: Fifteenth New York Battery Monument

39° 48.063' N, 77° 14.891' W

The Fifteenth New York Battery, formerly known as Light Battery B of the Irish Brigade, was commanded by Captain Patrick Hart, which gave rise to its later name, Hart's Battery. The monument marks the position of Hart's Battery on the afternoon of July 2.

The battery arrived on June 30 at Taneytown, Maryland, where it encamped during the first day of the battle. The next morning at daybreak, it began the march to Gettysburg. The battery arrived around ten-thirty that morning and was placed in a reserve position between Taneytown Road and Baltimore Pike. It passed the day quietly until four that afternoon, when it was ordered to the Peach Orchard. Its guns pointed southward, it began an artillery duel using shot and shell, causing a Confederate battery

to withdraw. The Confederates brought in fresh batteries, however. Their fire proved deadly to the Fifteenth, taking a toll on both men and horses.

When General Joseph Brevard Kershaw's South Carolina brigade advanced, the battery repulsed two charges but eventually ran low on ammunition, necessitating a retreat. After replenishing its ammunition chests, the battery once again was ready for battle. Its chance came on July 3 in the huge artillery duel prior to Pickett's Charge. In that action, the Fifteenth exploded two enemy caissons and dismounted two guns with deadly accurate fire.

The battery counted three men killed and thirteen wounded, including Captain Hart. It also lost twenty-five horses killed or wounded.

When Hart fell, he was replaced by Lieutenant Edward M. Knox, who would be awarded the Medal of Honor for holding his ground after the other batteries fell back. Despite a fierce attack by Kershaw's South Carolina brigade, he kept the battery in position until his only choice was to remove his guns by hand. He was severely wounded in the process. Knox's men honored him by including his likeness on the monument.

The monument was sculpted by R. D. Barr and fabricated by Smith Granite Company. Dedication ceremonies were held July 2, 1888.

F-20: Monument to Battery B, First New Jersey Light Artillery
39° 48.081' N, 77° 14.833' W

Battery B of the First New Jersey Light Artillery fought at this location from midafternoon until evening on July 2, firing thirteen hundred rounds of ammunition. Its losses included one killed, sixteen wounded, and three missing. The battery also had seventeen horses killed and five badly injured.

Captain Adoniram Judson Clark commanded the battery at Gettysburg, having taken charge after the death of Captain John E. Beam a year earlier at Malvern Hill. A former medical student in Newark, Clark served as that city's chief of police after the war.

On July 2, the battery moved to a position near the base of Little Round Top. At nine-thirty that morning, it relocated to the front and left, then to a position to the left of the Trostle House.

That afternoon, the battle heated up. Battery B was ordered to hold its position as long as the men had shot in their limbers and soldiers to work the guns. Early in the evening, however, support was pushed back, leaving the battery dangerously exposed. It had

to pull back to avoid being overrun, leaving a caisson on the field because the horses needed to pull it had been killed. The caisson was recovered later.

The next day, Battery B joined other units of the Artillery Brigade at this location but did not participate in the fighting.

At various times, the unit was alternately known as the First New Jersey Volunteer Artillery, Battery B; Beam's Battery (until Beam was killed); and Clark's Battery.

The monument was fabricated by Frederick and Field and dedicated June 30, 1888.

F-21: Seventh New Jersey Infantry Monument
39° 48.089' N, 77° 14.805' W

Shaped like a large minie ball, the monument to the Seventh New Jersey stands on the site where the regiment's commander, Colonel Louis R. Fran-

The Seventh brought 331 men to the field and suffered 114 casualties, including 24 killed, 77 wounded, and 13 missing. When the Third Corps was dissolved in 1864 because of heavy losses, the Seventh was moved into the Second Corps. The men showed their displeasure by attaching the Second Corps emblem, the trefoil, to their backsides instead of replacing their Third Corps diamond insignias.

Their monument was designed and constructed by Frederick and Field and dedicated June 30, 1888.

F-22: Seventy-third New York Infantry Monument
39° 48.126′ N, 77° 14.890′ W

Often referred to as the Fourth Regiment of General Daniel Sickles's Excelsior Brigade, the Seventy-third New York was also known as the Second Fire Zouaves because many of its members had been New York City firefighters prior to enlisting. The connection is commemorated in the monument, which depicts a fireman holding a calling horn standing beside a soldier holding his weapon. The two are holding hands, symbolizing the unity between the fire department and the regiment. Despite the fact that the firemen were now in the army, the city kept them on the rolls as active firefighters throughout the war.

The regiment was commanded by Major Michael W. Burns, a city inspector and New York fireman who had been wounded during the Second Manassas Campaign. Major Henry E. Tremain, an

cine, was mortally wounded on the evening of July 2 while the Seventh supported Clark's New Jersey Battery in Excelsior Field. Francine lingered until July 16. When he fell, Major Frederick Cooper assumed command of the regiment.

Perfectly proportioned, the bullet is over three feet in diameter. The minie ball was developed by Claude-Etienne Minie, an officer in the French army. It replaced the old musket ball and proved much more accurate, thanks to its increased muzzle velocity and better aerodynamic stability.

The regiment was initially located three hundred yards northeast of the monument but was repositioned to reinforce Brigadier General Charles Graham's brigade.

officer on Sickles's staff, conducted the regiment to the position marked by the monument.

The Seventy-third arrived on the field near midnight on July 1 and held a line in the vicinity of Emmitsburg Road until the middle of the afternoon on July 2. At that time, it was ordered into a line of battle in the area around where the monument now stands.

When Brigadier General William Barksdale's Mississippi brigade launched its attack early in the evening (see F-10), the Seventy-third was rushed toward a gap in the Union line. The regiment temporarily slowed Barksdale's advance but was soon overwhelmed. Within a few minutes, the Seventy-third was forced to retreat to avoid being outflanked.

Although the regiment fought in some of the war's biggest battles, it suffered its worst losses on the second day at Gettysburg, when 51 men were killed, 103 wounded, and eight declared missing out of 324 engaged, for a 50 percent casualty rate. Those numbers included four officers killed and one wounded. Over the course of the regiment's service, 18 of its officers were killed or mortally wounded, a loss exceeded by only four other regiments in the army.

In the months following the September 11, 2001, terrorist attacks, this monument became one of the most popular on the battlefield. Visitors placed floral wreaths, individual flowers, and written messages at its base in a show of admiration for the firefighters of New York City.

The unique monument was designed by Hoffman and Prochazka and sculpted by Joseph Moretti. It sits at the approximate position where the Seventy-third fought on July 2. It was erected

in August 1897 and dedicated September 6 of that year.

The regiment is also honored on the Excelsior Brigade Monument just a short distance away (39° 48.107′ N, 77° 14.849′ W).

F-23: Monument to Ninth Massachusetts Battery and Cora
39° 48.102′ N, 77° 14.552′ W

The men of the Ninth Massachusetts Battery had never been in battle before, and their first experience was not going well. Positioned at the Trostle Farm, the Ninth fought ferociously after retreating from its original position along Wheatfield Road (39° 48.004′ N, 77° 14.737′ W). Commanded by Captain John Bigelow, the battery had been forced to withdraw when the Confederates broke through the Union lines around the Peach Orchard and the Wheatfield. As the guns were pulled back, the men stopped periodically to fire a round of canister toward their pursuers.

In this second position, the battery held its ground until it was overrun by troops from South Carolina and Mississippi. Four of its guns were captured, and Captain Bigelow received a serious wound. Bigelow, a Harvard graduate, had also been wounded at Malvern Hill. Charles W. Reed, the battery's bugler, rushed to Bigelow's aid and assisted him to safety. Reed would be awarded the Medal of Honor for his actions under fire. Lieutenant Richard S. Milton took command when Bigelow fell.

Three officers, six sergeants, and twenty-eight enlisted men became casualties, and eighty of the battery's eighty-eight horses were either killed or disabled. Five of the battery's guns were captured by the Twenty-first Mississippi Infantry. Those guns were later recaptured by the 150th New York Infantry.

This monument is one of three dedicated to the battery. One of the others marks the battery's original position along Wheatfield Road, while the third notes its position on July 3 and 4 in Ziegler's Grove (39° 48.958′ N, 77° 14.092′ W). The designs for all three monuments were by Boston artist Charles W. Reed—the same man who saved Bigelow's life. This monument was dedicated October 19, 1885.

The affection the men had for their battery is evident on the breech of one of the guns, where the name the soldiers gave the weapon, Cora, is plainly visible.

F-24: 120th New York Infantry Monument
39° 48.280' N, 77° 14.766' W

The monument to the 120th New York sits where the regiment held the line on the second day of fighting. The action became fierce as General William Barksdale's brigade drew closer. When the Mississippians threatened to break through, the 120th was ordered to bolster the line. Its presence slowed the Confederates only momentarily, and the line soon collapsed. The regiment was forced to engage in a fighting retreat.

Of the regiment's 30 officers and 397 men at Gettysburg, six officers and 24 men were killed, 10 officers and 144 men wounded, and 19 men declared missing, for a total of 203 casualties. Gettysburg proved the most damaging battle for the regiment throughout the entire war.

Also known as the Washington Guards, the regiment fought in twenty-two battles or skirmishes, all of which are listed on the back of the monument. The 120th was commanded at Gettysburg by Lieutenant Colonel Cornelius D. Westbrook. When Westbrook was wounded twice on July 2, Major John Rudolph Tappen took command.

During the fighting, several color bearers went down. When the national flag fell for the last time, Tappen ordered Sergeant John I. Spoor to pick it up and hold it aloft. Spoor did so proudly. At one point, the staff was shattered by a shell. Spoor grasped the part of the shaft above the damage and placed his other hand below it, literally holding the staff together with his hands. He carried the flag in this manner for the remainder of the fight. His actions earned him a recommendation for promotion for conspicuous gallantry.

Frederick and Field fabricated the monument, which was dedicated June 25, 1889.

Chapter 7
Area G

WHEATFIELD,
LOOP,
PLUM RUN

Area G

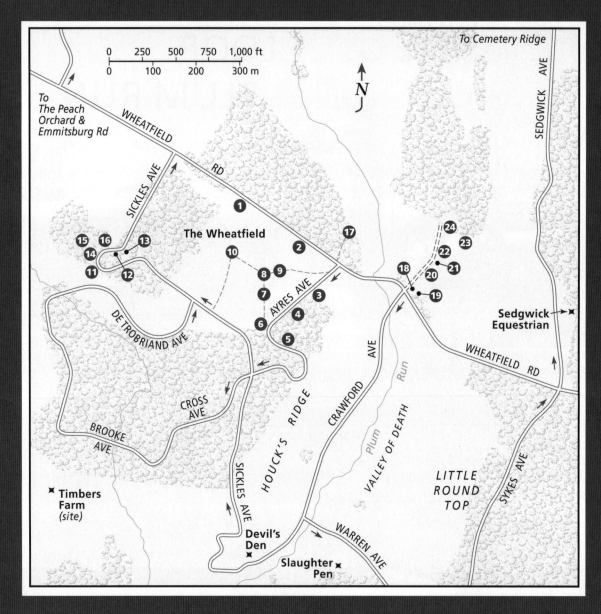

In late afternoon on July 2, 1863, the Confederate army launched an assault on several fronts, one of which was the Wheatfield. Under Brigadier General George T. Anderson, it met the Union army in an area of the Rose Farm called Stoney Hill, known today as the Loop, where the fighting became as fierce as any in the entire three days. Within a few hours, more than 30 percent of those fighting had become casualties and the twenty-six acres of George Rose's wheat had been destroyed.

The Union line initially extended from Emmitsburg Road to Devil's Den. As Anderson's Brigade entered the Rose Woods, the Third Arkansas and Fifty-ninth Georgia met the Union's Seventeenth Maine and Twentieth Indiana. Troops from the Eighth and Eleventh Georgia soon entered the fray, as did the Eighth New Jersey and the 115th Pennsylvania. The latter two Union regiments soon had to pull back toward the Trostle Farm, creating a gap in the Union line. The Eighth Georgia quickly moved into that gap, only to be met by the Seventeenth Maine, which had moved its right flank to a position where its monument now sits, lining up perpendicular to the stone wall. The Seventeenth Maine, with support from the Fifth Michigan and the Thirty-second Massachusetts, repelled the Eighth Georgia.

As the Eighth Georgia was driven back, the Eleventh Georgia moved into the area occupied by the Seventeenth Maine, and the fighting quickly became hand to hand. One of the Georgia color guards came running up. One of the Georgia color guards was captured in the fighting. The Ninth Georgia then pressed the attack but was pushed back into the Rose Woods. While both sides regrouped and replenished ammunition, the fighting temporarily lessened.

As Anderson planned his next move, he sought the assistance of Brigadier General Joseph Kershaw's brigade. In the meantime, the Fifteenth South Carolina moved into position to join the next assault. As Anderson worked his way through the Rose Woods to get back to his troops, he was struck in the thigh by a Union minie ball. His brigade was taken over by Lieutenant Colonel William Luffman of the Eleventh Georgia. Kershaw moved his South Carolina troops into position to initiate a second Confederate assault. That assault pushed the Union troops back, gaining the Southerners control of the Wheatfield.

Brigadier General John Caldwell's division of the Union's Second Corps rushed to the aid of the retreating Third Corps. The first two Union brigades in the fight were led by Colonel Edward Cross and Brigadier General Samuel Zook. Both were mortally wounded shortly after arriving. The Irish Brigade, commanded by Colonel Patrick Kelly, and Caldwell's reserve brigade under Colonel John Brooke also responded. The Union mounted a charge, pushing the Confederates back toward the Rose Farm. There, three brigades under Anderson, Kershaw, and Brigadier General Paul Semmes made their stand. Semmes was soon mortally wounded.

As more Confederate troops moved from the

Peach Orchard, Brooke was soon forced back, followed shortly by Zook's Brigade. The Fourth Michigan, Sixty-second Pennsylvania, and Thirty-second Massachusetts moved into the area to provide cover as the Union troops retreated. All three were soon overwhelmed. A dash for the rear was soon under way.

At the eastern edge of the Wheatfield, two brigades of United States Regulars under Colonel Hannibal Day and Colonel Sidney Burbank formed a defensive line. They were forced to hold their fire until the retreating Union troops passed through their line. By then, the pursuing Confederates were right behind. The Regulars held their positions for just a short time before they also were pushed back. In this action alone, one of every three Regulars became a casualty.

Although the Southerners now held the Wheatfield, the fighting was not yet over. Brigadier General Samuel Crawford arranged his troops into two lines of battle and ordered the Pennsylvania Reserves, who occupied the front line, to lead a charge into the Valley of Death to meet the onrushing Confederates. The exhausted Southerners were quickly pushed back by the fresher Union troops, who moved toward the Rose Woods.

As darkness fell, neither side had full control of the bloody Wheatfield. While soldiers quietly prepared for a restless night, wild hogs moved into the area to feed on the bodies that littered the field.

Monuments in Volume 1 located in this area include that to the Eleventh Pennsylvania Reserves. It is the first monument visible on the left side of Ayres Avenue after visitors enter from Wheatfield Road. As the road curves to the left, Little Round Top appears across the Valley of Death, followed closely by the monument to the famed Bucktails. Readers will learn the Bucktails' losing argument against other regiments using the same name.

At the intersection with Cross Avenue, a right turn takes visitors into the heart of the Wheatfield, at the far end of which sits the extremely popular monument to the Irish Brigade, whose marker features a reposing Irish wolfhound. Interested readers will learn why the name of the Fourteenth Independent New York Battery is included on the monument, though that unit was not part of the brigade. Visitors entering the Loop at the top of the hill will see a monument in the form of a pup tent, followed a short distance later by a plaque on a large boulder. Both honor the Thirty-second Massachusetts; the boulder and plaque signify the site of one of the first field hospitals ever on a battlefield. In the same general location is the monument to the Second Andrew's Sharpshooters. Readers will note the explanation of the vandalism that occurred several years ago. The actual vandalism is not what it appears to be!

Just after the sharp curve, visitors will reach the unusual monument to the 116th Pennsylvania Volunteers and learn the story of just what it depicts. Behind that marker and to the left sits a flank marker. Volume 1 reveals just what makes it unusual. Visitors will have a good view of the Rose Farm, one of the deadliest areas in the Wheatfield.

G-1: Brevet Major General Samuel Zook Monument

39° 47.905′ N, 77° 14.553′ W

When Samuel Zook was a small child, his family moved to Valley Forge to live with his grandmother. Growing up in the shadow of George Washington, and having ancestors who fought in the Revolutionary War, Zook developed a strong interest in military affairs. By the time he was nineteen, he joined a Pennsylvania militia regiment. He also served as adjutant in the Hundredth Pennsylvania Regiment.

In 1846, Zook moved to New York City to serve as superintendent of the Washington and New York Telegraph Company. He joined the Sixth New York, a ninety-day regiment, and held the rank of lieutenant colonel when the Civil War began. When the Sixth completed its commitment, Zook raised the Fifty-seventh New York. He served as its colonel for almost two years.

On the afternoon of July 2, 1863, Zook led his brigade into the Wheatfield. Suffering from rheumatism that made it difficult for him to walk, he advanced on horseback. This made him a conspicuous target. He soon was shot in the abdomen, which knocked him from his horse. He was taken to a nearby field hospital, where the surgeon declared his wound to be mortal. He was then moved to the G. F. Hoke tollhouse on Baltimore Pike, where he could rest more peacefully.

Zook lived less than twenty-four hours. His monument is approximately where he received his mortal wound, though the exact location is disputed by many historians.

On October 9, 1867, the War Department promoted Zook posthumously to brevet major general for "gallant and meritorious services at the battle of Gettysburg."

H. A. Dorr fabricated the marble shaft, which was dedicated July 25, 1882.

G-2: Lieutenant Colonel Henry Czar Merwin Monument

39° 47.857′ N, 77° 14.456′ W

Leading the Twenty-seventh Connecticut Infantry, which at Gettysburg consisted of only two

Merwin was one of those captured at Chancellorsville. He had been paroled just six weeks before Gettysburg. Major James H. Coburn took over command when Merwin was killed.

Easily overlooked, Merwin's marker was erected in 1880 to note where he was killed. One of the earliest monuments of any kind in the park, it was moved in 1897 to provide a place for the erection of the Twenty-seventh Connecticut's regimental monument. At that time, the inscription had to be recut because it indicated that Merwin fell "here," which was no longer where the marker sat. It was relocated again to its current site in 1987.

Merwin had previously served in the ninety-day Second Connecticut Infantry. He reenlisted when the call for additional troops went out in 1862. He is buried in Grove Street Cemetery in New Haven, Connecticut.

G-3: First Pennsylvania Reserves Monument
39° 47.799' N, 77° 14.437' W

By order of Governor Andrew Curtin, Pennsylvania raised thirteen regiments to form the state's Reserve Corps. As those units were pressed into service, they received official regiment numbers that were twenty-nine higher than their reserve designations. Thus, the First Pennsylvania Reserves became the Thirtieth Pennsylvania Infantry, and so on.

When the First Pennsylvania Reserves were activated, they were sent to Baltimore. Approaching

companies due to the capture of eight companies at Chancellorsville, twenty-four-year-old Henry Czar Merwin was killed at the approximate location of the regiment's monument in the Wheatfield (see G-9). This small marker commemorating Merwin's death is one of five monuments to the regiment. Ironically,

the city, they were warned by police that Confederate sympathies were rampant and that they should take a different route for their own safety. Refusing to be intimidated, the regiment's officers ordered ammunition to be issued. The regiment passed through the crowded streets with no problems beyond a great deal of verbal abuse from the crowds.

On the evening of July 2, the regiment mounted a charge from the rear to this location, capturing many prisoners in the process. The next day, it struck Confederate troops on their flank, catching them by surprise and capturing more than a hundred prisoners, a battle flag, and a large number of weapons. On July 5, the regiment participated in the pursuit of Lee's army.

Colonel William C. Talley commanded the First

Pennsylvania Reserves, who suffered eight killed and 38 wounded at Gettysburg of the 444 troops brought to the field. Five of the wounded ultimately died, bringing total deaths in the regiment to 13.

The monument, dedicated in September 1890, marks the general location of the regiment on the afternoon of July 2. The inscription "Co. K Recruited at Gettysburg" was a later addition. The sculptor is unknown.

Because the men of Company K were from Gettysburg, a separate marker in their honor was erected in town on Lincoln Square (39° 49.835′ N, 77° 13.878′ W). Many members of the regiment found themselves fighting within sight of their own homes.

G-4: Second Pennsylvania Reserves Monument
39° 47.776′ N, 77° 14.473′ W

The Second Pennsylvania Reserves, also known as the Thirty-first Pennsylvania Infantry, had just

been formed when the men were ordered to report to Camp Curtin in Harrisburg, Pennsylvania. Reserve regiments were normally mustered into Federal service before being sent out of state, but in the interest of time, Colonel William B. Mann secured permission from the governor to immediately move to Baltimore. However, upon arriving there, the regiment was refused by General John Adams Dix, who said he could not accept it until it had been properly sworn in and given official orders.

The regiment then proceeded to Sandy Hook, near Harpers Ferry, where General Nathaniel Banks also refused to accept it. Banks did, however, allow it to camp there and apply to the War Department for official orders. Until receiving those orders, the regiment could not draw rations for the men. The lack of adequate food, coupled with the idea among the ranks that they could not be held because they had not been officially mustered in, led to a refusal of nearly 25 percent of the men to muster in when the orders finally came.

The morning after this large-scale refusal, the regiment was called together. Those who had sworn in already were told they would have to do so again. This time, an even larger number of men refused. At that point, those who refused were ordered to surrender their weapons and uniforms. A detail of officers was ordered to escort them to Philadelphia.

When the officers returned, they were shocked to hear that those who had already taken the oath twice had been ordered to take it a third time. Deciding it apparently was easier to get out of the service than to stay in, many of those men refused and mustered in with other organizations. By now, the regiment was down to about four hundred of its original thousand men. This prompted many to say they should have been issued Bibles instead of guns, since they took the oath more often than they fought.

Ultimately, Companies B, F, G, and I were disbanded because they fell below the standard number for acceptance. The officers of those companies were discharged from service and the men transferred to other companies.

When the Confederate army moved into Pennsylvania, the regiment petitioned the brigade to allow it to defend its home state. The regiment was ordered to Gettysburg, arriving July 2. It held its position throughout the night and into the afternoon of July 3, when it moved forward with the brigade and cleared the Wheatfield of Confederates, capturing many prisoners.

The regiment had a force of 147 at Gettysburg. It lost 10 men killed and 30 wounded. Its commander during the battle was Lieutenant Colonel George A.

Woodward, a native of Wilkes-Barre, Pennsylvania, who had moved to Milwaukee to practice law.

The monument to the Second Pennsylvania Reserves marks the approximate position the regiment held on the evening of July 2 after it charged an advancing Confederate regiment. Its actual position was about a hundred feet behind where the monument stands.

The monument was dedicated in September 1890. Its sculptor is unknown.

G-5: Colonel Charles Frederick Taylor Monument
39° 47.741' N, 77° 14.480' W

Colonel Charles Frederick Taylor responded to President Lincoln's initial call for troops after Fort Sumter was fired on, organizing his own Pennsylvania company and serving as its captain. Without waiting for state acceptance, Taylor took his men to Harrisburg and had them placed into the famed Bucktail Regiment. His men were also known as the First Rifles or the Kane Rifles.

Taylor was captured at Harrisonburg, Virginia, on June 6, 1862, as he attempted to remove a wounded officer while under fire. He was paroled two months later and fought at Antietam, after which he was promoted to the rank of colonel in the Thirteenth Pennsylvania Reserves, also known as the Forty-second Pennsylvania Infantry. At the age of twenty-three, he was the youngest commissioned colonel in the Army of the Potomac.

At Gettysburg, he was still in command of the Thirteenth Pennsylvania Reserves. On July 2, while leading a charge across the Valley of Death toward the Wheatfield, he was struck in the heart by a ball from a sharpshooter's gun and was killed instantly.

The original marker for Colonel Taylor, one of the first placed at Gettysburg, was dedicated in 1878 and stood closer to the ridge facing Little Round Top. That marker resembled a headstone. It was replaced by this larger monument, which his comrades placed here in 1905 to more accurately reflect where he received his mortal wound.

Taylor is buried in Longwood Cemetery in his hometown of Kennett Square, Pennsylvania.

G-6: 148th Pennsylvania Infantry Monument
39° 47.757' N, 77° 14.518' W

On the morning of July 1, the 148th Pennsylvania Infantry was twenty-three miles from Gettysburg.

As the men drew closer, they could hear artillery fire. Stepping up their pace, they arrived on the field as darkness gathered. Weary from their march, they slept without leaving their ranks.

The regiment was commanded by Colonel Henry Boyd McKeen, who had been wounded at Fredericksburg and would be killed at Cold Harbor a year after Gettysburg. McKeen had been transferred from the Eighty-first Pennsylvania to the 148th by the brigade commander, Colonel Edward Cross, when the regular commander, Colonel James Beaver, had gone on sick leave. Cross chose McKeen over Lieutenant Colonel Robert McFarlane, who was deemed too inexperienced to be in charge in such a large battle. McFarlane got his chance to lead the regiment on the second day of the battle, when Cross was mortally wounded and McKeen was elevated to command the brigade.

In the early hours of July 2, Private George Osman became the 148th's first casualty when an artillery shell burst above the regiment, killing him instantly.

Fighting in the Wheatfield, the 148th played a significant role in the back-and-forth flow of the battle. It reached the far edge of the Wheatfield but was eventually forced out by the final Confederate attacks, re-forming behind a stone wall as the sun set. The regiment had 468 men at Gettysburg, of whom 19 were killed, 101 wounded, and five declared missing. Of those wounded, eight would die of their injuries.

On July 3, the regiment moved to Cemetery Ridge, where it captured more than four hundred Confederates as they came over the breastworks during Pickett's Charge.

The 148th fought in every battle of the Army of the Potomac from Chancellorsville to Appomattox, where it was present for the surrender of Robert E. Lee's Army of Northern Virginia. The monument sits where the regiment was engaged on the afternoon of July 2. Fabricated by P. F. Eisenbrown and Sons, it was dedicated September 11, 1889.

A second monument to the regiment is on Hancock Avenue (39° 48.327′ N, 77° 14.090′ W). It marks the position the 148th held on the third day of the battle, when it sat in support of artillery batteries.

G-7: Eighty-first Pennsylvania Infantry Monument

39° 47.795′ N, 77° 14.518′ W

As the Eighty-first Pennsylvania approached Gettysburg, it encountered an escort of cavalry bearing the body of General John Reynolds. With this vision in their minds, the men arrived on the field the evening of July 1 after an exhausting march. They immediately built breastworks.

Lieutenant Colonel Amos Stroh had taken charge just one day before the battle when the regiment's regular commander, Colonel Henry McKeen, was transferred to the command of the 141st Pennsylvania Infantry. Late in the afternoon on July 2, Stroh moved his men to the left, where heavy fighting

was in progress. The regiment took a position in the open field, firing on Confederate troops hidden behind the stone wall visible in the distance in front of the monument. The Eighty-first fought until late evening, finally expending all its ammunition, at which time it was relieved and moved to the rear.

The monument to the Eighty-first, fabricated by P. F. Eisenbrown and Sons, was dedicated June 13, 1888. It sits at the general location the regiment occupied during the fighting on July 2. From there, it advanced across the Wheatfield toward Confederate troops protected by the nearby stone wall.

The regiment suffered sixty-two casualties in the fighting, including nine killed or mortally wounded, five officers and forty men wounded, and eight men captured or missing. The losses represented 67.4 percent of the available men, placing the Eighty-first in the top fifteen of all regiments on both sides for percentage losses in a single battle.

The regiment had already lost 176 of its 261 men at Fredericksburg. Following the additional heavy losses at Gettysburg, it faced the possibility of not being able to continue due to a lack of personnel. That problem was averted in January 1864, when most of those eligible chose to reenlist.

G-8: Sixty-first New York Infantry Monument

39° 47.819′ N, 77° 14.518′ W

Led by its Swedish-born commander, Lieutenant Colonel Knut Oscar Broady, the Sixty-first New

York Infantry formed near Cemetery Hill upon its arrival on the morning of July 2. At approximately six that afternoon, the regiment moved to this location, where it fought for about thirty minutes, sustaining heavy casualties. When they were relieved, the men were given the duty of escorting a hundred prisoners approximately two miles to the rear. They stood guard over the prisoners all night.

On the morning of July 3, Broady detached sixteen men and one officer to continue as a guard over the prisoners, taking the rest of his regiment back to the brigade, where it was exposed to heavy artillery fire.

The Sixty-first was also known as the Clinton Guards, having been formed by the merger of the old Clinton Guards and the Astor Rifles. Because the original Clinton Guards made up eight of the ten companies of the newly formed regiment, their name was retained.

The regiment's casualties at this location included six killed and fifty-eight wounded, one of whom was an officer who soon died. Many of the men's wounds were so severe that they had to be discharged from service. Although no one from the regiment was captured at Gettysburg, many were captured on other battlefields. Over the course of the war, forty-six members died as prisoners of war.

The regimental history contains a story illustrating the spirit of the men of the Sixty-first. Lieutenant Charles A. Fuller, who had lost his leg and arm, was annoyed by the groans of a wounded Confederate soldier who was housed in the same hospital tent. Finally having enough, and despite the pain from his own wounds, Fuller is said to have quieted the unfortunate Confederate by threatening to get up and throw him out of the tent.

The dedication of the monument, which marks the regiment's position on the afternoon of July 2, was held July 1, 1889. The fabricator is unknown.

G-9: Twenty-seventh Connecticut Infantry Monument
39° 47.823′ N, 77° 14.494′ W

At Gettysburg, the Twenty-seventh Connecticut, a nine-month regiment, was only a fraction of its original strength. A full eight of its companies had been captured just two months earlier at Chancellorsville. As a result, only about seventy-five men and officers remained to represent the regiment. Those troops were combined as three companies and

placed under the command of Lieutenant Colonel Henry C. Merwin. Fighting as part of Brooke's Brigade, the Twenty-seventh drove Confederate troops across the Wheatfield toward what is now Brooke Avenue. In the process, thirty-eight of the seventy-five were either killed or wounded.

A smaller monument marks the position of the Twenty-seventh at the Brooke Avenue location (39° 47.721′ N, 77° 14.826′ W). In all, five monuments to the Twenty-seventy have been erected at Gettysburg, giving the regiment the distinction of having the most monuments to the fewest men on the battlefield. The regiment's advanced position was on Stoney Hill near the Rose Farm (see H-11). In addition, the markers for Lieutenant Colonel Henry Czar Merwin (see G-2) and Captain Jedediah Chapman on DeTrobriand Avenue (39° 47.773′ N, 77°

14.729′ W) honor the Twenty-seventh; the latter is featured in Volume 1 of *So You Think You Know Gettysburg?* Both Merwin and Chapman were killed in the Wheatfield.

The monument at this location, erected by the Survivor's Association, stands on the approximate spot where Merwin was killed while leading his men in the charge across the Wheatfield. The base contains a time capsule placed by the regiment's survivors. Although difficult to see from ground level, the eagle with its wings outstretched is standing on two crossed artillery tubes. The back of the monument features Connecticut's coat of arms and the motto "*Qui Transtulit Sustinet*," or "He who transplanted still sustains."

Designed and constructed by St. Johnsbury Granite Company, the monument was dedicated

October 22, 1885. The unveiling was conducted by Ruby Merwin Oswald, niece of Lieutenant Colonel Merwin.

The regiment was discharged from service two weeks after the battle. In just nine months, it lost 533 of the 829 men who originally mustered in.

G-10: Monument to Battery D, First New York Light Artillery
39° 47.845' N, 77° 14.569' W

Battery D was en route to Gettysburg early in the morning on July 2 when it stopped for a brief rest about three miles from town. Local citizens warned the battery that Confederate skirmishers were only a mile in front. With that news, the battery immediately resumed its march, reaching the battlefield around eleven that morning and going into a line of battle with the rest of the corps.

The unit was also known as Winslow's Battery, after Captain George B. Winslow. The monument marks the battery's position on the afternoon of July 2. Battery D was the only artillery unit for either side in the Wheatfield. As Confederate troops pushed toward Winslow's position from his front and right, Union troops in retreat made it impossible for him to fire his guns. He was forced to withdraw them to avoid capture.

Fabricated by Frederick and Field, the monument was dedicated July 2, 1888. The battery of six guns was posted here until around six o'clock in the afternoon on July 2. Advancing Confederates in

Brigadier General George T. Anderson's brigade hastened Battery D's withdrawal. Ten members suffered wounds in the fighting, and eight more were declared missing. Battery D had no fatalities at Gettysburg, although ten horses were killed.

The monument fell victim to vandals in 1982, when the right cannon tube was stolen. It was replaced in 1989. Capped by a polished stone cannonball, the monument features bronze depictions of gun tubes, a spoked wheel, pyramids of cannonballs, and artillery implements. The diamond symbol of the Third Corps appears on the upper front. The state seal of New York is in the lower center.

G-11: Twenty-second Massachusetts Infantry Monument
39° 47.826' N, 77° 14.785' W

The Twenty-second Massachusetts Infantry marched through the night of July 1 to reach the bat-

ricated by Smith Granite Company and dedicated October 8, 1885. It marks the position the regiment held on July 2 as the Confederates attacked from the direction of the Rose Farm.

Lieutenant Colonel Thomas Sherwin Jr. commanded the regiment at Gettysburg. He was in charge because the regiment's colonel, William S. Tilton, had been placed in temporary command of the First Brigade, First Division, Fifth Corps.

The regiment saw eight of its men killed, twenty-seven wounded, and one declared missing. While those numbers may seem small in comparison to the losses experienced by other regiments, the thirty-six casualties represented nearly 54 percent of the sixty-seven men brought to Gettysburg.

Known for its skirmishing skills, the Twenty-second was utilized in that capacity in various battles throughout the war. Many of its officers and some of its enlisted men had previously served in three-month regiments and had signed up with the Twenty-second when their original enlistments expired.

The Twenty-second was also known as Henry Wilson's Regiment, after its first colonel. Wilson later served as vice president under Ulysses Grant.

G-12: Eighteenth Massachusetts Infantry Monument
39° 47.841' N, 77° 14.755' W

Like several other Massachusetts monuments, this one was fabricated by Smith Granite Company and dedicated October 8, 1885. Its inscription reflects

tlefield at dawn on July 2. Not immediately needed, the men took advantage of their situation and slept for a couple of hours, even as the battle raged not far from where they lay.

In late afternoon, the regiment moved to this point not far from the Rose Farm. Expecting to be in that position for some time, the men stacked paper cartridges on the ground in front of them. However, they were ordered to withdraw as Brigadier General Joseph Kershaw's South Carolina brigade approached. Their withdrawal to the Trostle Farm was heavily criticized by brigade commanders, as it was made without their knowledge.

On the final day of the battle, the regiment was posted between Little Round Top and Big Round Top and saw no appreciable action.

The monument to the Twenty-second was fab-

the wishes of most men in the regiment, and likely in all regiments: "Let us have peace."

The Eighteenth Massachusetts missed the first day's fighting, arriving at Gettysburg on the morning of July 2. Its involvement was limited to the area in and around the Wheatfield. The regiment suffered one killed, twenty-three wounded, and three declared missing.

The national flag the Eighteenth carried into the battle was relatively new, having been received just four months earlier. It replaced the regiment's original banner, which had been so badly torn in battle that it could no longer be properly tied to its staff. The state flag was also a replacement, this one for the flag captured by the Twenty-seventh Virginia at Second Manassas in August 1862. On April 14, 1905, the original state flag was returned to Massachusetts.

The regiment was commanded by a Harvard graduate, Colonel Joseph Hayes, who would be wounded at the Wilderness less than a year after

Gettysburg. When the regiment mustered out in September 1864, those men who still had time remaining on their enlistment were absorbed by the Thirty-second Massachusetts Infantry.

G-13: Twenty-eighth Massachusetts Infantry Monument
39° 47.845′ N, 77° 14.739′ W

The Twenty-eighth Massachusetts formed in 1861. Its first two years were marked by internal feuding among the officers, primarily between those Irish factions recruited from New York and those recruited from Boston. The tensions were so high that at least one commander resigned. Several other officers were reduced in rank for incompetence and neglect of duty. In October 1862, when Colonel Richard Byrnes was appointed commanding officer, the choice proved so unpopular that seven subordinate officers sent a petition to Governor John A. Andrew of Massachusetts expressing their outrage. The governor was not swayed, however, and Byrnes went on to become a well-respected leader.

Part of the Irish Brigade, the Twenty-eighth arrived on the field on July 2, missing the first day's fighting. The regiment was not at full strength, as it had suffered greatly two days earlier when a grueling thirty-two-mile march in extreme heat had resulted in 185 of the 224 men falling out with heat exhaustion. The regiment rested less than a full day before resuming its march to Gettysburg. By then, all the

could not be brought off the field.

The remainder of the regiment stood on the line the next day during Pickett's Charge. Although a significant distance from the focus of the attack, it still captured several Confederate troops.

The monument sits in the general area where the regiment fought on July 2. The large eagle perched on top is shown with folded wings, a sign of peace. Near the top is the Irish Brigade's Gaelic motto: "*Faugh A Ballaugh*," or "Clear the Way." Other symbols on the monument are an Irish harp, the crossed flags of the United States and the Irish Brigade, and the Second Corps trefoil.

The monument, sculpted by Boston artists A. Ford and T. M. Brady, was dedicated July 2, 1886.

G-14: First Michigan Infantry Monument
39° 47.841' N, 77° 14.793' W

The First Michigan left Hanover, Pennsylvania, on the evening of July 1 and reached the battlefield on July 2, taking a reserve position. It remained there until late in the afternoon, when it was ordered forward. It had no sooner established its position in the line of battle when the skirmishers were driven in and Confederate troops appeared two hundred yards in the regiment's front. The men fought a thirty-minute skirmish and drove the assault back, only to have to repeat its actions a short time later. It again repelled the attack.

The commander of the First, Colonel Ira C. Abbott,

men were back, albeit weaker.

On July 2, the regiment was ordered into the Wheatfield. Prior to its advance, Father William Corby pronounced a general absolution for the troops of the Irish Brigade, an act discussed in Volume 1 and commemorated by a monument to the priest (39° 48.205' N, 77° 14.063' W).

Moments later, led by Colonel Byrnes, the regiment caught the Confederates by surprise and took numerous prisoners before Southern reinforcements flanked it and forced a retreat. In that segment of the fighting, the Twenty-eighth lost 100 of its 224 men, many of them wounded and captured when they

fighting at First Manassas, its flag was captured, not to be returned for twenty-five years. The regiment's unofficial slogan, "From the first to the last," reflected its service from the time it entered Alexandria, Virginia, on May 24, 1861, until Lee's surrender at Appomattox on April 8, 1865. During that time, it fought in fifty-four skirmishes and general engagements.

G-15: 118th Pennsylvania Infantry Monument
39° 47.858′ N, 77° 14.809′ W

This monument sits at the position the 118th Pennsylvania Infantry held on the right of the brigade line on the afternoon of July 2. Dedicated September 12, 1889, it was fabricated by Ryegate Granite Company. The cornstalks signify the unit's designation as the Philadelphia Corn Exchange Regiment, a name given because the funds needed for raising the regiment were furnished by the Philadelphia Corn Exchange, a brokerage house that also provided a payment of ten dollars for each man who signed up. The commander was Lieutenant Colonel James Gwyn, a Philadelphia merchant who would be wounded a year later at the Wilderness.

Reaching Gettysburg on the morning of July 2, the regiment initially was placed in reserve. Late in the afternoon, it was moved to support Major General Daniel Sickles's Third Corps. The 118th Pennsylvania was soon heavily engaged in the fighting, losing two killed, five wounded, and two missing in this segment of the battle. Overall, it had three killed,

was shot in the face in this action. His command was taken over by Lieutenant Colonel William A. Throop, even though he had already been wounded himself. At about seven-thirty that night, the regiment was relieved and fell back to a rear position.

The monument to the First Michigan was dedicated October 8, 1885. Sitting on a boulder, it features a Maltese cross on two sides and a stand of arms and a variety of military accouterments on the front. The monument is located at the position the regiment held on July 2. The sculptor is unknown.

The regiment had 21 officers and 240 men present for duty at Gettysburg. Of those, one officer, First Lieutenant Amos Ladd, and four men were killed, six officers and 27 men were wounded, and four men were declared missing.

The regiment was the first raised in Michigan after President Lincoln called for volunteers. In the

nineteen wounded, and three declared missing.

The next day, it moved to Big Round Top. Another monument marks its position there (see I-6). That monument was dedicated September 8, 1884.

On the morning of July 4, the regiment came under fire from Confederate skirmishers who had stayed behind to cover the retreat of Lee's army. Small skirmishes continued for the next nine days until Lee crossed the Potomac.

G-16: 140th Pennsylvania Infantry Monument
39° 47.859' N, 77° 14.773' W

Entering the fight in the early-evening hours on July 2, the 140th Pennsylvania quickly found itself in a fight against troops from Brigadier General Joseph Kershaw's South Carolina brigade. Taking shelter among the surrounding boulders, the men of the 140th saw two of their number receive the Medal of Honor for their actions. Sergeant James Pipes of Company A and Lieutenant James Purman retreated with the rest of the regiment on July 2. The two stopped to pick up and carry a wounded comrade to a place of safety. In the process, both were severely wounded; Purman had his leg amputated. A year later, Pipes, by then a captain and in command of a skirmish line, voluntarily assisted in checking a Confederate flank movement at Reams Station, Virginia. He was again severely wounded, losing his arm. For those two acts of bravery, Captain Pipes was awarded the Medal of Honor. Purman received the Medal of

ible on the boulder (39° 47.900′ N, 77° 14.283′ W). His story is discussed in Volume 1.

The monument is located at the 140th's position on the afternoon of July 2. It was fabricated by P. F. Eisenbrown and Sons and dedicated September 11, 1889. A second monument to the regiment sits across the road (39° 47.856′ N, 77° 14.736′ W). It was sculpted by John Flaherty and dedicated August 11, 1885. It also indicates the general position of the 140th on the afternoon of July 2. It served as the regimental marker until this larger monument was placed.

G-17: Sixth Pennsylvania Reserves Monument
39° 47.868′ N, 77° 14.383′ W

The Sixth Pennsylvania Reserves reached Gettysburg at two in the afternoon on July 2. Shortly after arriving, they made a short charge from Little Round Top. They remained at their new position throughout the night. Skirmishing began early in the morning on July 3 and continued all day. As evening approached, the Sixth made another charge. This effort resulted in the capture of several prisoners, the recapture of a Union gun, and the freeing of several Union prisoners.

The monument is located at the approximate position the regiment held on the evening of July 2. The sculptor is unknown. Dedication ceremonies were held in September 1890.

Six men of the regiment received the Medal of

Honor for his bravery at Gettysburg.

The regiment had 590 officers and men at Gettysburg and lost 37 killed, 144 wounded (16 of whom died), and 60 missing. Among the dead on July 2 was Colonel Richard P. Roberts, the regimental commander. Lieutenant Colonel John Fraser took command when Roberts fell.

Also killed was Captain David Acheson of Company C. His body was temporarily buried adjacent to a boulder on the John Weikert farm. The companions who buried him scratched his initials, *D. A.*, into the boulder so his family could find his body. A few years later, survivors of the regiment added *140 P.V.* Acheson's family reinterred his body in Washington, Pennsylvania, but the markings are still vis-

Honor for a single action in which all took part. Sergeant George W. Mears and Corporal Chester S. Furman of Company A, Sergeant John W. Hart and Corporal J. Levi Roush of Company D, Sergeant Wallace W. Johnson of Company G, and Corporal Thaddeus Smith of Company E all volunteered to charge a log house near Devil's Den on July 2, capturing a squad of Confederate sharpshooters.

An interesting fact surrounding the awarding of the Medal of Honor to these six men was that only one received it initially. Sergeant Mears got the award on February 16, 1897. Six months later, Corporal Furman, Sergeant Hart, and Corporal Roush were awarded the medal. On May 5, 1900, Corporal Smith received his. Not until August 8, 1900, did Sergeant Johnson receive his. Thus, it took three full years before all six citations were approved, despite the fact that the men took part in the same action.

The Sixth Pennsylvania Reserves was also known as the Thirty-fifth Pennsylvania Infantry. Lieutenant Colonel Wellington H. Ent commanded the regiment. He was killed a year later in the Overland Campaign. At Gettysburg, the regiment suffered two men killed and twenty-two wounded.

G-18: Third Massachusetts Battery Monument
39° 47.803' N, 77° 14.286' W

The Third Massachusetts Battery arrived at Gettysburg at about four in the afternoon on July 2 with the rest of the Artillery Brigade. It was left in the rear of the First Division to await orders. When those orders went out for the battery to move to the front, it could not be found, having already been moved to the rear of the Third Corps by someone on General

Daniel Sickles's staff. Battery I of the Fifth United States Artillery had been commandeered in the same manner, leaving the Fifth Corps, where the Third Massachusetts Battery belonged, short of artillery. The battery remained in position until dark, then moved in the middle of the night to the extreme left of the Union line, where it stayed until the end of the battle.

Dedicated October 8, 1885, the monument was fabricated by Smith Granite Company. It sits at the position of the regiment late in the afternoon on July 2.

The Third was also known as Martin's Battery or as Battery C, Massachusetts Light Artillery. It was commanded at Gettysburg by Lieutenant Aaron Francis Walcott. It brought 124 men to the field, six of whom were wounded in the fighting. In addition, two horses were killed and four wounded.

G-19: 139th Pennsylvania Infantry Monument
39° 47.796′ N, 77° 14.273′ W

The 139th Pennsylvania arrived at Gettysburg at midafternoon on July 2, following a thirty-six-mile march that took all night. That evening, the regiment moved with the brigade to support the Union left, taking a position on the right of Big Round Top. From there, it moved into the Wheatfield, pushing the enemy ahead of it. The regiment then returned to the position marked by this monument, where it remained until the next evening.

On the evening of July 3, the 139th advanced

again, recapturing a gun and three caissons lost by the Ninth Massachusetts Battery (see F-23), before returning to this location. The advanced position is marked by a monument near the intersection of Sickles Avenue and Wheatfield Road (39° 48.067′ N, 77° 14.821′ W). That monument was dedicated in 1886.

The regiment joined in the pursuit of the Confederate army on July 4, engaging Lee's rear guard at nearby Fairfield, Pennsylvania, in a brief skirmish.

The 139th had 511 present at Gettysburg. Of those, four were killed or mortally wounded, including Captain Jeremiah M. Sample. Another 16 were wounded. The regimental commander, Colonel Frederick H. Collier, reportedly was wounded and forced out of action when he accidentally shot

himself in the foot. Lieutenant Colonel William H. Moody took his place.

The monument was erected by the commonwealth of Pennsylvania on September 11, 1889, following fabrication by Smith Granite Company. The regiment held this position from the evening of July 2 until the end of the battle.

G-20: Ninety-third Pennsylvania Infantry Monument
39° 47.821' N, 77° 14.254' W

After a grueling nineteen-hour march in oppressive heat, the Ninety-third Pennsylvania launched an attack into the Wheatfield that resulted in the capture of several prisoners. A relocated monument marks that site (see J-5). On its return, the regiment moved to this position, where it remained for the rest of the battle.

The regiment originally served as a three-month unit, the Fourteenth Pennsylvania Volunteer Infantry. Methodist minister James M. McCarter was the chaplain. When the regiment re-formed, Colonel McCarter was the man responsible for bringing it together. Because the men were organized at nearby Lebanon, Pennsylvania, they were referred to as the Lebanon Infantry.

Fabricated by P. F. Eisenbrown, this monument marks the position the Ninety-third held after its counterattack in the Wheatfield on the evening of July 2. It was dedicated October 3, 1888.

The boulder on which the monument sits is

Remains of original base

the same one that supported the original regimental monument. Just a few yards away, the broken remains of the original base are visible, complete with inscriptions. That base was removed when the original monument was moved in 1888. The new monument was placed on top of the original base's lower section.

Of the 270 men in the regiment, eight were killed and 21 wounded.

G-21: Sixty-second New York Infantry Monument
39° 47.831' N, 77° 14.244' W

This monument was sculpted by Byron M. Pickett, fabricated by Maurice J. Power, and dedicated July 2, 1888. It sits where the Sixty-second New York was positioned just before it mounted a countercharge into the Wheatfield with the Ninety-third and 139th Pennsylvania infantries and recaptured two of Captain George B. Winslow's guns. That charge is depicted on a plaque on the rear of the monument.

The Sixty-second was commanded at Gettysburg by Colonel David J. Nevin. When Nevin became brigade commander on July 1, Lieutenant Colonel Theodore B. Hamilton assumed temporary command of the regiment.

Also known as Anderson's Zouaves, after Major Robert Anderson, the unit's organizer, the regiment had one man killed and 11 wounded at Gettysburg out of a force of 237. Anderson is best known for being the commander of Fort Sumter when it was bombarded in 1861, initiating the war.

Three of the regiment's men—Corporal Edward Brown of Company G, Private James R. Evans of Company H, and Sergeant Charles E. Morse of Company I—received the Medal of Honor, although not for their actions at Gettysburg.

G-22: 102nd Pennsylvania Infantry Monument
39° 47.846' N, 77° 14.244' W

A detachment of only three officers and a hundred men represented the 102nd Pennsylvania Infantry in the battle. While that detachment accompanied an ammunition train to Gettysburg, the bulk of the regiment was on picket duty, guarding the roads between the town and Westminster, Maryland.

On July 2, the detachment and the supply train undertook a thirty-six-mile journey at top speed to get the badly needed ammunition to the battlefield as quickly as possible. They reached Gettysburg at daybreak on July 3. Its mission of protecting the ammu-

G-23: Ninety-eighth Pennsylvania Infantry Monument
39° 47.855' N, 77° 14.199' W

The Ninety-eighth Pennsylvania Infantry was on duty in Manchester, Maryland, when the fighting in Gettysburg began on July 1. That evening, it undertook a forced march to the battle.

Arriving on the field late in the afternoon on July 2, it formed on the right front of Little Round Top (see I-22). Almost immediately, the men were ordered to charge into the Wheatfield and the surrounding woods in support of Major General Daniel Sickles's Third Corps. This action gave them the distinction of being one of the few regiments in the Sixth Corps to see actual fighting at Gettysburg. They rejoined the rest of the brigade as darkness fell, reassembling in the area marked by the monument.

The regiment's total casualties for the battle were two officers and ten men wounded, most of them by sharpshooter fire.

nition train completed, the detachment was immediately assigned to the Sixty-second New York Infantry and spent the day on skirmish duty.

On July 5, the detachment participated in the pursuit of Robert E. Lee, rejoining the main body of the regiment at Middletown, Maryland.

The monument marks the position the detachment held on July 3. Fabricated by H. Oursler and Sons, it was dedicated September 11, 1889.

The regiment was commanded at Gettysburg by Lieutenant Robert W. Lyon, a blacksmith in civilian life. Prior to taking command, Lyon had served as the regimental adjutant. In 1864, he was wounded twice within a month—at the Third Battle of Winchester in September and at Fair Oaks in October.

The regiment suffered no casualties at Gettysburg.

One company of the Ninety-eighth spent July 4 burying the dead, while the other nine performed picket duty. On July 5, the entire regiment took part in the pursuit of Lee's army.

The men were originally mustered in as the Twenty-first Pennsylvania Infantry, a three-month regiment. When they reorganized at the end of their enlistment, their new regiment was designated the Ninety-eighth Pennsylvania Infantry. At Gettysburg, the regiment was commanded by Major John B. Kohler, a native of Germany who would be killed at Cedar Creek, Virginia, in October 1864.

G-24: John Weikert Farm
39° 47.874' N, 77° 14.229' W

This farm was the home of newlyweds John T. and Sarah Weikert at the time of the battle. John Weikert, a journeyman carpenter, was probably not at home, having enlisted in Company B of the 138th Pennsylvania Infantry a year earlier. He most likely was with his regiment guarding railroads in the vicinity of Baltimore. He was wounded at Mine Run, Virginia, four months after Gettysburg.

The buildings currently on the farm were not there during the battle. The house and barn were constructed in the late 1800s. The Weikert Farm was eventually occupied by Francis Althoff and his family; the property is occasionally referred to as the Althoff Farm. It was acquired by the Gettysburg Battlefield Memorial Association and turned over to the War Department in 1896.

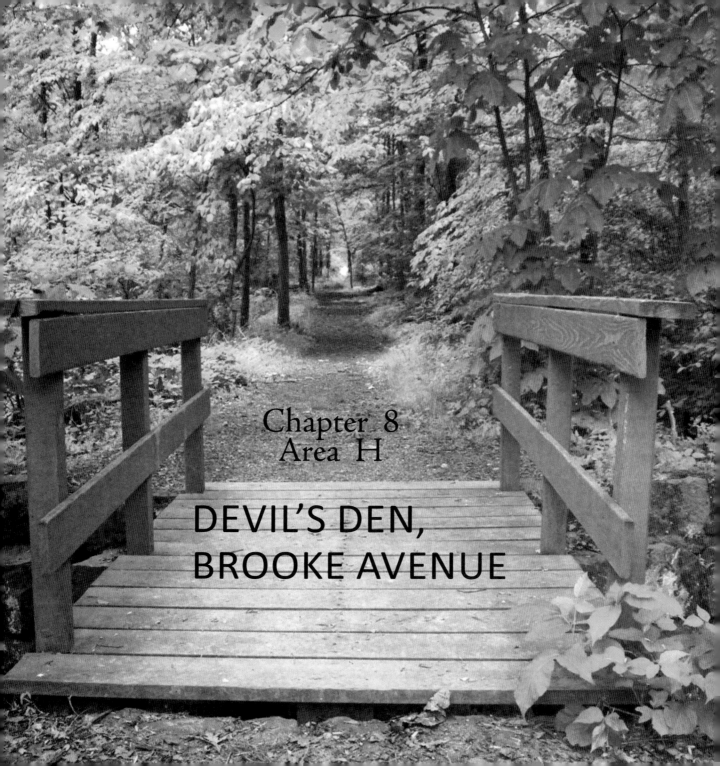

Chapter 8
Area H

DEVIL'S DEN,
BROOKE AVENUE

Area H

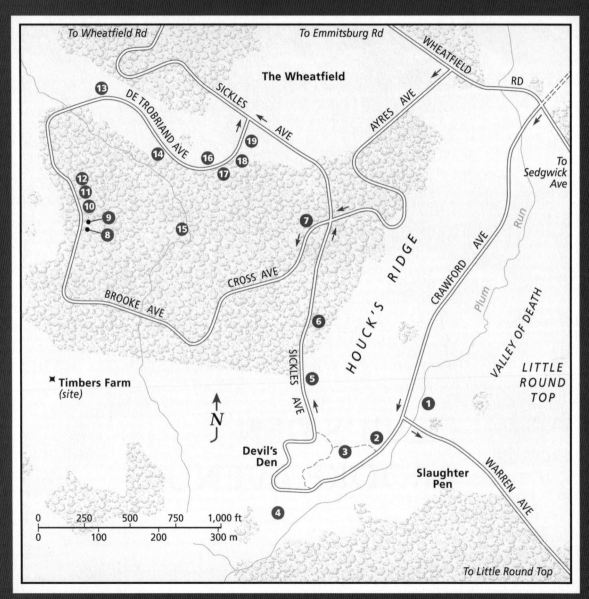

To Wheatfield Rd

To Emmitsburg Rd

WHEATFIELD

The Wheatfield

SICKLES AVE

DE TROBRIAND AVE

AYRES AVE

RD

To Sedgwick Ave

13

19

14

16

18

17

12
11
10
9
8

15

7

CROSS AVE

HOUCK'S RIDGE

CRAWFORD AVE

Plum Run

VALLEY OF DEATH

BROOKE AVE

SICKLES AVE

6

LITTLE ROUND TOP

✶ Timbers Farm
(site)

N

5

1

Devil's
Den

2

3

Slaughter
Pen

WARREN AVE

0   250   500   750   1,000 ft
0   100   200   300 m

4

To Little Round Top

On the afternoon of July 2, 1863, the fighting in the Wheatfield saw Union troops pushed back. Confederate forces fought their way through the area of what is now Brooke Avenue, sweeping across Seminary Ridge toward an outcropping of huge granite boulders known as Devil's Den.

Meanwhile, the men of the Fourth New York Battery held their position on the upper side of Devil's Den. The rock formation provided a good defensive position, but it also made bringing in ammunition difficult. Ammunition limbers could not reach the guns, so ammunition had to be hand-carried. Also, two of the battery's six guns could not be brought into position, due to the rocky terrain. Worse, the presence of the boulders meant there was only a small avenue of escape, should the need arise.

At the base of Devil's Den, a large field of similar boulders provided cover for attackers. This area saw such carnage that day that it would become forever known as "the Slaughter Pen."

A short distance from Devil's Den sat a triangular field. It was across this field that troops from the First Texas Infantry and the Fifteenth Georgia Infantry rushed toward the guns of the Fourth New York Battery. The 124th New York launched a coun-terattack that slowed the assault. Troops from the Fourth Maine Infantry and the Ninety-ninth Pennsylvania Infantry joined in, but Southern reinforcements from the Third Arkansas Infantry, coupled with additional attackers arriving behind the Union rear, overwhelmed the Federal troops. In the fighting, Colonel A. Van Horne Ellis and Major James Cromwell of the 124th New York were killed.

Once Devil's Den was in Confederate hands, sharpshooters moved in and made their presence known by firing at any Union troops unfortunate enough to make themselves visible on Little Round Top.

Cross Avenue, which becomes Brooke Avenue after the sharp curve, is the site of the remains of the Timbers Farm. Volume 1 tells the tragic story of Mr. Timbers. Past the Rose Farm, the 110th Pennsylvania Monument comes into view, followed by a small stone marker on the left that appears to be a grave headstone. In reality, it marks the general location where Captain Jedediah Chapman of the Twenty-seventh Connecticut Infantry fell. No other monuments from Volume 1 are in this general area.

H-1: Fortieth New York Infantry Monument

39° 47.542′ N, 77° 14.427′ W

The makeup of the Fortieth New York was unusual, as only four of the ten companies were from New York. The others came from Massachusetts and Philadelphia. This led to funds for the monument being appropriated from two states, Massachusetts and New York. This is the only monument on the field with such a distinction.

Formed under the direction of New York mayor Fernando Wood, the regiment was instrumental in repelling the Confederate assault on Little Round Top. The Fortieth arrived just about the time that General Evander M. Law's and Brigadier General Henry L. Benning's brigades were about to flank the Union positions from the south. Although it helped stabilize the Union line, the Fortieth could do little to recapture the guns of Captain James Smith's Fourth

New York Independent Battery on top of Devil's Den.

The monument features a soldier peering from behind a large rock, much as the men of the Fortieth must have done in the fighting at Gettysburg. Viewed from the front, the monument has a large rock to its right with the regiment's name carved on it. The markings have faded over the years and are nearly impossible to see unless someone has marked them in, as has been done in the accompanying shot.

The sculptor of the monument was R. D. Barr. The contractor for the granite portion was Smith Granite Company, while that for the bronze tablet was Bureau Brothers. The monument was dedicated July 2, 1888. The regiment held this position on the second day of fighting.

Also known as the Mozart regiment, after the Mozart Hall Committee, which helped organize the regiment, the Fortieth was commanded by Colonel Thomas W. Egan. It had 23 killed, 120 wounded,

was flanked on its left when Georgia troops under Brigadier General Henry L. Benning broke through the United States Sharpshooters in their assault on the Slaughter Pen and Little Round Top.

Adjacent to the monument sits a large boulder bearing the inscription "4th ME" and the diamond insignia of the Third Corps. This boulder is believed to have served as the regiment's marker until the monument was erected.

and seven declared missing at Gettysburg. Among the wounded was Colonel Egan.

Along with a number of other Gettysburg markers, this monument was vandalized on March 1, 1913.

H-2: Fourth Maine Infantry Monument
39° 47.512′ N, 77° 14.485′ W

The monument to the Fourth Maine Infantry was unveiled October 10, 1888, and dedicated a year later, on October 3, 1889. It marks the position the regiment held during the afternoon on July 2 in support of the Fourth New York Battery. The regiment

The regimental commander, Colonel Elijah Walker, was wounded in this area on July 2 and was replaced by Captain Edwin Libby. Walker and Libby would have another connection in 1864 at the Wilderness, where Walker was wounded and Libby killed. At Gettysburg, the regiment counted twenty-two killed, thirty-eight wounded, and fifty-six missing.

It moved to a position near the Angle the next day.

The Fourth Maine had gained a measure of notoriety in September 1861 when the men were told that their enlistment was for three years, rather than the three months they claimed. The resulting mutiny led to the transfer of a hundred men to another command. One company was completely disbanded and replaced two months later by new recruits. Other regiments also reported similar complaints. Michael Shaara dramatized the mutiny of the Second Maine Infantry in his Pulitzer Prize–winning novel, *The Killer Angels*, which was made into the movie *Gettysburg*.

H-3: Table Rock
39° 47.501' N, 77° 14.521' W

More than 180 million years ago, shale, sandstone, and siltstone were deposited in the Gettysburg area. Those deposits became known as the Gettysburg Formation. The surrounding hills were formed when two large dikes and a slab of molten rock, called the Gettysburg Sill, intruded into the Gettysburg Formation as a result of geologic activity. One of the results of this geologic activity was the collection of rocks and boulders known today as Devil's Den.

Although this particular rock formation at Devil's Den is officially known as Table Rock, it is just as often referred to as Duck Rock. A close examination reveals the reason behind the alternate name. From certain angles, such as the one shown, the boulders take on the likeness of a duck sitting on a nest.

H-4: Elephant Rock
39° 47.448' N, 77° 14.599' W

Much as Table Rock is often called Duck Rock, this unusual rock formation received its name because of its likeness—in this case, to an elephant when viewed from a certain position.

For the adventurous who dare to climb to the top, the rock carving "D. Forney 1849" is the reward. David Forney was a native of Gettysburg and a graduate of Pennsylvania College (now Gettysburg College). He moved to Virginia, where he became quite successful as a developer of zinc mines. Although he

who is shown casually standing with his arms folded across his chest, the pose he supposedly struck as he observed the Texas Brigade advancing toward his position.

In a desperate attempt to save the guns of the Fourth New York Independent Battery, the 124th launched a counterattack through the Triangular Field against the Texas Brigade. As it faltered, Major James Cromwell rode through the heavy fire in an attempt to rally his men. His effort was so heroic that many of the Texans refused to shoot at him and exhorted their companions to refrain as well. It was

lived in Virginia throughout the war, he did not serve in either army. When he died in 1911, his remains were returned to Gettysburg for burial in Evergreen Cemetery.

H-5: 124th New York Infantry Monument
39° 47.563' N, 77° 14.560' W

The men of the 124th New York were recruited in Orange County, New York, giving rise to their nickname, "the Orange Blossoms." The men showed pride in their home by wearing small orange ribbons on their uniforms. Citizens of Orange County contributed much of the funding to construct the monument at Gettysburg, the first erected to honor a New York regiment.

The monument marks the position the regiment held the afternoon of July 2. The figure depicts Colonel A. Van Horne Ellis, the regimental commander,

not to be, however, and both Cromwell and his horse were killed, as was Colonel Ellis. Ellis had led the attack on horseback, against the advice of his men, who feared he would be an inviting target. Ellis, who had predicted on the march to Gettysburg that he would not survive the battle, refused their advice. Legend has it that the regiment's monument sits on the very rock on which Ellis's body was placed.

Ellis was replaced by Lieutenant Colonel Francis Cummins, who had been dismissed from the Sixth Iowa Infantry for being drunk at Shiloh. Cummins was wounded in the fighting around Devil's Den and again a year later at the Wilderness.

Dedicated July 2, 1884, the monument was designed by two separate individuals. The granite portion was designed by Peter B. Laird, the bronze by Maurice J. Power. The scabbard and sword are replacements for the originals, which were vandalized many years ago. The current sword is actually a second replacement, made in 1989 by Karkadoulias Bronze Art.

The regiment brought 18 officers and 220 enlisted men to the battle, losing seven officers and 85 men either killed, wounded, or missing. The names of the 33 killed are listed on the monument. The remainder of the regiment moved on July 3 to a position near the Jacob Hummelbaugh farm, where its position is noted by a small stone marker at the intersection of Pleasonton and Hancock avenues (39° 48.52′ N, 77° 14.117′ W).

H-6: Eighty-sixth New York Infantry Monument
39° 47.614′ N, 77° 14.557′ W

In late afternoon on July 2, the Eighty-sixth New York Infantry played an important role in the fight for Devil's Den. As the Third Arkansas Infantry pushed across the Triangular Field, it was met by a barrage from the Union defenders. Then the Eighty-sixth charged down the hill with the Twentieth Indiana and Ninety-ninth Pennsylvania infantries and forced the Arkansas troops back. The regiment fought in the area for the rest of the afternoon until the Union line was forced to retreat.

The Eighty-sixth's monument was fabricated by Frederick and Field and dedicated July 2, 1888. It marks the regiment's position the afternoon of

H-7: Twentieth Indiana Infantry Monument
39° 47.695' N, 77° 14.561' W

The monument in the background of this photo is that to the Twentieth Indiana Infantry. Just as significant is the large rock in the foreground. It was at this boulder that the regiment's commander, Colonel John Wheeler, was killed instantly when he was shot in the temple as he rallied his troops against the Third Arkansas, the Fifty-ninth Georgia, and part of the First Texas during the fight for nearby Devil's Den. Known as Wheeler Rock, the boulder for

the second day of fighting. The plaque shows a scene commonplace at many homes on both sides during the war. A woman—presumably a mother or wife—grieves over the body of a fallen soldier. The inscription reads, "I yield him unto his Country and to his God."

The Eighty-sixth was also known as the Steuben Rangers. The regiment was commanded by Lieutenant Colonel Benjamin Higgins, who was the chief engineer in the Syracuse Fire Department. When Higgins was wounded in this general area, Major Jacob H. Lansing took his place.

The regiment had eleven killed, fifty-one wounded, and four declared missing at Gettysburg.

On July 3, Private Oliver Rood of Company B rushed through heavy fire to capture the flag of the Twenty-first North Carolina Infantry, an action that led to his receiving the Medal of Honor.

The fabricator of the monument was A. A. McKain. Dedication ceremonies were conducted October 28, 1885. The monument represents the position the regiment held late in the afternoon on July 2.

H-8: Second Delaware Infantry Monument
39° 47.691' N, 77° 14.819' W

Although the Second was designated a Delaware regiment, four of its companies were actually recruited from Philadelphia and Maryland. This was done so the state could quickly fill its quota and expedite getting the regiment into service.

Fighting at the Sunken Road at Antietam nine months earlier, the Second Delaware had been one of the Union regiments that broke through the Confederate line. Having captured the colors of the Sixteenth Mississippi, it prepared to charge one last time, only to receive orders to retire. Objecting strongly, the regiment began such a slow retreat that it was cheered by other Union regiments that also disagreed with the order. That subtle act of defiance led several New York troops to shout to the men of the Second that they were crazy, resulting in the nickname that followed the regiment until the end of the war: "the Crazy Delawares." While there are other versions of how the nickname came about, this is the

many years after the war bore a painted inscription that said, "Col. John Wheeler, 20th Ind. Vols., Killed in Action July 2, 1863." Wheeler is buried in Maplewood Memorial Cemetery in Crown Point, Indiana.

Colonel Wheeler had a premonition he would die at Gettysburg, expressing that concern in a letter to his wife just before the battle. He said the letter might be his last but that he believed the Union would win the battle before the sun went down.

Including Wheeler, the regiment had 32 killed, 114 wounded, and 10 declared missing. When Wheeler was killed, Lieutenant Colonel William C. L. Taylor assumed command until he was wounded, at which time Captain Erasmus C. Gilbreath took over.

most recognized. However the name originated, it became a badge of honor for the men, who embraced it proudly.

The regiment arrived at Gettysburg early on July 2 and formed along Cemetery Ridge. That evening, it made a charge through the Wheatfield, reaching this location in the Rose Woods. While fighting in this area, the regiment captured several prisoners. Heavy fighting forced its withdrawal to the area of the Trostle Farm. It was at that location that Colonel William P. Baily was wounded by artillery fire, after which Captain Charles Christman assumed command.

The next day, living up to the nickname, part of the regiment made a charge of its own after Pickett's Charge was defeated. The men captured a large number of Confederates.

On July 5, the regiment participated in the pursuit of Lee's army.

Of the 280 men brought to Gettysburg, eleven were killed, sixty-one wounded, and twelve declared missing.

The monument was fabricated by Thomas Davidson. The contractor for the installation was William N. Miller. Dedication of the monument, which originally sat in the Wheatfield, took place June 10, 1886. The monument was moved to its present location August 17, 1909.

H-9: Sixty-fourth New York Infantry Monument
39° 47.698′ N, 77° 14.819′ W

On July 2, the Sixty-fourth New York arrived at Gettysburg with 185 men and 19 commissioned officers. The regiment quickly advanced with the brigade across the Wheatfield under heavy fire. In the assault, it captured a number of Confederates.

This is one of ninety monuments dedicated to New York troops in the Gettysburg Campaign. It sits at the point of the regiment's position on the evening of July 2, following its charge across the Wheatfield. Sculpted by W. B. Archibald and carved by M. G. Cannon, the monument was dedicated July 2, 1890.

On July 3, the regiment built breastworks and fought tenaciously against Pickett's Charge. July 4 was devoted to burying the dead. Services were conducted by the chaplain of the 145th Pennsylvania Infantry, John H. W. Stuckenberg. After an inspection

one of the casualties took place on July 3, when a man was wounded on picket duty. The rest occurred in the charge across the Wheatfield on July 2. Among the officers killed was Captain Henry Fuller, whose death is commemorated by a marker discussed in H-15.

H-10: Fifty-third Pennsylvania Infantry Monument
39° 47.711' N, 77° 14.819' W

The Fifty-third Pennsylvania was instrumental in forcing the Confederates across the Wheatfield, reaching and holding this position until a counterattack broke the Union line. The regimental veterans' association chose this location and design for the monument, which is curious because the figure is shown wearing a winter uniform, even though the battle was fought in the heat of July. The monument is titled *The Sentinel*.

Arriving the morning of July 2, the men lined up on the extreme left of the Second Corps, connecting with the right flank of the Third Corps. When a Confederate battery in the Wheatfield began finding its mark, the Fifty-third was part of a bayonet charge led by Colonel John R. Brooke, who was carrying the Pennsylvanians' regimental colors. The intent of the charge was to either capture the battery or drive it from the field. The charge was successful in scattering not only the battery but also a large number of infantry troops. Unfortunately, the lines on either side of the Fifty-third did not drive as far, so the regiment's

on July 5, the regiment marched with the brigade to Frederick, Maryland.

The regiment originated as the Sixty-fourth New York Militia but reorganized as a volunteer infantry unit in the autumn of 1861. The Sixty-fourth New York Infantry was also known as the First Cattaraugus Regiment because so many of its members came from Cattaraugus County. Its commander at Gettysburg was Colonel Daniel G. Bingham, who was wounded in this area on July 2. He would die of an unrelated disease a year later. When advised that his illness was terminal, he refused to leave his regiment, serving until he became so weak he could no longer lead his command into battle. Major Leman W. Bradley replaced Bingham.

The regiment had four officers and eleven men killed at Gettysburg, seven officers and fifty-five men wounded, and eighteen men declared missing. Only

exposed flanks were in danger of being overrun. The Fifty-third was forced to return to its original position, suffering numerous casualties in the process, including Colonel Brooke. Following his wounding, command fell to Lieutenant Colonel Richard Mc-Michael, a veteran of the war with Mexico.

The next day, despite not being actively engaged, the regiment came under heavy artillery fire. It held its position until the afternoon of July 5, when it moved out in pursuit of Lee's army, bivouacking at nearby Two Taverns, Pennsylvania, along Baltimore Pike.

Represented by only three companies—A, B, and K—the Fifty-third brought 135 men to the field, of whom seven were killed, 67 wounded, and six captured or missing, for a 59 percent casualty rate.

The monument's granite portion was built by H. Oursler and Sons. The sculptor was A. Wagner. The bronze work was done by Henry Bonnard Bronze Company. First Lieutenant and Adjutant Charles P. Hatch gave the address when the monument was dedicated September 1, 1889. It marks the advanced position of the regiment late in the afternoon on July 2.

H-11: Twenty-seventh Connecticut Infantry Monument
39° 47.721' N, 77° 14.826' W

Only seventy-five men and officers of the Twenty-seventh Connecticut were available for duty at Gettysburg, eight full companies having been captured

at Chancellorsville just a few weeks earlier. The regiment's commander, Lieutenant Colonel Henry Czar Merwin, was killed in the Wheatfield, where the tallest monument to the regiment now stands (see G-9). Major James H. Coburn took command when Merwin was killed.

This monument, one of five honoring the Twenty-seventh, marks the regiment's farthest advance on the afternoon of July 2. No other regiment at Gettysburg has as many monuments to such a small number of men. Another of the monuments to the Twenty-seventh is a small positional marker (39° 47.718′ N, 77° 14.815′ W) not far from this monument; the two were dedicated together. The others are a marker for Captain Jedediah Chapman on DeTrobriand Avenue (39° 47.77′ N, 77° 14.729′ W) and a similar marker for Lieutenant Colonel Merwin (see G-2).

Dedication of this monument took place October 27, 1889. Discerning readers will note that the regiment's main monument in the Wheatfield was dedicated in 1885. Why the four-year delay until this monument was erected?

In truth, no plan existed for another monument after the regiment's other markers had been dedicated. But in the late 1880s, the state of Connecticut appropriated funds for the regiment to erect a new monument. Since its other positions were already marked, this location was chosen as representative of the farthest point the men reached in the charge across the Wheatfield. Thus, anyone wishing to follow the Twenty-seventh's charge can get a fairly accurate idea of its route by following the regimental markers.

H-12: 145th Pennsylvania Infantry Monument
39° 47.736′ N, 77° 14.826′ W

During the afternoon on July 2, the 145th Pennsylvania charged into the Wheatfield, capturing several prisoners. This monument to the regiment marks the position it held as it fought General Joseph B. Kershaw's brigade at the edge of the field. It held the position for only a short time before being outflanked and forced back.

Commanded by Colonel Hiram Brown, the 145th held the extreme right of the brigade in the fight and suffered severely. It brought 228 officers and men to Gettysburg, of whom three officers and 21 men were either killed or mortally wounded. An additional six officers, including Colonel Brown, and 50 men were wounded, and 10 men were captured or

Dedicated September 11, 1889, the monument was fabricated by Ryegate Granite Company. The figure stands in combat stance.

H-13: Trolley Line
39° 47.808' N, 77° 14.803' W

Twenty-one years after the war, a trolley line was constructed despite the protests of many veterans, who feared that the clearing of land would desecrate the ground on which many of their comrades had died. When completed, the line ran from the town of Gettysburg through the Wheatfield and Devil's Den to Little Round Top, where a park was established. Smaller parks also sprouted along the trolley

missing. When Colonel Brown suffered his wound, command fell to Captain John W. Reynolds, who would also be wounded. Captain Moses Oliver assumed command when Reynolds fell.

Later in the summer, when the regiment began receiving drafted soldiers, discipline problems quickly arose. The newcomers were not accepted well by the veterans. Desertions became increasingly common. Over the winter, the regiment sent recruiting detachments in hopes of finding additional men. Their efforts were successful. By spring, the regiment again had more than seven hundred men. Following the addition of those volunteers, discipline returned, and the regiment went on to serve faithfully until May 31, 1865.

line near Devil's Den and the Rose Farm, as entrepreneurs sought to capitalize on the early years of Gettysburg's tourist trade. A spur of the Gettysburg and Harrisburg Railroad also ran across the battlefield, passing through the fields of Pickett's Charge on its way to Little Round Top.

The park on Little Round Top proved hugely popular, boasting a dance pavilion, a saloon, several eating establishments, a merry-go-round, and a small museum. More people visited the amusement park than came to see the battlefield, according to some contemporary accounts. A victim of its own success, however, the park soon began to attract unsavory visitors. Vandalism, gambling, alcohol abuse, and prostitution all took place in the park on what is now one of the most visited parts of the battlefield. Guard shacks soon had to be built to monitor the activities (see I-20). The trolley went out of business in 1915 after considerable legal wrangling.

This trail, now used by visitors on foot or horseback, is the old trolley line roadbed. Remnants of the line are still visible on many parts of the battlefield.

H-14: Eighth New Jersey Infantry Monument
39° 47.759′ N, 77° 14.735′ W

The Eighth New Jersey sat waiting at this location on the afternoon of July 2. It soon was struck by Brigadier General George Anderson's brigade of Georgia troops. Having little support, the men quickly were forced back. As they retreated, their colors became snagged in a tree. As the men of the Eighth struggled to free their flag, the onrushing Georgians poured a horrendous fire into their midst, causing many casualties, including Colonel John Ramsey, who commanded the regiment. His position was taken by Captain John Langton. Ramsey would be wounded again at Petersburg.

During the battle, Lieutenant Andrew J. Mandeville of Company D was accused of attempting to leave his company while actively engaged with the enemy. Although stopped by Ramsey's drawn pistol, Mandeville left again when the colonel was wounded. Mandeville said he had been wounded and went to Littlestown, Pennsylvania, for treatment. The un-

lucky Mandeville encountered Ramsey again when the colonel was taken to the same location for treatment of his wound. When ordered back, Mandeville refused and was declared to be absent without leave. He would return to the regiment in August. Mandeville's claim was supported by the regimental surgeon. He was found not guilty at a court-martial.

On July 3, the regiment supported batteries on Cemetery Ridge. Its monument was dedicated June 30, 1888. It sits where the regiment fought on July 2. The sculptor is unknown.

The regiment had seven killed, 38 wounded, and two declared missing of the 170 brought into the battle. Among the wounded were seven officers.

H-15: Captain Henry Fuller Monument
39° 47.692' N, 77° 14.71' W

Because of its location, this is one of the least-visited monuments on the battlefield.

Captain Henry Fuller of the Sixty-fourth New York's Company F fell here. Fuller's first lieutenant, John Manley, who himself was wounded, wrote that Fuller was killed leading his command in a charge with the rest of the Second Corps. The regiment had broken through the first two lines of the Confederate defense when the captain was struck in the chest by a bullet as the men attacked the third line. Manley said

Fuller died within a few moments. Another version of Fuller's death says that, after his wounding, he was being carried to safety by one of his men when he was shot again, this time fatally. Whichever version is correct, Fuller's men chose to honor him by placing this marker where he drew his last breath. It was dedicated in July 1894.

Fuller had joined the Sixty-fourth at age twenty as a private and quickly rose through the ranks. His promotions to first lieutenant and to captain came in recognition of his bravery in battle.

The twenty-two-year-old captain left a young wife and infant son, in addition to his parents, two brothers, and a sister. One of his brothers, Benjamin, was a member of the Thirty-seventh New York Infantry. The Thirty-seventh was not at Gettysburg, having mustered out of service just a week earlier.

H-16: 115th Pennsylvania Infantry Monument
39° 47.748′ N, 77° 14.679′ W

The 115th Pennsylvania, commanded by Major John P. Dunne, arrived on the morning of July 2 with only nine companies, rather than the customary and official ten. The reason? J. H. Vosberg, the officer responsible for recruiting Company H, resigned before completing his task, saying he was "otherwise and more satisfactorily employed." As a result, the 115th had no Company H.

On their arrival at Gettysburg, the men were immediately positioned in front of the Round Tops.

This position, however, was too far ahead of the main line of battle. Heavy fire forced the regiment to fall back.

That afternoon, a Confederate assault breached the line and flanked the 115th, again pushing the regiment back. Forming in support of a battery in danger of being captured, the regiment held off the assault long enough for the guns to be moved. It then was ordered to kneel in the wheat and hold its ground, despite the lack of any protective cover. The men did so until they were relieved.

On the afternoon of July 3, the regiment was sent to support the Irish Brigade but did not arrive in time to be of much assistance. When Lee retreated on July 4, the men joined the pursuit.

A year after the battle, the 115th was consolidated with the 110th Pennsylvania Infantry.

The regiment's losses at Gettysburg were three killed, eighteen wounded, and three missing. Its monument was dedicated September 12, 1889. The sculptor is unknown.

H-17: Seventeenth Maine Infantry Monument
39° 47.744' N, 77° 14.665' W

The men of the Seventeenth Maine Infantry fought at this position on the second day, having reached the battlefield without eating in more than twenty-four hours. Like many of the Confederate

troops, a number of men in the Seventeenth had no shoes. Despite these hardships, the men from Maine fought valiantly, suffering more than a hundred casualties that afternoon.

The monument is located where the regiment's colors stood during the fighting. More than twenty feet high, it features a soldier peering from behind a stone wall much like the one that protected the regiment during the fighting, which can still be seen behind the monument. A trampled stand of wheat lies beside the soldier, symbolizing the Wheatfield, where the regiment fought. The red diamonds on the shaft are also symbolic. The diamond was the symbol of the Third Corps, while red was the color of the First Division. Designed and constructed by Hallowell Granite, the monument was dedicated October 10, 1888.

When the 115th Pennsylvania and Eighth New Jersey were forced back, the Seventeenth Maine's flank was exposed to heavy fire from the Eighth, Ninth, Eleventh, and Fifty-ninth Georgia infantries. In response, Lieutenant Colonel Charles Merrill, a lawyer and farmer, moved several companies to form a right angle with the stone wall, a move called "refusing the line." The fighting became hand to hand. The color bearer of the Eighth Georgia succeeded in placing his flag on the wall, only to be driven back. As the fighting grew more intense, the regiment was ordered to fall back to the high ground in the Wheatfield. During the severe fighting there, the regiment lost 133 of the 350 men engaged, for a casualty rate of 38 percent. Of those, 18 were killed or mortally wounded, 112 wounded, and three declared missing.

A second monument to the regiment (39° 48.477′ N, 77° 14.165′ W) sits near the Pennsylvania State Memorial.

H-18: Sixty-second Pennsylvania Infantry Monument
39° 47.753′ N, 77° 14.645′ W

The Sixty-second Pennsylvania Infantry faced toward the stone wall in the latter stages of the battle for the Wheatfield. Thus, its monument faces the wall as well, requiring viewers to leave the road-

way to read the front inscription. The monument indicates the position the regiment held on the evening of July 2.

The Sixty-second provided covering fire for retreating troops when General Samuel K. Zook's brigade was overrun. As Confederate reinforcements moved in, the Sixty-second found itself in danger. Soon, the men joined the rush to the rear.

The monument was fabricated by H. Oursler and Sons and dedicated September 11, 1889.

The regiment brought 26 officers and 400 men into the battle and lost four officers and 24 men killed, 107 men wounded, and 40 men captured or missing, for a total loss of 175. Lieutenant Colonel James C. Hull commanded the regiment. He would be killed at Spotsylvania in May 1864.

H-19: Fourth Michigan Infantry Monument
39° 47.772′ N, 77° 14.636′ W

As other units pulled back during the second day's fighting in the Wheatfield, the Fourth Michigan remained in position, providing cover for the troops in retreat. Because the men of the Fourth stayed behind, seventy-six of their number were captured, more than the total for any other regiment in the fight for the Wheatfield.

The men of the Fourth engaged in fierce hand-to-hand combat at this location. When several Georgia troops attempted to wrest the regiment's flag from the color bearer, the Fourth's commander, Colonel

Harrison H. Jeffords, rushed to the color bearer's aid. Brandishing his sword, Jeffords fought off the Rebel troops and grabbed the colors. As he pulled back, his regimental colors still in his possession, he was bayoneted several times. The mortally wounded Jeffords was unable to gather the strength to hold on to the flag, and the Confederates temporarily gained control of it. Several members of the Fourth entered the fray and, after a short but bloody struggle, regained possession.

When the regiment decided to place a monument where it had fought, the members chose to

honor their colonel by showing him holding the flag he died defending. To ensure that future visitors would know what happened here, they added the inscription, "Colonel Harrison H. Jeffords fell mortally wounded at this point."

The regiment had 27 officers and 376 men at Gettysburg. Of those, Colonel Jeffords and 24 of his men were killed, nine officers and 55 men were wounded, and one officer and 75 men were declared missing.

The granite work was done by Mitchell Granite Company, while the bronze was done by American Bronze Company. The monument was dedicated June 12, 1889.

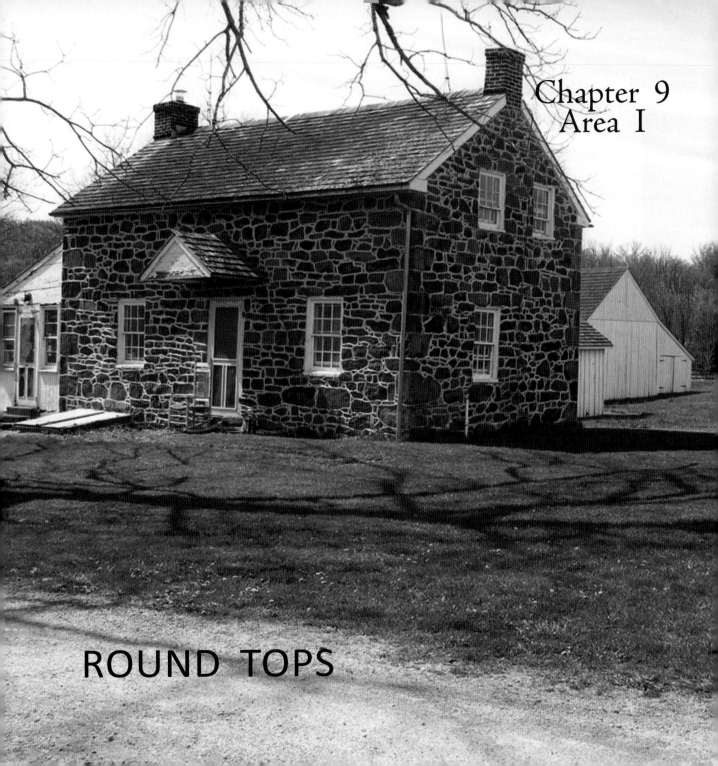

ROUND TOPS

Area I

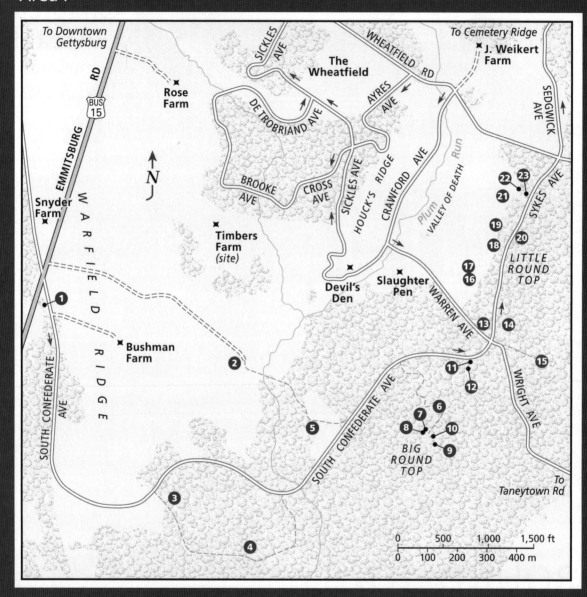

Brigadier General Gouverneur Warren, standing on Little Round Top, saw that General Daniel Sickles had moved his troops forward, leaving a gap in the Union line. Without Sickles's corps in its assigned position, Little Round Top became vulnerable. Losing it would mean the Union would lose its anchor on the left of the line, not to mention that a key observation post would no longer be available.

Warren ordered a small crew of signalmen to hold its position, then rushed to get Union troops to the crest of the hill. Warren's action ultimately saved Little Round Top for the Union. The 140th New York responded first. In a race for the hill, Colonel Strong Vincent of the Fifth Corps got his men to the front face just as Alabama troops began to move in. The fight began in earnest.

Action on the north slope and front face of Little Round Top became brutal, as Vincent's troops and those of Brigadier General Stephen Weed desperately fought off the advancing Fourth and Fifth Texas infantries and the Forty-eighth Alabama Infantry. Captain Augustus Martin, chief of artillery for the Union's Fifth Corps, ordered a battery of six guns moved onto the hill, a task that could be done only by hand because the terrain made using horses impossible. The Fourth Texas momentarily broke through the lower defenses and threatened to take the hill but was pushed back by the 140th New York.

Weed, Lieutenant Charles Hazlett of the Fifth United States Artillery's Battery D, and Colonel Patrick O'Rorke of the 140th New York were killed in the fighting. Lieutenant Colonel Benjamin Carter of the Fourth Texas fell, badly wounded. Vincent was mortally wounded as he rallied the Sixteenth Maine.

On the extreme left, the Twentieth Maine Infantry faced Colonel William Oates and his exhausted Fifteenth Alabama Infantry, who had just arrived at the hill and had no water and little ammunition. Both sides scavenged ammunition from their dead and wounded until Colonel Joshua Chamberlain ordered the men from Maine to mount a bayonet charge. As the Alabamans retreated from the onrushing Federals, they were met with a hail of bullets from their flank, delivered by the Twentieth Maine's Company B, which had been posted a short distance away to defend against a flanking movement. The Eighty-third Pennsylvania Infantry, which had been commanded by Strong Vincent, joined the Twentieth Maine at the end of the charge and assisted in the capture of more than four hundred men from the Fifteenth and Forty-seventh Alabama infantries. Oates's brother, Lieutenant John Oates, fell mortally wounded, struck eight times by enemy fire.

Skirmishing continued throughout the evening,

but the chance of a Confederate victory at Little Round Top was gone.

For visitors willing to leave the battlefield for a mile or two, the picturesque Sachs Covered Bridge is the reward. Volume 1 tells how the bridge played a role in the battle. Returning to the battlefield by way of Millerstown Road, visitors will see on the right the farm on which President Dwight D. Eisenhower lived after he left office.

Following the right turn on to West Confederate Avenue, the upturned cannon marks the general location of General James Longstreet's headquarters. The tower across the road provides a panoramic view of the southern end of the battlefield. Just past the tower sit the monuments to troops from Georgia and South Carolina, followed shortly by those for Arkansas and Texas. Across the road from the modest Texas Monument sits the Bushman Farm. Volume 1 explains why this farm was so deadly for the Texans.

The marker placed by the Confederacy to honor all its soldiers and sailors stands where the road gently curves to the right. A short distance past this marker, on the left behind a scenic rail fence, is the field that was part of the ill-fated charge led by General Elon Farnsworth. Just ahead on the right is the figure of Major William Wells, who earned a Medal of Honor in that charge. On the front of his monument is an intricate plaque depicting the actions of Major Wells and the First Vermont Cavalry, described in detail in Volume 1.

Across the intersection where South Confederate Avenue becomes Sykes Avenue, one of the more popular monuments on the battlefield—that to the Twentieth Maine Infantry— sits on the right above the road. To the left is the monument to the Eighty-third Pennsylvania, where readers will learn an interesting story about the figure on top. Moving up Sykes Avenue toward the crest of Little Round Top, visitors will pass the marker indicating the area where Strong Vincent died, along with the boulder marking where he was wounded. The large castle-like monument to the Forty-fourth and Twelfth New York infantries also sits nearby. Volume 1 tells why both regiments are honored by the same monument. Most of the monuments on Little Round Top require visitors to park and walk, an easy prospect because the markers are close together.

Leaving the "castle," visitors will first see the monument to the 140th New York. Volume 1 tells who the figure is and why his nose is so shiny. A small marker commemorating the deaths of Brigadier General Stephen Weed and Lieutenant Charles Hazlett appears next. Here, readers will learn the unusual story of how the two died. Looking down the face of Little Round Top, visitors will see an unusual rock formation. Known as the Curious Rocks, the formation served as a shield for Union soldiers during the battle.

The figure standing on the large boulder that dominates the northern end of Little Round Top is that of Brigadier General Gouverneur Warren. Volume 1 describes why he is often referred to as "the Savior of Little Round Top." Just behind Warren is Signal Rock, where signalmen performed heroic duty during the battle.

Looking down the northern face of Little Round Top, visitors will see the monument to the 155th Pennsylvania. Volume 1 tells why the figure is wearing a uniform that was not adopted until 1864, many months after the battle.

―――――――――――

I-1: Hood's Texas Brigade Monument
39° 47.421' N, 77° 15.266' W

Hood's Texas Brigade was made up of the First, Fourth, and Fifth Texas infantries and the Third Arkansas Infantry. The brigade was named for Lieutenant General John Bell Hood, the commander of the Texas Brigade from February 1862 through July of that year, when he was promoted to major general and relinquished command of the brigade. Hood's Texas Brigade was commanded at Gettysburg by Brigadier General Jerome Bonaparte Robertson, a doctor and Indian fighter.

The brigade had been on the field only a few minutes when it was ordered into action late in the afternoon on July 2, having had little time to rest from a long march. Advancing across Plum Run toward Little Round Top, the brigade came under heavy artillery fire, taking many casualties. The Fourth and Fifth Texas participated in the attack on Little Round Top, where for nearly two hours they engaged in heavy fighting. Meanwhile, the First Texas and Third Arkansas attacked Devil's Den, capturing a number of prisoners and taking three guns of the

Fourth New York Battery. The brigade eventually retired to a position south of Devil's Den, then finally to a point near where its monument stands today.

The marker for Hood's Texas Brigade was paid for through private contributions from all parts of Texas, solicited by Mrs. Mable Bates. It sits where the brigade formed prior to its attack on the Round Tops on July 2. It was dedicated September 17, 1913.

In the fighting, the brigade suffered 604 casualties out of approximately 1,100 men brought to the field. Among the fallen was General Robertson, who suffered a wound above his knee that took away his

mobility. When he retired to the rear, Lieutenant Colonel P. A. Work took his place.

The First Texas, commanded by Lieutenant Colonel Work, had twenty-nine men killed, forty-six wounded, and twenty-two missing or captured.

The Fourth Texas was commanded by Colonel J. C. G. Key until he was wounded, at which time Lieutenant Benjamin F. Carter took over. When Carter was wounded, command fell to Major J. P. Banelt. The Fourth had twenty-eight men killed, fifty-three wounded, and thirty-one missing or captured.

The Fifth Texas was commanded by Colonel R. M. Powell. When Powell was wounded and captured, Lieutenant Colonel King Bryan took charge. Bryan was wounded almost immediately, after which Major S. C. Rogers became the regiment's third commander in only a few minutes. The regiment suffered 54 killed, 112 wounded, and 45 missing or captured.

Colonel Van H. Manning commanded the Third Arkansas, which had 43 killed, 101 wounded, and 40 missing or captured.

This was the first non-regimental Confederate monument at Gettysburg. It was dedicated September 17, 1913.

I-2: Slyder Farm
39° 47.329′ N, 77° 14.804′ W

On the second day of fighting, the Slyder Farm changed from a small family operation to an important part of one of the most important battles in our nation's history when the Second United States

Sharpshooters, under Colonel Homer R. Stoughton, clashed with Brigadier General Evander Law's Confederate brigade. The Federal troops took a stand on a small rise northwest of the house before being forced into a fighting retreat to Big Round Top and Devil's Den. Their actions produced the first Confederate casualties of the July 2 attack as the Southern troops passed through the farm on their way to Houck's Ridge and Little Round Top.

One Confederate officer remarked that the bullets were like a hornet's nest. The men of the Second United States Sharpshooters decided to include a depiction of a hornet's nest on their monument adjacent to the Slyder farmhouse (39° 47.338′ N, 77° 14.812′ W).

Although the Union men were forced back, their stand delayed the Confederate advance enough to allow the Federals to hold Little Round Top. Many of the sharpshooters ultimately joined Joshua Chamberlain's Twentieth Maine in the defense of the left flank of the Union army at that location.

On July 3, General Elon Farnsworth's cavalry brigade charged through the Confederate lines near the barn. Several of Farnsworth's men were wounded

Second U. S. Sharpshooters monument with its hornet's nest

or killed on the lane. After the battle, several of the dead from both sides were buried near the barn.

The house, barn, summer kitchen, and outhouse were here during the battle. The barn was used as a temporary field hospital for wounded Confederate troops.

I-3: Eighteenth Pennsylvania Cavalry Monument
39° 47.080′ N, 77° 14.959′ W

The Eighteenth Pennsylvania Cavalry, which also carried the name of the 163rd Pennsylvania Volunteers, had already fought in Pennsylvania at Hanover on June 30 and Hunterstown on July 2 before coming to Gettysburg. On the afternoon of July 3, it was positioned at this location until it made a charge with the rest of Brigadier General Elon Farnsworth's brigade against Confederate infantry firmly positioned behind a stone wall.

The First West Virginia Cavalry had launched the first wave of the attack. Unsuccessful, it was in full retreat when Brigadier General Judson Kilpatrick ordered the Eighteenth Pennsylvania's commander of only three months, Lieutenant Colonel William Penn Brinton, to move his troopers out. They were no more successful in ousting the Confederates from their position than were the West Virginians. The First Texas Infantry fended off the attack, which was shortly followed by the failure of the First Vermont Cavalry's assault.

The Eighteenth Pennsylvania Cavalry suffered two killed, eight wounded, and four missing of its force of 599 troops at Gettysburg. Over the course of the war, the unit saw 131 of its number die in Confederate prison camps.

The Eighteenth often claimed it had been issued equipment that was inferior to that of other Pennsylvania troops. That claim was given validity when a squad was captured in Virginia early in 1863 by the famous John Singleton Mosby. Looking for weapons and horses for his guerilla war against the Union, Mosby found nothing he could use and immediately paroled his captives, sending them back to Lieutenant Colonel James Gowan with a note requesting the squad be given better arms because it didn't pay for him to bother capturing the men with their existing weapons.

The monument was fabricated by Smith Granite Company and dedicated September 11, 1889. The horse's ear was damaged in an act of vandalism in 1992.

The Eighteenth joined with the Twenty-second Pennsylvania Cavalry in July 1865 to form the Third Provisional Pennsylvania Cavalry.

I-4: Fifth New York Cavalry Monument
39° 46.993' N, 77° 14.777' W

Sculpted by Caspar Buberl and fabricated by New England Monument Company, this monument now sits at the position of the Fifth New York Cav-

alry on July 3 while in support of Captain Samuel Elder's Battery B of the Fourth United States Artillery. The original location was said to be on ground occupied by the enemy. The monument was moved to its current site in 1893 at the request of the veterans. Because it had been dedicated so recently (July 3, 1888), no rededication was deemed necessary.

The Fifth New York Cavalry was also known as the First Ira Harris Guard, in honor of Senator Ira Harris of Albany, and the DeForrest Cavalry, after Colonel Othneil DeForrest, who had formed the unit. Companies A, B, K, and M were made up of recruits from the Bliss Cavalry, which had been absorbed into the Fifth when the latter was formed.

Just a few days prior to arriving at Gettysburg, the men had fought at Hanover, Pennsylvania, where they were the first cavalry unit to exchange shots with General J. E. B. Stuart's men. They followed that skirmish with a fight at Hunterstown two days later. At Hanover, the unit had twenty-six men killed or wounded in hand-to-hand fighting but captured Lieutenant Colonel William Payne of the Second North Carolina Cavalry and seventy-five men. Payne was captured when he had to be rescued after falling into a vat at the Winebrenner Tannery.

Early in the morning on July 3, the Fifth took a position on the left in support of Elder's Battery. That afternoon, Brigadier General Elon Farnsworth's brigade was ordered to assault the well-entrenched First Texas Infantry, reinforced by troops from Georgia and Alabama. The First West Virginia Cavalry tried first and was forced back. The Eighteenth Pennsylvania Cavalry and a portion of the Fifth were the next to make the attempt, with the same results. This led to the charge of the First Vermont Cavalry (see I-5), which cost General Farnsworth his life and led to a Medal of Honor for Major William Wells.

Commanded by Major John Hammond, who would become a United States congressman after the war, the Fifth fought in 52 battles and 119 skirmishes and saw 114 of its number die as prisoners of war. At Gettysburg, it had one man killed, another wounded, and four declared missing.

I-5: First Vermont Cavalry Monument
39° 47.215′ N, 77° 14.626′ W

The First Vermont Cavalry participated in Brigadier General Elon Farnsworth's ill-fated charge on July 3. Ordered to charge by General Judson Kilpatrick, better known as "Kill Cavalry" for his recklessness, Farnsworth protested the order. Kilpatrick shamed Farnsworth into leading the attack, saying that if Farnsworth was afraid, Kilpatrick would do it himself. Farnsworth reluctantly agreed.

The Confederates were positioned behind a stone wall with wooden fence rails piled on top, rendering it too high for horses to jump. This required the Union troops to dismount and tear down the fence while under heavy fire. Numerous boulders and fences presented additional obstacles that hindered the charge.

The First West Virginia Cavalry, the first to

make the attempt, was quickly forced back by the First Texas Infantry, losing ninety-eight men in the process. The Eighteenth Pennsylvania Cavalry, with a few companies of the Fifth New York Cavalry, tried next but found the same result.

Farnsworth then divided the First Vermont Cavalry into three battalions and sent them into the fray. By now, the Ninth, Eleventh, and Fifty-ninth Georgia had reinforced the Texans, followed by the Fourth Alabama. The men from Vermont fared no better than their counterparts from West Virginia, Pennsylvania, and New York. Turned back, the three Vermont battalions did all they could to avoid the continuous fire. Major William Wells would receive the Medal of Honor for his efforts in leading the survivors to safety. The monument to Wells (39° 47.088′ N, 77° 14.716′ W) is discussed in Volume 1.

In the retreat, Farnsworth was struck in the leg, abdomen, and chest by fire from the Fifteenth Alabama Infantry. He fell mortally wounded near the stone wall about seventy-five yards southwest of where the First Vermont Cavalry Monument stands today.

The First suffered sixty-five casualties in this action. Its monument, fabricated by Wells, Lamson and Company, was dedicated in October 1889.

I-6: 118th Pennsylvania Infantry Monument
39° 47.243′ N, 77° 14.332′ W

On the morning of July 2, the 118th Pennsylva-

nia Infantry reached Gettysburg, where it was held in reserve in the rear of Cemetery Hill until late in the afternoon, when it was sent to the Wheatfield to assist against the Confederate assault. There, it lost two killed, five wounded, and two missing. Another monument notes the regiment's Wheatfield location (see G-15).

Early the next morning, the regiment moved here, where it remained behind breastworks. It saw no action that day other than occasional fire from Confederate sharpshooters.

On the morning of July 4, it engaged with Rebel skirmishers defending the rear of Lee's army, which was in retreat. The regiment joined in the pursuit but stopped when the Confederates crossed the Potomac

River. In that pursuit, the regiment fought a series of small skirmishes over the course of nine days.

The regiment's commander was Lieutenant Colonel James Gwyn, a Philadelphia merchant who would be wounded a year later at the Wilderness. The 118th was also known as the Philadelphia Corn Exchange Regiment, in honor of the Philadelphia brokerage house that provided the funds for raising it. The Corn Exchange also offered a payment of ten dollars for each man who signed up.

The monument was dedicated September 8, 1884, in conjunction with the dedication of the main monument discussed in G-15. The fabricator is unknown. The monument is located on an original War Department trail leading to the top of Big Round Top.

I-7: 119th Pennsylvania Infantry Monument
39° 47.202′ N, 77° 14.364′ W

The 119th Pennsylvania Infantry conducted a continuous march of thirty-seven miles to reach Gettysburg, arriving on the afternoon of July 2. The regiment initially formed its line behind Little Round Top. That location is marked by a monument at the intersection of Howe Avenue and Taneytown Road (39° 47.028′ N, 77° 13.760′ W). The regiment's role there was to defend against any Confederate flanking movements.

On the afternoon of July 3, the regiment moved to the position on Big Round Top marked by the monument in this photo. On July 4, with the rest of the brigade (the Sixth Maine, Forty-ninth Pennsylvania, and Fifth Wisconsin), it covered the Union's left. On the morning of July 5, it began the pursuit of Lee's army. The men engaged in a small skirmish with Lee's rear guard at nearby Fairfield, Pennsylvania.

The commander of the 119th Pennsylvania, also known as the Gray Reserves, was Colonel Peter C. Ellmaker, the regiment's organizer. Since the 119th had little contact with the Confederate army, its casualties were light at Gettysburg—only two men wounded.

Erected in 1885 by the regiment's survivors, the monument was dedicated October 3, 1885.

I-8: Twentieth Maine Infantry Monument

39° 47.197′ N, 77° 14.370′ W

Those who have seen the movie *Gettysburg* are familiar with the role the Twentieth Maine Infantry played in the defense of Little Round Top on July 2, 1863. The Twentieth, commanded by Colonel Joshua Chamberlain, had little or no ammunition remaining when it mounted a charge down the slope of Little Round Top, pushing back an equally depleted Fifteenth Alabama Infantry, led by Colonel William Oates. That daring charge, credited with protecting the left flank

of the Union army, ultimately brought the Twentieth to this location on Big Round Top, where it captured twenty-five prisoners. The monument on Little Round Top commemorates the men's action there (39° 47.366′ N, 77° 14.167′ W).

This monument on Big Round Top, dedicated October 3, 1889, marks the position the Twentieth held on the night of July 2 until relieved the next day. It also represents the regiment's advance during its countercharge from Little Round Top that evening. Keen-eyed observers will spot the incorrectly spelled "monumet" on the fourth line from the bottom of the inscription.

Two members of the regiment received Medals of Honor. Colonel Chamberlain, who would be wounded six times in the war, received the medal for his heroism and tenacity in holding the regiment's position. After the war, Chamberlain became governor of Maine and president of Bowdoin College, where he had been a professor before the war. Sergeant Andrew J. Tozier, color bearer for Company I,

received his medal for standing alone at an advanced position, where he defended his colors with a musket and ammunition picked up at his feet.

The regiment lost 29 killed, 91 wounded, and five missing out of the 386 men brought to Gettysburg. Of those killed or mortally wounded, three were officers: Captain Charles W. Billings of Company C, Second Lieutenant Warren L. Kendall of Company G, and First Lieutenant Arad H. Linscott of Company I, who fell mortally wounded not far from the site of the monument.

I-9: Twelfth Pennsylvania Reserves Monument
39° 47.175′ N, 77° 14.341′ W

The Twelfth Pennsylvania Reserves, also known as the Forty-first Pennsylvania Infantry, reached the battlefield at midmorning on July 2. When fighting intensified on the left of the Union army, the regiment was ordered to the vicinity of Little Round Top. Along the way, it passed wounded troops from General Daniel Sickles's corps as they were being carried back to hospitals, a sobering sight for even battle-tested veterans. After forming on the right side of Little Round Top, the men were eventually moved to the left, which was coming under heavy attack. There, they hurriedly built stone walls and breastworks for protection.

Just after dark, they were ordered with the rest of the Third Brigade to Big Round Top, where they took the position marked by this monument. In the dark-ness, unfamiliar with the terrain, the regiment became temporarily split, re-forming just before reaching the summit. Once there, the men constructed the stone wall now visible around their monument. After-battle reports indicated that the Confederates could be heard building similar walls just below the Twelfth's position.

On July 3, the regiment came under occasional sharpshooter fire but had little contact otherwise. Looking to their left, however, the men had a fine view of the ill-fated cavalry charge conducted by General Elon Farnsworth.

On the morning of July 4, a skirmish line noted the presence of a large number of enemy troops hidden behind a stone wall. As the regiment cautiously approached, it became apparent that the Confederates had placed the muskets of their dead and wounded against the wall, giving the appearance that it was occupied. In truth, the Confederates had already joined in the retreat southward. The ruse bought them some additional time.

The regiment took part in the pursuit, skirmishing briefly with the rear guard of Lee's army at Williamsport, Maryland, before the Confederates crossed the Potomac.

This monument, erected in 1890 by the commonwealth of Pennsylvania, was dedicated in September of that year. The sculptor is unknown. The monument sits at the position the regiment held on July 3.

The Twelfth had 26 officers and 294 men at the battle and suffered one man killed and another wounded. Its commander was Colonel Martin D. Hardin, an 1859 West Point graduate. Hardin would go on to attain the rank of brigadier general before retiring from the army in 1870 to become an attorney in Chicago.

I-10: Fifth Pennsylvania Reserves Monument
39° 47.189' N, 77° 14.344' W

Upon its arrival on the field, the Fifth Pennsylvania was for a time held in reserve in the vicinity of Little Round Top. Late in the afternoon on July 2, as fighting on Little Round Top slowed, the regiment was sent to Big Round Top.

The monument was fabricated by Smith Granite Company and dedicated in September 1890. It

indicates the position the Fifth held on Big Round Top from the night of July 2 to the close of the battle. During that period, it assisted in protecting the Union left.

Again following "the rule of twenty-nine" (see G-3), the Fifth Pennsylvania Reserves were redesignated the Thirty-fourth Pennsylvania Infantry. The regiment was commanded at Gettysburg by Lieutenant Colonel George Dare, a shopkeeper from Huntingdon. Dare, who had already been wounded at Fredericksburg, would be killed at the Wilderness in May 1864.

The regiment saw little action at Gettysburg, experiencing only limited skirmishing on July 3. Two of its men were wounded out of a force of 334.

I-11: Tenth Pennsylvania Reserves Monument

39° 47.321′ N, 77° 14.259′ W

The unusual dark appearance of this monument is the product of its construction material. Cast in bronze, it represents the Tenth Pennsylvania Reserves, also known at the Thirty-ninth Pennsylvania. It is one of only two Pennsylvania monuments on the battlefield constructed entirely of bronze. The other is that to the Fifty-sixth Pennsylvania Infantry (see A-15).

The Tenth Pennsylvania Reserves occupied this location along the stone wall on the evening of the

second day of fighting. The regiment's assignment was to hold the position should the Confederates launch any further attacks on that end of the line. Nearby Little Round Top had been the scene of ferocious fighting just a short time earlier, and Union officers had no way of knowing if the Confederates planned to attack again. The figure on the monument is in the "trail arms" position, stooped and leaning forward. He would be expected to assume that position as he scaled Big Round Top.

The commander of the Tenth was Colonel Adoniram J. Warner, who had been wounded the previous September at Antietam. As did many Gettysburg veterans, he became a congressman after the war.

The regiment engaged in heavy skirmishing throughout July 3. It had two men killed and three wounded out of its 420 at Gettysburg.

The monument was designed by J. H. Buck and manufactured by Gorham Manufacturing Company. It was dedicated in September 1890.

I-12: Ninth Massachusetts Infantry Monument
39° 47.310′ N, 77° 14.263′ W

Two days after the attack on Fort Sumter that launched the war, President Abraham Lincoln called for seventy-five thousand volunteers to put down the rebellion. Irish immigrant Thomas Cass immediately began recruiting others like himself in the Boston area. Within a few weeks, he enlisted more than seventeen hundred men. Those enlistees formed the Ninth Massachusetts Infantry. Being predominantly Irish, the regiment sought and received permission to carry an Irish flag in addition to the flags of the United States and Massachusetts. Named colonel, Cass served in that capacity until he was mortally wounded at Malvern Hill on July 1, 1862.

At Gettysburg, the Ninth, detached from the Second Brigade, held this position at the base of Big Round Top. Erected in June 1885, the monument marks the regiment's location from the night of July 2 through July 3. During the battle, the regiment took shelter behind the rock wall adjacent to where the monument now stands.

Colonel Patrick R. Guiney commanded the

Ninth at Gettysburg. Guiney would be seriously wounded less than a year later, when he lost an eye at the Wilderness.

Casualty figures for the Ninth are unknown with any degree of certainty. Most sources agree that one man was killed and another was missing, but beyond that, total casualties vary from one source to another. The monument says the regiment suffered twenty-six total casualties, but other sources indicate the number could be as low as seven. Whatever the case, the Ninth's losses were relatively light compared to other regiments at Gettysburg.

I-13: Ninth Pennsylvania Reserves Monument

39° 47.381′ N, 77° 14.232′ W

The Ninth Pennsylvania Reserves, or Thirty-eighth Pennsylvania Infantry, arrived on the field at about five in the afternoon on July 2. When the Confederates threatened to take the strategic Little Round Top, the Ninth received orders to clear and hold the line between the two Round Tops. Once they accomplished that, the men gathered rocks and built the stone wall visible near the monument, then took cover behind it from Confederate sharpshooters in Devil's Den.

Lieutenant Colonel James Snodgrass, a farmer in civilian life, commanded the regiment, which had five men wounded of the 377 available at Gettysburg.

The monument was designed and constructed by Smith Granite Company. Dedicated in September 1890, it sits where the regiment was positioned the evening of July 2. The bas-relief shows a soldier gazing sadly downward at the grave of a fallen friend, giving rise to the monument's title, *By a Comrade's Grave*. The scene could have been from either side at any battlefield.

The regiment joined the pursuit of Lee's army on July 5.

I-14: Oates's Ledge of Rocks

39° 47.388′ N, 77° 14.169′ W

On the afternoon of July 2, the Fifteenth Alabama launched an assault on Little Round Top, which was defended by the Twentieth Maine. Colonel William C. Oates, who had just been promoted to the rank less than two months earlier, led the Alabamans in the attack, which was featured in the movie *Gettysburg*.

Oates would write in his report that he saw no enemy troops until he came within forty to fifty steps of an irregular ledge of rocks. Believing the rocks provided a natural shelter, he worked his men toward them, only to see the Twentieth Maine rise and pour a vicious volley into his ranks. Both sides fought valiantly. The Fifteenth Alabama was driven back with heavy casualties, losing thirty-three killed, seventy-six

wounded, and eighty-four captured.

As the Fifteenth Alabama was pushed back, Colonel Michael J. Bulger was badly wounded and was found lying against a tree. A captain from the Forty-fourth New York Infantry demanded his sword, but Bulger refused when he learned that his antagonist was only a captain. Although in great pain, Bulger said he would surrender his sword only to someone equal in rank, despite threats that he would be killed. Bulger ultimately won the argument. Colonel James Rice of the Forty-fourth New York was summoned to accept Bulger's surrender. Taken captive, Bulger survived his wounds.

Years after the war, Oates returned to Gettysburg and identified this rock as being part of the ledge. More specifically, he said it was the rock where his brother, Lieutenant John Oates, was mortally wounded. Oates proposed that a monument to the Fifteenth Alabama be placed here. However, Joshua Chamberlain, who during the battle had been colonel of the Twentieth Maine and who was awarded a Medal of Honor for his actions against Oates, opposed the effort to place a monument where Oates wanted it. Chamberlain said he was not opposed to a monument to the Alabamans, but he didn't want it there. He said that the Fifteenth Alabama had not reached that rock. Doing so would have meant either that the Twentieth Maine had turned its line back, which he said had not occurred, or that the Alabamans had gotten behind the Union line. Chamberlain was adamant that the Fifteenth Alabama had not reached that point. Ultimately, the War Department's Gettysburg National Park Commission denied Oates's request, and the monument never was erected.

Both Chamberlain and Oates became governors of their respective states.

I-15: Monument to Company B, Twentieth Maine Infantry
39° 47.322′ N, 77° 14.091′ W

As the main body of the Twentieth Maine fought against the Fifteenth Alabama on Little Round Top in late afternoon on July 2, Company B was dispatched to this location, where it took a position behind the stone wall visible in back of the marker. Under Captain Walter Morrill, the company had only forty-three officers and men, plus a few sharpshooters who were unaffiliated with the regiment. Their assignment was to act as skirmishers and watch the Confederate right for a flanking movement. As the Fifteenth Alabama

posted on the right flank of Colonel Strong Vincent's brigade. With no other Union troops on their right, the Confederates moved up the slope to take advantage of the opening. Part of the Sixteenth Michigan fell back to higher ground as the fighting intensified. However, Vincent quickly rallied the men and directed them back. Vincent was mortally wounded while in the process of moving the Sixteenth back into position.

Also referred to as the Stockton Independent Regiment, the Sixteenth was commanded by Lieutenant Colonel Norval Welch, who would be killed in the fighting at Peebles Farm, Virginia. The Sixteenth brought 356 officers and men to the battle, making it the smallest regiment in the brigade. It had 23 killed, 34 wounded, and three declared missing.

The monument to the Sixteenth was erected by the state of Michigan. It sits at the regiment's position during the afternoon and night of July 2. It was fabricated by Smith Granite Company and

retreated ahead of the charge by the rest of the Twentieth Maine, Company B poured a heavy fire into its midst, causing many casualties and sending the startled Alabamans into confusion.

The nearby monument to the main body of the Twentieth Maine (39° 47.366′ N, 77° 14.167′ W) is discussed in Volume 1. A second monument to the Twentieth sits on Big Round Top (see I-8).

I-16: Sixteenth Michigan Infantry Monument
39° 47.469′ N, 77° 14.260′ W

The Sixteenth Michigan was one of the earliest regiments to reach Little Round Top. It initially

dedicated June 12, 1889. The monument originally sat at ground level but was later moved to its present location on this large boulder.

The monument contains a great deal of symbolism. The Maltese cross at the top is the symbol of the Fifth Corps. The palms forming the wreath around the cross represent peace. The musket points toward Devil's Den, the direction in which the regiment focused its attention. The regiment is believed to have constructed many of the breastworks around the site of the monument.

The Sixteenth had the honor of being one of the regiments selected to receive the arms and flags of the Army of Northern Virginia when Lee surrendered at Appomattox on April 9, 1865.

I-17: Michigan Sharpshooters Monument
39° 47.487' N, 77° 14.263' W

Dedicated informally on June 12, 1889, the monument to the Michigan Sharpshooters was fabricated by Smith Granite Company. No formal dedication took place, and the sculptor is unknown. The monument honors four companies in Colonel Hiram Berdan's sharpshooters and sits at the location they occupied on July 3. Their role was to fire at enemy troops positioned across the Valley of Death on Houck's Ridge and in Devil's Den.

The four companies fought independently of each other on July 2. Companies C and K of the First Regiment of United States Sharpshooters saw action in the vicinity of the Sherfy House. Company C counted six wounded and one missing, while Company K's casualties included four wounded. Company I, also of the First Regiment, had one officer killed and another officer and three men wounded while fighting near Pitzer's Run. The fourth unit was Company B of the Second United States Sharpshooters. It fought near the Slyder farmhouse (see I-2) and had four men wounded.

On July 3, the four companies were detached from their respective regiments and deployed at this location on the face of Little Round Top in support of several nearby batteries. Corporal Wellington Fitch of Company C was singled out in post-battle reports for making a reconnaissance alone and returning with an entire squad of Confederate sharpshooters he had captured with no assistance.

I-18: Ninety-first Pennsylvania Infantry Monument

39° 47.527′ N, 77° 14.204′ W

Under the command of Lieutenant Colonel Joseph H. Sinex, the Ninety-first Pennsylvania arrived at Gettysburg late in the morning on July 2, moving into position on the right of the Union army. In midafternoon, it was ordered to Little Round Top, moving up the backside while the Confederates began to move up the front. After some brief maneuvering and position changes, the regiment located here in support of Battery D of the Fifth United

States Artillery and soon began skirmishing with the Confederates.

Brigadier General Stephen Weed and Lieutenant Charles E. Hazlett, commanding Battery D, were killed during this period. The Ninety-first honored them by dedicating its first, smaller monument to their memory. That monument (39° 47.524′ N, 77° 14.197′ W) sits a few feet away but was originally on this site. In 1889, the smaller monument was moved and the larger one erected. The rock on which the smaller monument sits has a carving identifying the location as that where Hazlett was killed. The carving has weathered to the point that it is now extremely difficult to read.

The regiment got little sleep the night of July 2, instead using the many stones lying in the area to construct protecting walls. However, little fighting took place in this area on July 3, and the walls were not utilized to any great extent.

On July 4, the regiment sent out a skirmish line, which succeeded in capturing some prisoners. In that engagement, two officers and thirteen men became casualties. Overall, the regiment had four killed and fifteen wounded, including the two officers.

The Ninety-first participated in the pursuit of the Confederate army when it retreated southward.

This impressive structure was fabricated by Ryegate Granite Company and dedicated September 12, 1889. A state seal originally adorned the monument but has been missing since it was taken by vandals on August 23, 1985.

I-19: 146th New York Infantry Monument
39° 47.563' N, 77° 14.199' W

The 146th New York, commanded by Colonel Kenner Garrard, was also known as the Halleck Infantry, in honor of Major General Henry Wager Halleck of Oneida, New York. When Garrard assumed command of the brigade after Brigadier General Stephen Weed was mortally wounded, Lieutenant Colonel David Jenkins took control of the regiment. Jenkins would be killed a year later at the Wilderness. Garrard, a West Point graduate who had also been the commandant there, was a stern disciplinarian

who insisted on "soldierly enthusiasm." Despite complaints about the discipline, the men of the regiment took it as a badge of honor, referring to themselves as the Garrard Tigers.

The regiment's records indicate that it took up a position here on July 2, arriving just in time to engage in hand-to-hand combat with Lieutenant General John Bell Hood's division of Longstreet's Corps. Other units in the area disputed the claim that the 146th was among the first regiments to reach Little Round Top. Those regiments claimed the 146th arrived late in the battle, and that its men spent most of their time protecting an artillery battery and erecting stone breastworks for protection. Whichever version is true, the men remained in this position through the rest of the battle.

The regiment gained the envy of many others when General George Meade observed the battle from the vicinity of the monument on July 3. It was those observations that led Meade to consider a counterattack after Pickett's Charge was repulsed.

The regiment had four men killed and twenty-four wounded in the fighting.

Frederick and Field fabricated the monument, which was dedicated in late 1888. It marks the position the regiment held on July 2 and 3.

I-20: Guard Shack Foundation
39° 47.542′ N, 77° 14.144′ W

Following the establishment of Gettysburg National Military Park in 1895, the War Department assumed control of the battlefield. It didn't take

long for that body to make it known that commercial enterprises on the battlefield would no longer be tolerated. Among the steps taken was the condemnation of the trolley line (see H-13) and the amusement parks that had sprouted around the battlefield. While eliminating commercialism was the primary goal, a hoped-for side benefit was the eradication of much of the unsavory activity that had begun to take over the parks, particularly the largest one on Little Round Top.

While the legal proceedings dragged on, a guard corps was established. Small guard shacks were scattered around the battlefield. Their purpose was to provide shelter for the guards who monitored the park's roads and monuments, looking for damage or vandalism. The guards also watched for relic hunters and tried to curb gambling and prostitution, an effort that was only marginally successful. For their efforts, guards were paid forty dollars monthly.

When the amusement parks eventually closed and the trolley shut down, illegal activity on the battlefield decreased dramatically. Within a few years, it was apparent the guards were no longer needed. The shacks were closed around 1920. These three slabs of concrete are all that remain of the foundation for the guard shack that sat on Little Round Top. Before the construction of modern-day Sykes Avenue, the shack was at the edge of a visitor parking area and a small road that provided access to Little Round Top and its amusement park. The foundation sits in the woods fifty feet below Sykes Avenue on the opposite side of the road from the monuments.

I-21: Monument to Battery L, First Ohio Light Artillery
39° 47.615′ N, 77° 14.182′ W

After marching nearly all night on July 1, Battery L of the First Ohio Light Artillery went into position to the right of Baltimore Pike about eight in the morning on July 2. After fighting for about an hour, the battery moved across the pike. In midafternoon, it received orders to move to the assistance of the Fifth Corps and was placed in the general position where the monument now stands. The terrain was so rugged that the battery was forced to move its guns into position by hand after unhitching the horses. This delayed the placement of the guns.

Seeing the chaotic retreat of the United States Regulars, the men of the battery waved their hats to the onrushing Union men, signaling them to get close to the ground. They then fired canister after canister over the heads of the retreating Federals into the Confederate troops in pursuit, opening huge holes in the Southern line. The guns fired so rapidly that battle reports stated they became too hot to touch.

Battery L was also known as Gibbs's Battery, after its commanding officer, Captain Frank C. Gibbs. The area where its monument sits is known as Gibbs's Ledge and marks the position of the battery on the afternoon of July 2.

Ryegate Granite Company fabricated the monument, which was dedicated September 14, 1887. The battery had two men wounded in the fighting.

I-22: Ninety-eighth Pennsylvania Infantry Monument
39° 47.627′ N, 77° 14.145′ W

The Twenty-first Pennsylvania Volunteers were organized as a three-month regiment at the beginning of the war. When the men's enlistment was up, they were reorganized as the Ninety-eighth Pennsylvania Infantry, a three-year regiment.

After a forced march of thirty-six miles from Manchester, Maryland, with the rest of the Sixth Corps, the regiment arrived on the battlefield on the evening of July 2. It had proudly led the corps in the march. The men formed a line of battle in the vicinity of where the monument now stands. Because they were among the first of the corps to arrive on the field, they were ordered into battle almost immediately, charging into the Wheatfield and the surrounding woods. Two officers and nine men were wounded. As darkness fell, the Ninety-eighth re-

The regiment's monument was erected and dedicated in 1885 by the commonwealth of Pennsylvania. The Ninety-eighth was commanded at Gettysburg by Major John B. Kohler, who would be killed at Cedar Creek, Virginia, in October 1864.

I-23: 121st New York Infantry Monument
39° 47.619′ N, 77° 14.128′ W

The 121st New York arrived at Gettysburg on the afternoon of July 2 after a difficult seventeen-hour march with the rest of the Sixth Corps. The regiment took a position in the area of the monument,

turned to the brigade, where its position is marked by another monument (see G-23).

The next day found the regiment in an advanced position, where it came under fire from both artillery and Confederate sharpshooters. One officer was wounded in this action.

The men spent July 4 retrieving the wounded and removing them to field hospitals. That evening, nine companies served on picket duty while the tenth was assigned the less enviable detail of burying the dead.

The following morning, the Ninety-eighth joined in the pursuit of Lee's army.

overlooking the Valley of Death. It was held in reserve the evening of July 2 and all of July 3 and did not participate in any of the fighting at Gettysburg. However, the 121st did do some heavy fighting on other battlefields. Over the course of the war, it saw 14 officers and 212 men killed and another 27 officers and 596 men wounded, for a casualty rate of 61 percent.

The medallion on the rear of the monument depicts Colonel Emory Upton, commander of the regiment. Upton eventually was promoted to brigadier general.

For more than a year and a half, the monument was missing the figure of the soldier on top. An unusual early snowstorm in October 2011 caused a tree limb to fall, striking the figure. It was removed for repair and replaced in the spring of 2013. The accompanying photos show the monument both with and without the soldier.

The monument's sculptor was S. J. O'Kelley. Fabrication was by Frederick and Field. Dedication took place October 10, 1889. The regiment was positioned here the night of July 2 through July 3.

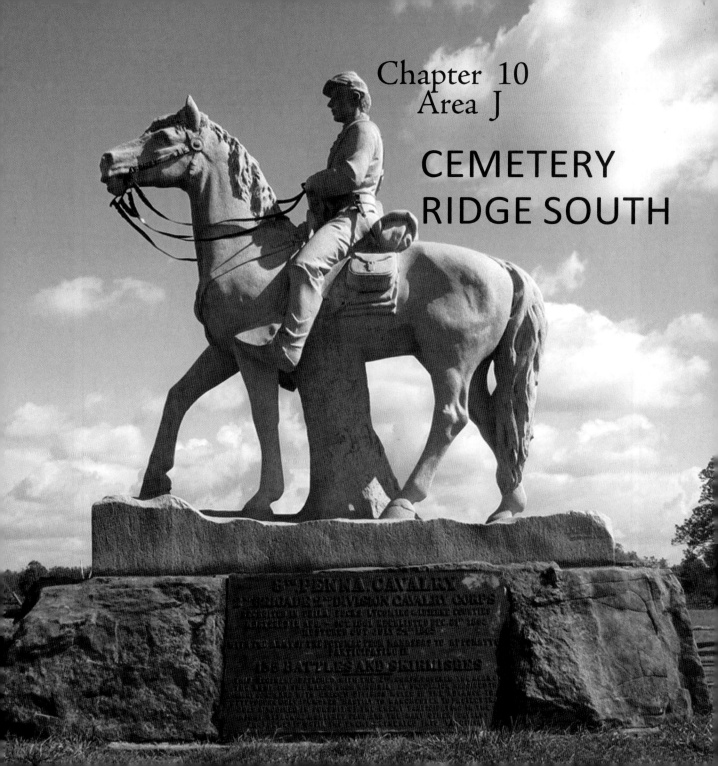

8TH PENNA. CAVALRY

188 BATTLES AND SKIRMISHES

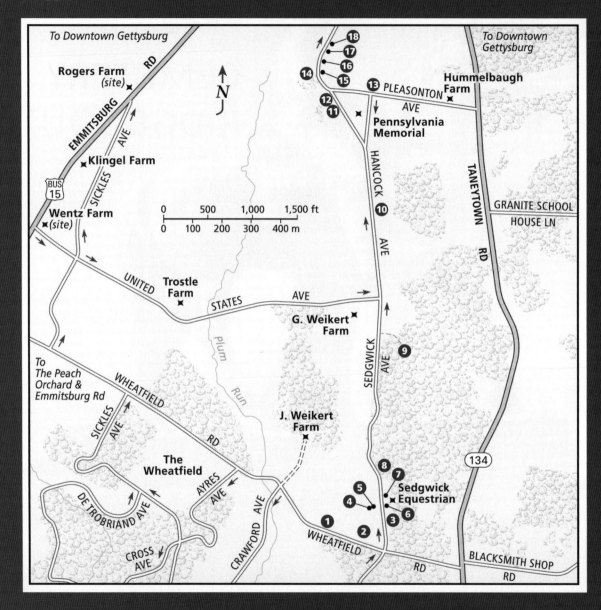

Late in the night on July 2, 1863, the commander of the Union army, Major General George Meade, assembled his corps commanders at his headquarters in a council of war. The purpose was to devise a plan of action for the coming day. The consensus was to hold the established positions and wait for Lee to attack.

On July 3, that attack came. The assault began with an artillery barrage unlike any ever seen on this continent before or since. When the cannonade was over, Robert E. Lee's Confederate army stepped off in a march across nearly a mile of open field. Its destination: a small clump of trees, or copse, on Cemetery Ridge, where the Union army waited. The most famous charge of the war was under way. Officially Longstreet's Assault, it would be forever known more commonly as Pickett's Charge.

Initially holding their fire, the Union men watched as the gray-clad troops drew closer. Then they let loose a deadly fire. Each volley from the Union guns thinned the Confederate line a little more. Reaching Emmitsburg Road, the Confederates had to slow their attack to remove fence rails. Those on the right of the line found themselves under fire from artillery on Little Round Top as they crossed the Codori Farm. By now, the attackers' ranks had been thinned by about half.

Just past the Codori Farm, Brigadier General James Kemper's men swung to their left so the attack could be concentrated at the copse of trees. This movement exposed Kemper's right flank, and troops from Vermont took advantage. Advancing through the smoke of battle, the Thirteenth and Sixteenth Vermont fired into the ranks of the Eleventh and Twenty-fourth Virginia, tearing large holes in their lines. Kemper was felled by a bullet in his groin just yards short of his goal.

Both sides fought furiously, often in hand-to-hand struggles. Whole lines fell from artillery fire. Union troops who were behind the line and unable to fire their weapons hurled rocks over the heads of those in front, doing anything they could to halt the advance. Ultimately, the attackers were overpowered and driven back.

Reaching Seminary Ridge, they found a distraught Robert E. Lee waiting. The general told them the failure of the attack was his fault. Expecting Meade to counterattack, Lee ordered Major General George Pickett to re-form his division to prepare. Choking back tears, Pickett famously replied, "General Lee, I have no division."

Returning to their cars after visiting the monuments on Little Round Top, visitors will pass down the north side of the hill and cross Wheatfield Avenue at the bottom. The mounted figure just ahead on the right is that of General John Sedgwick, who complained that he "might as well go home" when he realized that, with his troops being held in reserve, he wouldn't have much to do in the battle. At the intersection with United States Avenue is the historic George Weikert farm. Just ahead on the right stands the figure of Father William Corby, chaplain of the Eighty-fourth New York Infantry, who gained fame for his absolution of the troops of the Irish Brigade at this site, just before they went into battle. The next marker in this area that appears in Volume 1 is the New York Auxiliary Monument, often jokingly referred to as "the Monument to Every New Yorker Who Doesn't Have a Monument Somewhere Else."

The large monument ahead is the Pennsylvania State Memorial, which features bronze tablets extending around its perimeter. The story of those tablets and the figures adorning the corners of the columns is told in Volume 1, as are the stories of the easily missed monoliths sitting above the archways. Just before the Pennsylvania State Memorial is the monument to the First Minnesota Infantry. Volume 1 describes that regiment's suicidal charge, which resulted in 82 percent of its men becoming casualties.

A short distance down Pleasonton Avenue sits the impressive monument to the Fifteenth and Fiftieth New York Engineers. The reason it appears as a small turreted castle is explained in Volume 1.

J-1: Ninety-fifth Pennsylvania Infantry Monument
39° 47.725′ N, 77° 14.192′ W

The Ninety-fifth Pennsylvania left Westminster, Maryland, the evening of July 1, marching all night to reach Gettysburg on July 2. Late that afternoon, the regiment went into action in the right front of Little Round Top. One man was killed and six wounded, according to regimental battle reports. This is contrary to the numbers on the monument. The regiment then went into reserve until July 4, when it was sent to reconnoiter the Confederate position.

The monument to the Ninety-fifth marks the position the regiment held in a reserve capacity until joining the pursuit of the Army of Northern Virginia on the morning of July 5. For the next nine days, the regiment skirmished sporadically with Lee's rear guard.

Also known as the Gosline Zouaves, the regiment was commanded by Lieutenant Colonel Edward Carroll, who had been a carpenter in Philadelphia when war broke out. Carroll would be killed in the fighting at the Wilderness in 1864.

The monument's sculptor is unknown. The dedication was held July 2, 1888. The bronze inscription was added in 1901.

J-2: Fifth Maine Infantry Monument
39° 47.718' N, 77° 14.1' W

The Fifth Maine Infantry made a march of forty miles in nineteen hours to reach the battlefield in late afternoon on July 2. This monument indicates the regiment's approximate position on the afternoon of the second day's fighting. It stayed here through the rest of the battle. The remains of the walls erected by the regiment are visible around the monument.

Commanded by Colonel Clark S. Edwards, a farmer in civilian life, the regiment had no casualties at Gettysburg among its 340 members. Just five weeks after the battle, however, Thomas Jewett of Company D was executed for aggravated desertion. Born in England, Jewett had been accused of leaving the ranks just as the fighting at Salem Church, Virginia, began on May 3, 1863. He was returned by the provost guard on July 17, two weeks after Gettysburg. He was promptly court-martialed and, despite being described as a good soldier by his commanding officers, was found guilty. On August 14, near Warrenton, Virginia, he was shot by a firing squad

made up of ten men from the Ninety-sixth Pennsylvania. The entire First Division of the Sixth Corps was forced to watch.

The Fifth Maine also went by the name of the Forest City Regiment. It participated in nearly every major battle in the Eastern theater. Nearly half the regiment would be lost in a single advance at the Bloody Angle at Spotsylvania in May 1864.

When the regiment mustered out in 1864, those whose enlistments had not expired were transferred into a battalion with similar members of the Sixth Maine Infantry. Those soldiers were later combined with the Seventh Maine Infantry to form the Maine Veteran Volunteer Infantry.

The monument's sculptor is unknown. Dedication took place October 3, 1889.

J-3: Second Rhode Island Infantry Monument
39° 47.734' N, 77° 14.046' W

Dedicated October 12, 1886, the monument to the Second Rhode Island was fabricated by Smith Granite Company. It marks the regiment's location in

the second line of the brigade on the night of July 2.

The regiment was commanded by Colonel Horatio Rogers Jr., an attorney before the war. Rogers would subsequently serve Rhode Island as a state legislator and state attorney general. However, two other members of the regiment became more widely known.

The first was Major Sullivan Ballou, killed at First Manassas. Ballou was the author of one of the most famous letters of the war, to his wife, Sarah. That letter, featured prominently in the popular Ken Burns *Civil War* series on PBS, is presented in Appendix C.

The Second Rhode Island was also the home regiment of Elisha Hunt Rhodes, who began his career as a private in Company D. By the end of the war, he had risen to command the regiment. His diary was also quoted extensively in the Ken Burns series.

The regiment had a rich history. It fired the opening volley at First Manassas and was present at Lee's surrender at Appomattox. At Gettysburg, it did little fighting. As a reserve unit on the third day of the battle, it was moved to the locations where the fighting was heaviest and where it was needed most.

The Second had one man killed, Private Charles Powers of Company C. Five additional men were wounded and one was declared missing out of 409 engaged in the battle.

A secondary monument to the regiment sits along Emmitsburg Road near the Codori Farm (39° 48.588′ N, 77° 14.53′ W).

J-4: Monument to Battery C, First New York Light Artillery

39° 47.760' N, 77° 14.083' W

This monument marks the position of Battery C of the First New York Light Artillery from late afternoon on July 2 until early the next morning, when it moved to the left to support Brigadier General Albion P. Howe's division.

The unit was also known as Barnes's Battery, after Captain Almont Barnes, a prewar journalist. The battery arrived at Gettysburg with the rest of the Artillery Brigade of the Fifth Corps before dawn on

the second day of fighting and quickly took a position in a wheat field near Rock Creek. At about four that afternoon, Captain A. P. Martin, chief of the artillery corps, ordered Captain Barnes to "follow the Regulars," and added the warning, "Don't let Sickles get you!" referring to General Daniel Sickles, whose Union troops were coming under heavy fire.

The battery assumed a position on the right of Little Round Top, where it suffered no casualties but did see some of its horses' harnesses cut by bullets. The men found themselves frustrated, unable to fire their guns because of the presence of the Pennsylvania Reserves as they made their charge across the Wheatfield. Only when the Confederates had been driven back could the battery begin to fire.

The next morning, it moved to the extreme left of the line, where it remained until the end of the battle.

The monument's fabricator was Frederick and Field. Dedication took place July 2, 1893.

J-5: Ninety-third Pennsylvania Infantry Monument

39° 47.762' N, 77° 14.077' W

The Ninety-third Pennsylvania, also known as the Lebanon Infantry, arrived on the field in midafternoon on July 2 after a forced march with the Sixth Corps from Manchester, Maryland, in oppressive heat. What should have been a thirty-seven-mile march was made even longer when the corps took several wrong turns in the darkness. The march took

This monument was the original regimental marker. In 1888, it was moved from the John Weikert farm to this location, where it indicates the regiment's position prior to moving into the Wheatfield. The monument's sandstone was quarried on the Coleman Farm near Lebanon, Pennsylvania, and donated by that family.

A second monument reflects the regiment's position after returning from the Wheatfield (see G-20).

J-6: First Massachusetts Cavalry Monument
39° 47.764′ N, 77° 14.051′ W

The First Massachusetts Cavalry was not in action at Gettysburg. Rather, it served as the headquarters guard for Major General John Sedgwick. Among its duties was assisting the provost marshal in guarding prisoners. This monument commemorates the

nineteen hours. An hour after their arrival, the men were ordered to their left in support of the Third and Fifth corps.

Major John Nevin, a former schoolteacher, commanded the regiment. The movement to the left was led by General John Sedgwick himself. From that position, the regiment fought its way forward, taking twenty-five prisoners.

As evening fell, the regiment was ordered to move forward and recapture a battery that had been lost earlier in the day. Arriving where the battery should have been, the Ninety-third learned that the guns had already been removed from the field. It then returned to its earlier position. For most of that night, the regiment buried the dead and brought wounded men to a nearby field hospital.

On July 5, the regiment participated in the pursuit of Lee's army, guarding the corps' artillery and assisting it across the mountains.

At Gettysburg, the regiment suffered eight killed and twenty-one wounded.

regiment as it carried out those duties.

The light duty was welcomed by the First, which had suffered greatly just two weeks earlier at Aldie, Virginia, where it had twenty-four men killed, forty-two wounded, and eighty-eight taken prisoner. No other engagement in the war cost the First so dearly.

Lieutenant Colonel Greely S. Curtis commanded the First, which suffered no losses among its 292 officers and men at Gettysburg. Of its three battalions, only two were at Gettysburg. The third was serving in South Carolina.

The monument was fabricated by Boston Marble and Granite Company and dedicated October 8, 1885.

J-7: Tenth Massachusetts Infantry Monument
39° 47.782' N, 77° 14.051' W

The Tenth Massachusetts Infantry reached the battlefield on July 2 after a thirty-five-mile, eighteen-hour march in oppressive heat. Originally placed behind the Round Tops in a support position, the regiment moved to this location on July 3.

The monument marks the position the Tenth occupied on July 3. It was designed by Captain J. K. Newell of Company I. The sculptor was Melzar Hunt Mosman. Fabrication was by Chester Granite Company. The monument was dedicated October 6, 1885. At one time, the three muskets forming a stack on top of the monument were removed. Those muskets have been replaced and are visible in the photo.

Commanded by Lieutenant Colonel Joseph B. Parsons, the regiment brought 416 men into the battle, four of whom fell wounded and five of whom were declared missing. Ironically, the regiment never fired a shot at Gettysburg. All those who became casualties fell in the artillery barrage that preceded Pickett's Charge.

J-8: Thirty-seventh Massachusetts Infantry Monument
39° 47.83' N, 77° 14.059' W

The Thirty-seventh Massachusetts Infantry undertook a forced march with the rest of the Sixth

J-9: First New Jersey Brigade Monument
39° 48.036' N, 77° 14.002' W

Corps on the night of July 1. After thirty-five miles and nearly eighteen hours, the regiment arrived at Gettysburg late in the afternoon on July 2, just as the fighting on the left of the Union line was ending. The monument sits about a hundred yards in front of the regiment's actual July 2 position, which was nearer the ridge line.

On July 3, the regiment, under Colonel Oliver Edwards, took heavy casualties from Confederate artillery fire in advance of Pickett's Charge. Of the Thirty-seventh's 593 men at Gettysburg, two were killed, 26 wounded, and 19 declared missing.

The monument was fabricated by Milles and Luce and dedicated October 6, 1886. It marks the position the regiment held throughout the battle. The monument depicts a tree trunk with muskets leaning against it and a knapsack hanging on the side, along with a stand of colors. Like a number of other monuments in the southern area of the battlefield, this piece was vandalized on March 4, 1913.

The First New Jersey Brigade was comprised of the First, Second, Third, Fourth, and Fifteenth New Jersey infantry regiments at Gettysburg. The Twenty-third New Jersey Infantry had also served with the brigade but had mustered out a few weeks before the battle. Two additional regiments, the Tenth New Jersey Infantry and the Fortieth New Jersey Infantry, would be added to the brigade in 1864 and 1865, respectively. The First enjoyed the honor of being the only Union brigade to consist entirely of regiments from one state.

Held in reserve during the battle, the regiments

chose to erect a single monument to the brigade, rather than individual regimental monuments. This impressive tower was the result. Also known as Kearney's New Jersey Brigade, after its former commander, Major General Philip Kearney, the First purchased the entire George Weikert farm to ensure that its positions could be preserved. It placed its monument near the center of, but just slightly behind, its battle line. Tucked away on this small knoll in a wooded area, however, the monument is passed by most visitors, who don't take the short walk from the road to view it.

Standing forty feet tall, the monument honors with small bronze plaques both General Kearny and the brigade's commander at Gettysburg, Brigadier General Alfred T. A. Torbert. Small individual markers at the base of the knoll note each regiment's approximate position. The monument was designed by New England Monument Company and contracted by Bureau Brothers. It was dedicated June 30, 1888.

Lieutenant Colonel William Henry Jr. commanded the First New Jersey at Gettysburg, Lieutenant Colonel Charles Wiebecke the Second New Jersey, Colonel Henry W. Brown the Third New Jersey, Major Charles Ewing the Fourth New Jersey, and Colonel William H. Penrose the Fifteenth New Jersey. The brigade's casualties were light. The First and Fourth suffered no losses, while the Second had six wounded, the Third had two wounded, and the Fifteenth had three wounded. The brigade suffered no fatalities.

J-10: Fourth Pennsylvania Cavalry Monument
39° 48.286′ N, 77° 14.072′ W

The Fourth Pennsylvania Cavalry, commanded by Lieutenant Colonel William E. Doster, arrived at Brinkerhoff Ridge on July 2 after a nine-hour ride. The troopers could hear the sounds of heavy fighting from nearby Gettysburg. The Fourth, also known as the Sixty-fourth Pennsylvania Volunteers, received orders to proceed to Gettysburg and protect the left flank of the Union army, where it would remain until late in the evening as the guard for Brigadier General Alfred Pleasonton. The men also were called on to support a battery for a short time. Their monument marks the position they held in support of that battery. Several men and horses were wounded in this action.

The men spent the night of July 2 performing picket duty. On July 3, they moved to East Cavalry

Field, where they came under heavy fire but suffered no casualties. Their total loss for the entire battle was one man killed out of the 307 engaged.

On July 4, the Fourth was relatively inactive. On the morning of July 5, Doster and his men advanced toward the York Pike/Hanover Pike crossroad, finding a Confederate picket line along the way. The Confederates quickly surrendered and came into the Fourth's lines. The unit also captured five hospitals and three hundred wounded Confederates. The Fourth participated in the pursuit of Robert E. Lee later in the day. In that capacity, it engaged in numerous skirmishes with Lee's rear guard.

The monument, dedicated September 11, 1889, was fabricated by Dalbeattie Granite Works.

J-11: Ninth Michigan Battery Monument
39° 48.469′ N, 77° 14.159′ W

This monument marks the position the Ninth Michigan Battery held from early afternoon on July 3 until the next morning. Within an hour of taking its position, the battery silenced a Confederate gun. Not long after that, however, the men were ordered to fall back. Captain Jabez J. Daniels, in command of the battery, refused, saying he would not retreat as long as he had a gun left to fight with.

When a second Confederate gun was trained on the battery, four of the Ninth's guns were quickly disabled. The battery used double charges of canister to repulse two charges by enemy infantry. Bloodied but

still fighting, Daniels and his men held their position until the next morning, when the attacks ended. During that time, they fired 322 rounds of shot, shell, and canister.

Despite the heavy fighting, their losses were relatively light. One man was killed and four wounded. The battery also had twenty-three horses killed.

A merchant in civilian life, Daniels was in command throughout the battle. The Ninth was also known as Daniels's Battery.

Smith Granite Company fabricated this work, which was dedicated June 12, 1889.

J-12: Monument to Companies E, F, and G, New Hampshire Berdan Sharpshooters
39° 48.484′ N, 77° 14.171′ W

Company E of this regiment belonged to the First United States Sharpshooters, while Companies F and G were part of the Second United States Sharpshooters. The monument sits at the position Company E held on July 3.

The three companies were led by Major Homer R. Stoughton. On the morning of July 2, a detachment was sent forward to determine Confederate positions. That detachment spent the entire day delivering a constant fire into the ranks of the enemy until it ran out of ammunition and was forced back.

Meanwhile, a second detachment was sent to the left with the Third Maine Infantry under orders to do the same as the first detachment. Its line ran parallel to Emmitsburg Road. When that detachment also encountered Confederate troops, a short skirmish broke out that forced the sharpshooters back under the cover of some nearby woods. The remainder of the regiment moved forward and engaged until expending its ammunition.

On July 3, the sharpshooters undertook a similar action, a detachment again harassing Confeder-

ate skirmishers. Before withdrawing, the detachment captured a total of eighteen prisoners.

Together, the three companies had five men killed, twenty-three wounded, and fifteen missing out of the two hundred engaged.

All three companies were part of the Berdan United States Sharpshooters, arguably the best-known regiment in the army. Standards were so high for acceptance into Colonel Hiram Berdan's group that most states could raise only a few companies. Those who became part of the elite unit had to demonstrate extreme shooting proficiency by scoring ten consecutive hits within a circle ten inches in diameter. This had to be done from a distance of two hundred yards from a kneeling or standing position. Many of Berdan's men could hit the center of the target with all ten shots.

Initially, the sharpshooters were not highly thought of by other soldiers, who considered their tactics of shooting their victims at great distances to be cowardly and immoral. Berdan himself was also considered by many to be militarily inept and cowardly. He was twice unsuccessfully court-martialed in an attempt to remove him from command. Berdan would take an unauthorized leave of absence a few months after Gettysburg and never return to command.

Under the leadership of their line officers, the sharpshooters eventually gained the respect that had been lacking the first few years of their existence.

The monument, dedicated in 1886, was fabricated by Thomas Nahn.

J-13: Eighth Pennsylvania Cavalry Monument
39° 48.499' N, 77° 14.077' W

This striking monument is said to be the first effort in the United States to produce a granite equestrian monument. It sits in the general vicinity of General Alfred Pleasonton's headquarters.

Captain William A. Corie commanded the Eighth Pennsylvania Cavalry, also known as the Eighty-ninth Pennsylvania Volunteers. The Eighth had suffered heavy losses at Chancellorsville two months earlier in a gallant charge in which thirty men and three commissioned officers were killed. That same charge resulted in the loss of eighty horses.

From 1861 to 1865, the Eighth participated in 135 battles and skirmishes, serving from First Manassas to Lee's surrender at Appomattox. Interestingly, the unit was originally raised as a rifle regiment, rather than cavalry.

Its impressive monument notwithstanding, this unit was not physically at Gettysburg during the battle, having been assigned to protect the trains at Manchester, Maryland. The Eighth did participate in the pursuit of the Confederates back to Virginia after the battle, however, helping capture 250 supply wagons and six hundred prisoners near South Mountain in Maryland.

The decision to erect the monument came during a reunion on the battlefield in July 1887. John M. Gessler and Sons fabricated the monument, which was dedicated September 1, 1890. The monument has been vandalized many times over the years. Some of the bronze work has been lost. The bronze carbine was stolen, returned in 1953, and stolen again in 1954. The latest act of vandalism occurred January 18, 2005, when the sword was stolen. Total damage in that incident was estimated at three thousand dollars.

Visitors often ask why a tree trunk is beneath the horse. The answer, while not obvious, shows a certain amount of ingenuity on the part of the sculptor. This is the only freestanding stone equestrian monument at Gettysburg. Other stone cavalry monuments have the horses carved into larger supporting structures. A freestanding stone monument, however, proved to be unstable. The sculptor solved the problem by adding support in the form of the tree trunk.

J-14: Wounding of Hancock
39° 48.527' N, 77° 14.224' W

Nicknamed "Hancock the Superb," Major General Winfield Scott Hancock was ordered by Major

General George Meade to take temporary command of the First, Second, Third, and Eleventh corps after Major General John Reynolds was killed on the first day of fighting. Major General Oliver O. Howard, a more senior officer, protested, but Hancock won the argument, having the direct backing of Meade.

During the heavy artillery bombardment that began Pickett's Charge on July 3, Hancock calmly rode through his lines encouraging his men. Shortly after stopping to talk with Brigadier General George J. Stannard, Hancock received a severe wound when a bullet struck the pommel of his saddle and sent wood fragments and a large nail into his right thigh. Aides eased him from his horse and applied a tourniquet. Seeing the nail protruding from his thigh, Hancock removed it himself. Looking at it, he famously said, "They must be hard up for ammunition when they throw such shot as that." Despite the severity of his wound, he refused to be transported to the rear until the battle was over. The wound never completely healed. Hancock felt its effects the rest of his life.

After the war, his fame as a military hero prompted supporters to urge him to run for president. Finally talked into it, he ran unsuccessfully against James Garfield in 1880. Hancock died February 9, 1886, and is buried in West Norristown, Pennsylvania.

This marker noting Hancock's wounding was dedicated in 1892. It was fabricated by Smith Granite Company.

J-15: Fourteenth Vermont Volunteers Monument
39° 48.529′ N, 77° 14.195′ W

The Fourteenth Vermont, a nine-month regiment, had almost reached the end of its enlistment. Prior to reporting to Gettysburg, its men had occupied their time on picket duty, practicing daily drills, building corduroy roads, and digging rifle pits. Untested in battle, the regiment endured a six-day march to Gettysburg. Arriving on the field too late for the first day's fighting, the Fourteenth took a position in a wheat field to the left of Cemetery Hill. The next day, it moved to a position marked by this monument, where it remained until the end of the battle.

In its first real test, the regiment was ordered to move forward under fire to the rear of a battery that had been abandoned when the Confederates overran the position. With the Thirteenth and Sixteenth Vermont infantries, the regiment attacked and overran Brigadier General Ambrose Wright's Georgia brigade, capturing several prisoners and saving the battery.

In General William Barksdale's advance (see F-10), it was men from the Fourteenth Vermont who found the mortally wounded Barksdale. Eight men from the regiment under Sergeant Henry Vaughan carried the Confederate general to a Union field hospital at the Jacob Hummelbaugh farm, where he died a few hours later. Barksdale's last known words, for his wife, were given to Sergeant Vaughan, who was killed the next day before he was able to deliver the message.

On July 3, the regiment moved slightly forward, taking advantage of some trees and brush for shelter from the ferocious artillery barrage. As the Confederate line began its march across the open field, the men from Vermont waited, under orders to hold their fire until the Rebels were close, then to fire a volley, then to follow it with a bayonet charge. When the Confederates changed direction in front of the Vermonters, the regiment participated in the famous flank attack that decimated Brigadier General Cadmus Wilcox's division and took several hundred prisoners.

The Fourteenth had to be content with its glory at Gettysburg, the only battle the regiment fought before being mustered out just two weeks later. Commanded by Colonel William T. Nichols, the Fourteenth suffered nineteen killed and seventy-four wounded on the second and third days of the battle. Of the wounded, eight would die, for a total of twenty-seven deaths due to the battle. This represented the heaviest loss in killed and wounded sustained by any regiment in the brigade.

After the battle, the regiment joined in the pursuit of Lee's army.

The obelisk was fabricated by Estabrook Granite Works and dedicated October 19, 1889. It marks the position the Fourteenth held prior to its advance on July 3 to counterattack Confederate troops during Pickett's Charge.

J-16: Sixteenth Vermont Infantry Monument
39° 48.548' N, 77° 14.193' W

The Sixteenth Vermont reached the battlefield late on July 2, forming on the left on Cemetery Hill for what would be the only battle it ever fought. It

was exposed to heavy enemy artillery fire as it took a position in support of an artillery battery. That night, it was detailed for picket duty.

The next day, the Sixteenth participated in the repulse of Pickett's Charge. When its skirmish line was driven back, the regiment rallied in the Codori thicket and mounted a charge on the flank of Pickett's Division, at which time it captured three flags and took several hundred prisoners. After flanking Pickett's Division, the Sixteenth turned and struck the flank of Brigadier General Edward Perry's Flor-

ida brigade, which had advanced with Wilcox's Brigade to support the withdrawal of Pickett's troops.

After the battle, the regiment pursued Lee's retreating army. During that pursuit, the regiment's enlistment period ended. Ordered home, the men assumed they were out of danger. Arriving in New York, however, they found themselves in the midst of the infamous draft riots, during which more than a hundred citizens were killed and extensive property damage took place. Initially, the rioters were members of the working class protesting that the wealthy could avoid being drafted into military service by paying a three-hundred-dollar fee for a substitute. However, the protests quickly turned into a race riot. Military intervention was required to put the riot down. The men of the Sixteenth assisted with riot control and remained in New York until peace was restored, effectively extending their enlistment by several days.

The monument, whose fabricator is unknown, was dedicated in September 1892. It originally marked the position the Sixteenth held on July 3 after their skirmish line was driven back. That point is approximately a thousand feet from this location. The monument was moved to its present site in 1907 at the request of Congressman Kittredge Haskins, who served in the regiment's Company I but did not fight at Gettysburg, having resigned five months earlier due to disabilities.

The Sixteenth was commanded by Colonel Wheelock Graves Veazey, who would be awarded the Medal of Honor for his bravery at Gettysburg. He earned the medal for organizing troops in their first battle and leading them in a charge while under heavy fire, destroying a Confederate brigade.

The regiment saw 16 of its members killed and 102 wounded. One man was declared missing.

J-17: Vermont State Memorial
39° 48.566' N, 77° 14.182' W

Vermont authorized the construction of this monument to honor all the state's regiments that fought at Gettysburg. This was the first large state memorial on the battlefield. The base has a replica of the state coat of arms on the front and brief accounts of the First Vermont Brigade, the Second Vermont Brigade, and the Vermont Sharpshooters and First Vermont Cavalry on the remaining three sides.

The monument consists of a column that stands fifty-five feet in height, topped by a statue of Brigadier General George Stannard, commander of the Second Vermont Brigade. Wounded in the right thigh on July 3 when he was struck by an artillery fragment, Stannard remained on the field. Close observation of the statue reveals that it also shows him missing his right arm. This did not occur at Gettysburg, but later

in the war in the assault on Fort Harrison, Virginia. Stannard would receive a brevet promotion to major general for his actions at Fort Harrison.

The memorial's designer and contractor was Henry Bonnard Bronze Company, and the sculptor was Karl Gerhardt. Fabrication was done by Frederick and Field. The monument was dedicated October 9, 1889.

J-18: Thirteenth Vermont Infantry Monument
39° 48.579′ N, 77° 14.175′ W

The monument to the Thirteenth Vermont brings with it one of the more unusual stories of the battle. It concerns the man represented on the statue, Lieutenant Stephen F. Brown of Company K.

The Thirteenth was part of a forced march to Gettysburg conducted in severe heat and with little food or water. Many men dropped out during the march, leading to orders that nobody was permitted to leave the ranks except during rest stops. When the march passed near a well outside Frederick, Maryland, Brown took several of his men's canteens and attempted to fill them, whereupon the troops guarding the well ordered him to return to his ranks. Brown refused and was arrested. His sword, the symbol of his position as an officer, was taken from him.

On July 3, with Pickett's Charge imminent, Brown was released from arrest and allowed to return to his men. Having no sword, he picked up a camp hatchet as his weapon and led a charge into

the advancing Confederates. Spying a Southern officer, he rushed to him and brandished the hatchet, demanding the officer's surrender. The officer immediately turned over his pistol and sword to the hatchet-waving Brown, becoming the lieutenant's prisoner.

When a design for the monument was submitted, it depicted Brown carrying the hatchet. The War Department withheld approval on the grounds that it honored the disobedience of orders. The final design showed Brown holding the captured sword, with the hatchet at his feet. This design was approved, and the

monument was then constructed as designed.

Brown himself was the model for the statue, which was sculpted by F. Moyneham and constructed by Gorham Manufacturing. The base was done by J. H. Walling Company. Dedication took place October 19, 1899. The monument sits at the position the regiment held from the evening of July 2 until the end of the battle.

Captain John Lonergan of Company A exhibited his own gallantry in the battle when he recaptured four guns and captured two additional guns, along with several prisoners. He would be awarded the Medal of Honor for his actions.

The Thirteenth was commanded by Colonel Francis V. Randall, an attorney and member of the Vermont state legislature. The regiment had 710 men at Gettysburg and suffered 10 killed, 103 wounded, and 10 declared missing. The Thirteenth was a nine-month regiment, and this was the only battle it ever fought. The regiment mustered out two weeks after Gettysburg.

Chapter 11
Area K

CEMETERY RIDGE NORTH

Area K

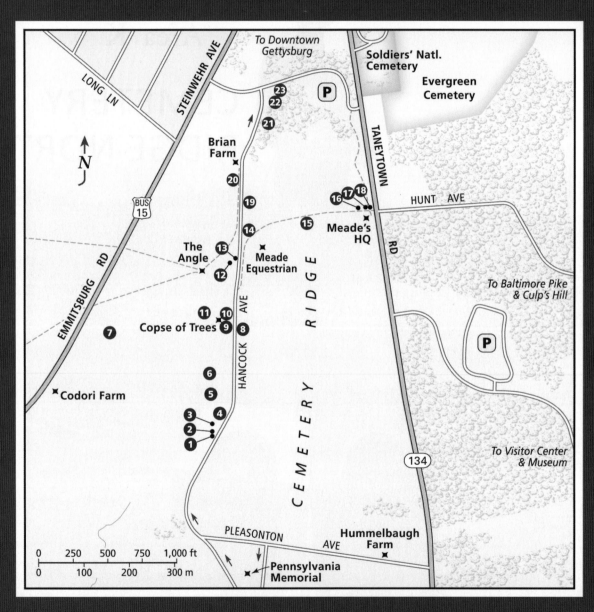

To Downtown Gettysburg

Soldiers' Natl. Cemetery

Evergreen Cemetery

P

LONG LN

STEINWEHR AVE

N

BUS 15

23
22
21

Brian Farm

20

19

TANEYTOWN RD

HUNT AVE

16 17 18

Meade's HQ

14

15

The Angle

13

12

Meade Equestrian

EMMITSBURG RD

To Baltimore Pike & Culp's Hill

CEMETERY RIDGE

P

11 10

Copse of Trees

9 8

7

6

HANCOCK AVE

5

3
4

2

1

Codori Farm

To Visitor Center & Museum

134

PLEASONTON AVE

Hummelbaugh Farm

0   250   500   750   1,000 ft
0   100   200   300 m

Pennsylvania Memorial

General Robert E. Lee's attacks on the Union left and right had not achieved much, leading him to recognize that further efforts on the ends of the Federal line would not be fruitful. His plan for the third day of fighting was to attack the Union center, where he thought the line would be weakest. General James Longstreet objected, saying that no fifteen thousand men ever assembled would be able to take that position. But Lee had made up his mind.

The morning of July 3, 1863, saw both Lee and General George Meade organizing their troops, Lee in an attack mode, Meade in a defensive one. In early afternoon, the scene was set.

By one o'clock, 140 Confederate guns had been moved into a line along Seminary Ridge. The signal was given, and the guns of both sides came to life in the largest artillery barrage ever seen on this continent. For an hour, the guns fired continuously. The noise was said to be audible fifty miles away.

Then, the artillery's job done, more than twelve thousand brave Confederates began the trek across the open field. The Union artillery resumed its deadly fire, and the troops massed along Cemetery Ridge opened up as well. Large holes developed in the Confederate line, but still the troops came.

Using a copse of trees as a landmark, the Confederates closed ranks as they got closer to the Union defenders. Approaching the stone wall that marked the Union line, the Confederates faced a deadly fire of double canister from the Union artillery. Major General James Kemper and Brigadier General Richard Garnett fell. Brigadier General Lewis Armistead reached the stone wall near the Angle and, placing his cap on the point of his sword, led his men across the wall and into the ranks of the Union defenders. Hand-to-hand fighting ensued. Armistead was mortally wounded and his men driven back.

A twenty-two-year-old lieutenant named Alonzo Cushing was in command of Battery A of the Fourth United States Artillery near the Angle. Battery A had taken heavy fire during the initial bombardment. As the Confederates reached the stone wall, Cushing was down to only two working guns and a skeleton crew of cannoneers. Already badly wounded, he ordered extra canister to be loaded. Willing his pain-racked body to continue the fight, Cushing fired one of the guns himself. Then, as he prepared to fire again, he was shot through the mouth, dying instantly. In an unprecedented act, the United States Congress is reviewing his actions 150 years later with the idea of awarding the Medal of Honor to the young lieutenant.

Just north of the Angle, two Confederate leaders, Brigadier General James Pettigrew and Major General Isaac Trimble, were wounded. The Eighth Ohio Infantry attacked the left flank of the charge, delivering a deadly fire. Seeing his troops fall, Pettigrew recognized that further attack would only add to the carnage while achieving nothing. He ordered the Southern troops to fall back.

Seeing the retreat, Brigadier General Alexander Hays dragged a captured Confederate flag behind his horse to the cheers of his Union men, many of whom had been among the group derisively referred to by other troops as "Harpers Ferry Cowards," having been captured there a year earlier. The "Cowards" felt more than vindicated for the role they had just played in defending the Union line.

Pickett's Charge had failed, fifty-five hundred Confederate and seventeen hundred Union soldiers had become casualties, and the Battle of Gettysburg was history. But the fight did not end the war. Battles remained to be fought at such places as Chickamauga, the Wilderness, Spotsylvania Court House, and Cold Harbor. The war was destined to go on for nearly two more brutal and bloody years.

Since Pickett's Charge dominated this area, it is no wonder so many monuments are clustered so closely. Monuments on Hancock Avenue described in Volume 1 include those to the United States Regulars, Brigadier General John Gibbon, and the Tammany Regiment, with its controversial figure on top. In short order, visitors will then pass the monuments to the First Pennsylvania Cavalry and Brigadier General Alexander Webb before arriving at the High Water Mark area of the battlefield.

There, as detailed in Volume 1, sits possibly the most controversial monument at Gettysburg: that to the Seventy-second Pennsylvania. Also in this area is the marker signifying the location of Brigadier General Lewis Armistead's heroic death, as well as the marker for the equally heroic Alonzo Cushing. The California Regiment's marker is unusual because no California troops fought at Gettysburg. Volume 1 tells why the monument to the Seventy-first Pennsylvania Infantry carries the California name.

Among the famous landmarks in this area described in Volume 1 are the Angle, the stone wall, and the field of Pickett's Charge. Across the field is a tall pine tree with a small marker related not to the Civil War but to World War II; Volume 1 tells its story. Moving toward the northern end of Hancock Avenue, visitors will pass the marker for the Eleventh Mississippi, followed by that for the 111th New York. A short distance down a path to the right of the road sits the equestrian statue of General George Meade.

In the area known as Ziegler's Grove is the marker for the Ninth Massachusetts, followed by the GAR Memorial and the monument to General Alexander Hays. Visitors who turn right at the intersection and pass through the parking lot (scheduled to be razed to return the area to its 1863 appearance) will see the state memorials of Maryland and Delaware where the lot exits on to Taneytown Road.

K-1: Twentieth New York State Militia Monument

39° 48.614′ N, 77° 14.165′ W

This marker to the Twentieth New York State Militia, also known as the Eightieth New York Infantry or the Ulster Guard, is one of the newer monuments on the battlefield, having been dedicated July 3, 1981. The sculptor and fabricator are unknown.

Under the command of Colonel Theodore Burr Gates, the regiment fought from a position south of the marker on July 3, hitting the right flank of the Confederate army as it advanced toward the copse of trees during Pickett's Charge. As the Confederates passed, the New Yorkers followed, firing into the ranks as they moved. Later, Colonel Gates explained that he feared the advancing Confederates would gain possession of the hill and the batteries positioned there.

Reaching the copse, the regiment mounted a charge, driving Confederate troops into the open from their position in the brush, which Union forces had created by felling trees to provide a clear field of fire for the artillery. Those Confederates who were not killed or wounded were taken captive by Gates and his men.

In the assault, Captain Ambrose N. Baldwin of Company K was mortally wounded. Major Walter A. Van Rensselaer was also seriously wounded in his successful attempt to capture an enemy battle flag. He would live in pain for sixteen years until he died in 1879 as a result of his wounds. In 2004, Van Rensselaer's grandson donated the flag to Gettysburg National Military Park.

The Twentieth suffered losses of 35 men killed, 111 wounded, and 24 missing. The regiment is also honored by a monument under the name of the Eightieth New York (see A-2).

K-2: Eighty-second New York Infantry Monument

39° 48.619′ N, 77° 14.165′ W

This monument marks the position the Eighty-second New York held on July 2 and 3.

On the evening of July 2, the Eighty-second and

Huston, commander of the regiment, was killed. Captain John Darrow assumed command.

On July 3, the regiment fought near the copse of trees to repulse Pickett's Charge. The Eighty-second captured the flags of the First and Seventh Virginia regiments. The man credited with taking the Seventh Virginia's colors was Sergeant Hugh Carey of Company E. He suffered two wounds in the effort. Carey, a native of Ireland, would be awarded the Medal of Honor for this action.

Also known as the Second Regiment New York State Militia, the Eighty-second took part in twenty-nine engagements before mustering out on June 25, 1864. The remaining recruits and reenlisted men were transferred to the Fifty-ninth New York Infantry.

At Gettysburg, the regiment had 24 officers and 331 men available. It counted 45 killed, 132 wounded, and 15 missing, for a 54 percent casualty rate. The Eighty-second's monument was sculpted by Maurice J. Power and dedicated July 2, 1890.

the Fifteenth Massachusetts were ordered into a gap in the Union line. The Eighty-second placed its left flank adjacent to the Codori House. The men quickly dismantled a fence and used it to build breastworks in their front. When the onrushing Confederates from Georgia struck their line, the New Yorkers could not hold their position. Falling back so quickly that they were unable to set fire to the Codori buildings, as they had been instructed to do in the event of a retreat, many were struck by friendly canister fire from Union artillery.

Finally able to reorganize, the regiment mounted a counterattack that took it back to its original position. It captured the colors of the Forty-eighth Georgia in this charge. During the fighting, Colonel James

K-3: First Minnesota Infantry Monument
39° 48.629' N, 77° 14.165' W

One of the legendary regiments at Gettysburg, the First Minnesota suffered heavily, losing 82 percent of its men on July 2 alone. Only one other regiment, the Confederate army's First Texas, lost a greater percentage in one battle, enduring a casualty rate of 82.3 percent at Antietam. The First Minne-

fall at Gettysburg. Colonel William Colville became the first such casualty when he was badly wounded during the charge of July 2. Captain Nathan Messick took over, only to be killed as the regiment fought against Pickett's Charge the next day. Messick's place was taken by Captain Wilson B. Farrell, who was killed shortly after taking command. Captain Henry C. Coates took charge for the remainder of the battle.

Two men of the First received Medals of Honor for their bravery at Gettysburg. Private Marshall Sherman of Company C received his for capturing the flag of the Twenty-eighth Virginia Infantry. Corporal Henry D. O'Brien of Company E picked up his company's fallen colors and ran ahead of the regiment to a position close to the Confederate guns, receiving a wound in the process. Despite this, he held the colors while fighting desperately until he was wounded a second time.

The monument was dedicated in 1897.

sota regained some strength on the morning of July 3 when Companies C, which had been detached, and L, whose men had been positioned as skirmishers, rejoined the regiment.

The First has three monuments at Gettysburg. The other two are at the intersection of Humphreys and Hancock avenues (39° 48.396′ N, 77° 14.102′ W) and in the National Cemetery (see D-11). The monument shown here notes the location where the regiment, already decimated in the previous day's epic charge, fought during Pickett's Charge, losing seventeen more men but capturing a Confederate flag.

As may be expected in a regiment that lost so many men, the First also saw several commanders

K-4: Monument to Battery B, First New York Light Artillery
39° 48.637′ N, 77° 14.147′ W

Battery B of the First New York Light Artillery held this position on the afternoon of July 3, the final day of the battle. The unit was also known as the Empire Battery or Pettit's Battery, after Captain Rufus D. Pettit, who resigned a month before Gettysburg.

Captain James McKay Rorty, a twenty-six-year-old New York City book canvasser who had been born in Ireland, commanded the battery after taking over

on July 2 for Lieutenant Albert S. Sheldon, who was badly wounded. After three of his guns and their crews were disabled in the artillery barrage that initiated Pickett's Charge, Rorty stepped in to work one of the remaining guns. The short-handed battery commander called on the Nineteenth Massachusetts Infantry to furnish additional men to help keep the guns working. A former ordnance officer for the Second Corps, Rorty had requested a combat command for this battle. He and nine of his men were killed in vicious hand-to-hand fighting when the battery was briefly overrun by Major General James Kemper's Virginia brigade. The Virginians temporarily placed their flag on one of Battery B's guns before being pushed back. Lieutenant Robert E. Rogers assumed command when Rorty was killed.

The battery served for about forty-six months, during which time it fought on seventy-eight separate days, an average of a battle every two to three weeks for nearly four years. It had 114 men at Gettysburg, of whom 10 were killed and 16 wounded.

The monument's fabricator was Frederick and Field. Dedication took place July 3, 1888.

K-5: Nineteenth Maine Infantry Monument
39° 48.663' N, 77° 14.167' W

Under the command of Colonel Francis E. Heath, the Nineteenth Maine fought in this area on the second day. The men initially lay prone as General Daniel Sickles's Third Corps ran over them in a disorganized retreat, until a corps officer ordered

Heath to have his troops stop the retreating men at the point of their bayonets. Heath refused the order and waited until the pursuing Florida Brigade appeared out of the smoke, at which time he told his troops to stand. They fired several rounds at the Floridians, captured their battle flag, took many prisoners, halted the Confederate advance in that area, and helped recapture four Union guns.

The next day, the regiment moved to the right and assisted in repelling Pickett's Charge. The Nineteenth was said to have captured two Confederate battle flags but had them taken away by other regiments.

The Nineteenth brought 405 men to the battle and saw 65 of their number killed or mortally wounded, 137 wounded, and four declared missing. Heath was wounded on July 3, leaving command of the regiment to Lieutenant Colonel Henry Whitman.

Dedication ceremonies for the monument were held October 3, 1889. The sculptor is unknown.

K-6: Twentieth Massachusetts Infantry Monument
39° 48.686′ N, 77° 14.169′ W

Perhaps no marker on the battlefield illustrates the old saying "Beauty is in the eye of the beholder" better than that to the Twentieth Massachusetts. Many say it is the least attractive monument they have ever seen, while others are captivated by its simplicity and meaning.

The Twentieth was known as the Harvard Regiment because so many of its officers were Harvard men. The most famous was a young lieutenant named Oliver Wendell Holmes, destined to become an associate justice of the United States Supreme Court.

Recruited in Roxbury, Massachusetts, the regiment had fought at such battles as Ball's Bluff,

Yorktown, Fair Oaks, Antietam, Fredericksburg, and Chancellorsville before arriving at Gettysburg. It had received many accolades and had seen many of its men fall. At Gettysburg, forty-four members of the regiment were killed, including two who bore famous names. Colonel Paul Joseph Revere, grandson of Paul Revere, was killed by artillery fire. Lieutenant Sumner Paine, whose great-grandfather was a signer of the Declaration of Independence, died during Pickett's Charge.

First Lieutenant Henry Ropes was also killed, but in his case it was by his own guns. As Ropes lay in position with the rest of his company in front of a Union battery, a bad shell traveled only a few feet after being fired and landed next to him, killing him and wounding several others.

A special monument was planned to honor those killed. But what would make it stand out? The decision was made to bring a large boulder from a playground in Roxbury. It was said that many of the soldiers had played around the boulder as youths. The bronze tablet on the monument's base honors Revere, Ropes, Paine, and the forty-one enlisted men who were killed or mortally wounded. Colonel Revere's daughter presented the tablet.

The monument is located where the regiment stood on July 2 and 3 until it moved to the copse of trees to assist in repelling Pickett's Charge. The designer and contractor was Smith Granite Company. The monument was dedicated in June 1886.

K-7: Colonel George H. Ward Monument
39° 48.734' N, 77° 14.325' W

Colonel George H. Ward commanded the Fifteenth Massachusetts Volunteer Regiment. In the fighting on July 2, he was wounded at this location by troops from the Third Georgia Infantry. Ward lay on the field for two hours before his brother, Lieutenant Henry C. Ward, found him. He died of his wounds the next day. The citizens of his hometown of Worchester, Massachusetts, and the regiment's survivors honored him with this memorial.

On October 14, 1868, Ward was posthumously

appointed to the rank of brevet brigadier general for his actions at Ball's Bluff, Virginia, in 1861, as well as his "gallant and meritorious services" at Gettysburg. He had been badly wounded at Ball's Bluff, resulting in the amputation of the lower portion of his left leg. Despite the loss, Ward actively recruited Union troops during his recovery and returned to his regiment before the wound fully healed. He was said to have been leaning on his cane when he was mortally wounded at Gettysburg. The former machinist, one of fifteen children of the Ward family, was thirty-seven years old.

The monument features a bas-relief of Ward on the front. Fabricated by Boston Marble and Granite Company, it was dedicated June 2, 1886. Colonel Ward's wife, Emily, and their two sons were present at the dedication.

Reaching the monument requires visitors to climb over or through a five-rail fence. That, combined with the marker's relatively isolated location along Emmitsburg Road, discourages many from visiting it.

K-8: Monument to Battery B, First Rhode Island Light Artillery

39° 48.738' N, 77° 14.124' W

This monument to Battery B of the First Rhode Island Light Artillery came perilously close to never being constructed. The Rhode Island state legislature's original plan was to build a single memorial to honor all the state's troops at Gettysburg. Only after

learning that other states were erecting monuments for each individual regiment or battery did the legislature change its mind and decide to do the same.

On the afternoon of July 2, Battery B sat between the Codori Farm and the copse of trees, approximately five hundred yard west of the site of the monument. A small marker designates that position. Brigadier General Ambrose R. Wright's Georgia brigade overran the Rhode Islanders' position and captured their guns, which were quickly recovered in a counterattack led by the 106th Pennsylvania Infantry (see K-10). However, Battery B still felt the effects of that fighting the next day, when only four of its guns were in condition to be fired.

When the fierce cannonade preceding Pickett's Charge began, Battery B, under the command of Captain T. Fred Brown, was part of the Union response. Situated where the monument now sits, the battery fired round after round. One gun was knocked out of service when a Confederate round struck it just as it was being loaded, denting the muzzle and killing two gunners. The remainder of the crew tried valiantly to continue firing the gun, but it was permanently disabled when another Confederate round struck nearby. The shot the crew was loading became lodged in the barrel, rendering it unable to fire. That gun, its shot still plainly visible in the muzzle, can be seen today in Providence, Rhode Island.

The monument, dedicated October 13, 1886, was designed and built by John Flaherty.

K-9: First New York Independent Battery Monument
39° 48.741′ N, 77° 14.138′ W

The First New York Independent Battery, commanded by twenty-three-year-old captain Andrew Cowan, reached the field at about three in the afternoon on July 2 and went into reserve duty immediately. Born in Scotland, Cowan had been studying at Madison University in New York City when the war began.

The monument marks the position the First held on July 3. More commonly referred to as Cowan's Battery, it had just moved here when Pickett's Charge began, having been ordered to the former position of Battery B of the First Rhode Island Light Artillery (see K-8). As the assault continued, the First fired continuously into the Confederate troops. Its last charge was double canister, as the Southern troops by that time had breached the Union line and were only ten yards away.

The First's officers noted that the battery suffered more at Gettysburg than in all the former battles in which it had engaged. Of the battery's 113 men, four

were killed and two lieutenants and six men wounded. Fourteen horses were also killed. The regiment's battle report gave detailed descriptions of some of the injuries received: "First Lieut. Wm. P. Wright was shot through the right lung, the ball entering his

breast and coming out at the back below the shoulder blade, severe hemorrhage resulted and he is considered dangerously wounded. First Lieut. [William H.] Johnson was wounded in the thigh. Privates [Edward] Peto, James Grey, [Jacob] McElroy and [Otis] Billings were killed outright, and Henry Hitchcock had a thigh so mangled by a shell that he died this morning. Privates [Charles] Gates and H. [Henry] Clark were slightly wounded, Serg't [Albert E.] Kimbark, also, but he is on duty now, Corporal [Alexander] McKenzie was wounded in the leg, not severely however. Capt. Cowan had holes shot through his coat, and when his men were shot down and both Lieutenants carried from the field wounded, threw off his coat and worked a gun himself."

The monument was sculpted by J. G. Hamilton and fabricated by Smith Granite Company. At the extreme right center of the plaque is a Confederate flag, indicated by the arrow in the second photo and circled in the close-up in the third photo. It is one of the few depictions of the Confederate flag on any Union monument on any battlefield. Dedication ceremonies were held July 3, 1887.

K-10: 106th Pennsylvania Infantry Monument
39° 48.755' N, 77° 14.137' W

Part of the Philadelphia Brigade, the 106th Pennsylvania has three monuments at Gettysburg. This one commemorates the regiment's charge on July 2, which resulted in the retaking of the guns of

Battery B of the First Rhode Island Light Artillery and the capture of 21 officers, including a colonel, and 250 men of the Forty-eighth Georgia Infantry. The regiment also was part of the assault that took the Bliss Farm. That charge is re-created on the plaque mounted on the side facing Hancock Avenue.

On the evening of July 2, the regiment moved to East Cemetery Hill to reinforce the Eleventh Corps, as indicated by a small marker at 39° 49.335′ N, 77° 13.765′ W. An interesting quote appears on that marker. To emphasize the importance of holding the position, General O. O. Howard pointed to the advancing enemy and said to Major Thomas Osborne, commander of the Eleventh Corps' artillery, "Your

batteries can be withdrawn when that regiment runs away."

The third marker sits at the Codori farmhouse (39° 48.696′ N, 77° 14.396′ W). It originally stood where the regimental monument is now located.

The regimental monument features three drums sitting on a base made of four knapsacks. The drums are stacked so they form the trefoil symbol of the Second Corps. Forty smaller trefoils form a border around the four sides of the monument shaft, symbolizing the number of rounds of ammunition each man carried into the fight.

The 106th Pennsylvania was commanded by Lieutenant Colonel William L. Curry, a Philadelphia paperhanger. Curry would be wounded at Spotsylvania and would die as a result on July 7, 1864.

The regiment had 23 officers and 312 men at Gettysburg. Two officers and 10 men were killed or mortally wounded, eight officers and 43 men wounded, and one man declared captured or missing.

The regiment was originally raised as the Fifth California. Many on the West Coast wished for California to be represented in the fighting in the East. Senator Edward D. Baker of Oregon was asked to raise a regiment to be credited to California. A regiment was subsequently recruited in Philadelphia and named the First California. Ultimately, three more such regiments—the Second, Third, and Fifth California—were raised. When Baker was killed at Ball's Bluff, Pennsylvania claimed the four regiments, renaming the First California the Seventy-first Pennsylvania, the Second California the Sixty-ninth Pennsylvania, the Third California the Seventy-second Pennsylvania, and the Fifth California the 106th Pennsylvania.

The monument's sculptor was John Walz. The granite work was done by John M. Gessler and Sons, while the bronze was done by Bureau Brothers. The monument was dedicated September 12, 1889.

K-11: Sixty-ninth Pennsylvania Infantry Monument
39° 48.756′ N, 77° 14.178′ W

The Sixty-ninth Pennsylvania Infantry, recruited from the Second Regiment (Irish Brigade), Second Division, Pennsylvania Militia, was originally designated as the Second California Regiment. The monument marks the position the regiment held on July 2 and 3. Over the course of the war, the Sixty-ninth would earn forty-five battle ribbons, never losing its colors.

Late in the afternoon on July 2, the regiment assisted in driving back a desperate attack by Brigadier General A. R. Wright's Georgia brigade, recapturing the guns of the Second Rhode Island Artillery in the process. But it was the men's valor the next day that garnered the regiment its fame.

On July 3, this position came under heavy artillery fire in the famous barrage that preceded Pickett's Charge. As the assault began, Colonel Dennis O'Kane ordered his men to stand strong, telling them that if any member of the Sixty-ninth failed to perform his duty, he was to be shot by the man beside him.

The section of wall to the Sixty-ninth's right had been manned by two companies of the Seventy-first Pennsylvania Volunteers during Pickett's Charge, but they had been driven back, leaving the Sixty-ninth's right flank unprotected. It was through this breach that Brigadier General Lewis Armistead led his Confederates. The fighting became hand to hand, many combatants using their muskets as clubs. Armistead was killed. O'Kane soon fell as well, shot through the abdomen. He would live only a few hours.

O'Kane had been involved in an ugly incident with his commanding officer, Colonel Joshua Owen, several months earlier. A drunken Owen had made a lewd remark to O'Kane's wife. When O'Kane pulled Owen from his horse, Owen's head struck solidly against the ground. Both men were court-martialed. O'Kane was acquitted, while Owen was convicted on two of three charges. He was sentenced to dismissal but reinstated by virtue of his distinguished military service.

Of its 258 men at Gettysburg, the regiment suffered a loss of 137. In addition to O'Kane, the dead included Lieutenant Colonel Martin Tschuby, who had been wounded the previous day but refused to leave the field. The regiment's major and adjutant were among the wounded. When Company F was overrun, every one of its members was either killed, wounded, or captured.

Part of the Philadelphia Brigade, the Sixty-ninth was the only regiment to carry the green regimental colors. Many of its members were Irish at a time when the Irish were looked down upon. When the men marched out of Philadelphia in 1861, many of the city's residents had pelted them with stones and bricks. Although none of the regiment lived to see it, the city made up for that treatment in 1999, when it presented the regiment with its highest honor, the Philadelphia Medal of Honor. The regiment was further recognized in March 2005 when the Pennsylvania State Senate passed a resolution honoring it for its "outstanding battlefield performance during the Civil War."

The monument, sculpted by Joseph E. Burk, was dedicated July 3, 1887. The small concrete posts on either side of the monument represent the relative positions of Companies G, K, B, E, C, H, D, F, A, and I, from left to right and in that order. The monument sits between the markers for Companies C and H.

K-12: Twenty-sixth North Carolina Infantry Monument
39° 48.814′ N, 77° 14.139′ W

The Twenty-sixth North Carolina, the largest regiment in the Army of Northern Virginia, suffered greatly on the first day of fighting around McPherson Ridge (see A-10) and earned a much-deserved day of rest on July 2. The next day, however, brought more fighting for the Tar Heels when they were pressed into action in Pickett's Charge.

In that assault, the Twenty-sixth was commanded by Captain H. C. Albright, who had taken command upon the death of Colonel Henry K. Burgwyn. The men advanced to within ten paces of the stone wall, where they were hit with canister fire. The regiment's color bearer and one sergeant actually made it to the stone wall, where Union troops showed their admiration for the two men's bravery by holding their fire and helping them to safe positions on the Union side of the wall.

This small monument marks the farthest point of the Twenty-sixth's advance. The price for the men's bravery was high. Only ninety troops made it back to the Confederate line on Seminary Ridge. The casualty rate of nearly 72 percent was the third-highest for any Confederate regiment in any battle, exceeded only by the First Texas at Antietam (82.3 percent) and the Twenty-first Georgia at Second Manassas (76 percent).

The monument is one of the newest on the field, having been dedicated in 1985. It includes the slogan, "The men of the Twenty-Sixth Regiment would dress on their colors in spite of the world."

K-13: First Company Massachusetts Sharpshooters Monument

39° 48.819' N, 77° 14.127' W

Affiliated with the Fifteenth Massachusetts Infantry, the First Company Massachusetts Sharpshooters were originally slated to serve with the famed Berdan Sharpshooters, headed by Colonel Hiram Berdan. When they learned they would have to forfeit their enlistment bounty if they joined Berdan, the Massachusetts men petitioned the governor of their state, John Andrew, to allow them to be a separate organization. Andrew granted that wish, and the men honored their governor by calling themselves the First Andrew's Sharpshooters, a name that followed them throughout the war.

Telescopic sights ran the length of the barrels of

sharpshooters' guns, affording a degree of magnification that enabled them to accurately place their shots even at long range. Civil War–era sharpshooters were the equivalent of modern-day snipers, as reflected in the figure of the sharpshooter on the monument.

The First Company Massachusetts Sharpshooters came from all walks of life. Their ages ranged from late teens to early fifties. They were engaged on July 2 against Brigadier General Ambrose R. Wright's Georgia brigade, but their real contribution came on July 3, when they poured deadly fire into the ranks of Lieutenant General A. P. Hill's corps during Pickett's Charge.

Captain William Plumer, an attorney and graduate of Harvard University, served as regimental commander. He had come to Gettysburg in an ambulance, due to wounds received a month earlier. Of the company's fifty men engaged in the battle, two were killed and six wounded.

The unit's slogan, "In God We Put Our Trust But Kept Our Powder Dry," appears on the front of the monument, which was sculpted by Fred M.

Torrey. It was erected in 1886 but not dedicated until 1913.

K-14: Thirty-ninth New York Infantry Monument
39° 48.849′ N, 77° 14.114′ W

The Thirty-ninth New York Infantry was raised by Colonel Frederick George D'Utassy in 1861. Also known as the Garibaldi Guards, after Italian general Giuseppe Garibaldi, the Thirty-ninth was truly a melting pot. Three of its companies were made up of

German immigrants, three others of Hungarians, one each of Italian, French, and Swiss immigrants, and another of a combination of Portuguese and Spanish immigrants. However, by the time the regiment reached Gettysburg, it had been reduced to only four companies because of disease and casualties.

The monument consists of a shaft of granite topped by the trefoil of the Second Corps. A plaque on the back describes the regiment's actions on the evening of July 2, when it mounted a charge with the 150th New York Infantry and recaptured the guns and equipment of Battery I of the Fifth United States Artillery from the Twenty-first Mississippi. A small marker notes the location where that action occurred (39° 48.171′ N, 77° 14.271′ W).

Commanded by Major Hugo Hillebrandt, the regiment suffered fifteen killed and eighty wounded at Gettysburg. Its monument was designed and built by Frederick and Field. Dedication took place July 1, 1888. The monument marks the position the regiment's four companies held on July 2 and 3.

A small secondary marker near the Trostle Farm (39° 48.171′ N, 77° 14.271′ W) indicates the actual location where the guns of Battery I of the Fifth United States Artillery were recaptured.

The Thirty-ninth had been the senior regiment at Harpers Ferry in the late summer of 1862 when Lee's Army of Northern Virginia captured the garrison. The 12,500 United States troops captured there (along with 73 pieces of artillery, 200 wagons, and 13,000 small arms) constituted the largest surrender of American troops until Bataan in World War II.

K-15: Second Pennsylvania Cavalry Monument

39° 48.861′ N, 77° 14.020′ W

The Second Pennsylvania Cavalry, also known as the Fifty-ninth Pennsylvania Volunteers, was attached to the provost guard. Its monument sits where it was positioned on July 3. During the battle, detachments from the Second also served on other parts of the field.

As provost guard, the Second was responsible for gathering stragglers and deserters and forcing them back into battle, as well as guarding and trans-

porting prisoners. At the end of the battle, it escorted three thousand prisoners to Westminster, Maryland. Once its prisoners were safely delivered, the Second returned to Gettysburg.

The commander of the Second was Colonel Richard B. Price. The regiment suffered no casualties in the battle among its 573 men engaged. The Second's enlistment ended six months after Gettysburg, at which time nearly every man reenlisted.

On June 17, 1865, the Second and Twentieth Pennsylvania cavalries consolidated to form the First Provisional Pennsylvania Cavalry.

Henry Jackson Ellicott sculpted the monument, which was dedicated September 11, 1889.

K-16: Oneida Cavalry Monument

39° 48.874′ N, 77° 13.939′ W

The forty-nine members of the Oneida Cavalry, commanded by Captain Daniel P. Mann, had the honor of serving as Major General George Meade's escort. Their primary function was to provide bodyguard protection to Meade throughout the war. They also served at the headquarters of every other Army of the Potomac commander over the course of the war, the only unit to do so. The men performed duties as headquarters orderlies as needed. The Oneida Cavalry was recognized by generals in the Union army as being dependable in delivering dispatches and for its prowess on raids, picket lines, and reconnaissance.

The regiment reported no casualties at Gettysburg.

In fact, the Oneida Cavalry suffered only two casualties in the entire war, when a pair of men were declared missing at Spotsylvania.

The monument, whose sculptor is unknown, was dedicated in 1904. It marks the location where the unit served as Meade's bodyguard at Gettysburg. This was the last New York monument erected on the battlefield.

K-17: Monument to Companies E and I, Sixth Pennsylvania Cavalry
39° 48.876′ N, 77° 13.927′ W

The Sixth Pennsylvania Cavalry was also known as the Seventieth Pennsylvania Volunteers, the Lanc-

ers, or Rush's Lancers. Companies E and I served as the headquarters escort for Major General George Meade during the battle. The main body of the Sixth stood on the left flank of the army along Emmitsburg Road. A large and detailed monument marks that location (39° 46.773′ N, 77° 15.643′ W). Meade specially detailed four companies of the Sixth for hazardous duty in the rear of Lee's army when the Confederates retreated after the battle.

The regiment received the "Lancers" nickname because it was the only cavalry unit in the Union army to carry lances. The men did not use the lances at Gettysburg, since they had proven impractical in wooded terrain in Virginia.

The regiment had 366 men engaged at Gettys-

burg, of whom three were killed, seven wounded, and two declared missing. Companies E and I had no casualties.

The monument was dedicated in 1891. The sculptor is unknown. The monument originally was placed in the front yard of the Leister House, about thirty yards from its present site. It was relocated in 1961.

K-18: Ninety-third New York Infantry Monument
39° 48.876′ N, 77° 13.921′ W

The Ninety-third New York Infantry was attached to army headquarters and served as provost guard for Major General George Meade, commander

of the Army of the Potomac, on July 2 and 3.

The regiment was split into detachments at Gettysburg and placed where needed in the rear areas, although some of the men did reach the field. One detachment went with General Meade on to the battlefield. Another performed the actual provost duty, picking up and escorting prisoners. A third served as guards for the medical purveyors, while a fourth remained at general headquarters. This monument marks the Ninety-third's position at the Leister Farm headquarters.

On July 3, the number of guards was reduced to the minimum, as all available men were ordered to the field to help in the battle. However, those members of the Ninety-third were all held in reserve, none seeing any action.

The regiment was also known as the Morgan Rifles, which often caused confusion with the Fifty-eighth New York Infantry, a unit that had the same nickname. Commanded at Gettysburg by Colonel John S. Crocker, the regiment suffered no casualties.

Fabricated by Frederick and Field, the monument was dedicated July 3, 1890.

K-19: 125th New York Infantry Monument
39° 48.883′ N, 77° 14.114′ W

The monument to the 125th New York, fabricated by Frederick and Field and dedicated October 3, 1888, marks the regiment's position on July 2 and 3. The bronze plaque on the front was added in 1902.

The regiment engaged in twenty-three battles throughout the war, which took a heavy toll. Regimental records showed a total of 547 men on the rolls at the beginning of the final campaign of 1865, but only 12 officers and 219 were actually present for duty.

The 125th was part of the Harpers Ferry garrison during the Antietam Campaign in 1862, when 12,500 men surrendered to Robert E. Lee's Army of Northern Virginia. That surrender was the largest of Federal troops during the Civil War. The regiment had been in service only eighteen days when it was taken captive. Those captured were referred to as the "Harpers Ferry Cowards" by others in the Union army. After spending the winter in a prison camp and being paroled and exchanged, the regiment was determined to erase its nickname at Gettysburg.

On July 2, the 125th and the rest of the brigade launched a counter assault on Brigadier General William Barksdale's Mississippi brigade. Many of the men shouted "Remember Harpers Ferry!" as the brigade turned back the Confederate assault, mortally wounding Barksdale in the fighting. In a touch of irony, the Mississippi troops had been among those who captured the brigade at Harpers Ferry.

After the assault against Barksdale's Brigade, the regiment returned to the stone wall, where it had been positioned prior to the charge. It participated in the repulse of Pickett's Charge the next day. The regiment lost 139 men at Gettysburg of the 500 who fought. Of those, 26 were killed, 104 wounded, and nine declared missing.

Lieutenant Colonel Levin Crandell, a bookkeeper in civilian life, commanded the regiment and Colonel George Lamb Willard the brigade. Willard was killed on July 2 as he led the brigade in the charge against Barksdale's Mississippians. The location where he fell is designated by a small marker (39° 48.381′ N, 77° 14.339′ W). Command fell to Colonel Eliakim Sherrill of the 126th New York (see K-22) until he was killed the next day during Pickett's Charge.

Corporal Harrison Clark of Company E was awarded the Medal of Honor for picking up the colors and advancing them after the color bearer was shot.

K-20: Twelfth New Jersey Infantry Monument
39° 48.908′ N, 77° 14.126′ W

The Twelfth New Jersey's participation at Gettysburg is noteworthy for its capture of the Bliss Farm

(see C-9) following two charges on July 2 and 3.

The monument was carved by M. Reilly and fabricated by Beattie and Brooks. It was formally dedicated May 26, 1886. The bronze relief plaque, depicting the regiment's fight at the Bliss Farm, was added six years later. The plaque was created by Beattie & Brooks and cast by Henry Bonnard Bronze Company. The monument sits at the approximate location of the regiment on July 3.

The top of the monument contains a musket ball sitting on three buckshot, a combination known as "buck and ball." The "buck and ball" issued to the regiment was the standard load for smoothbore mus-

kets. Knowing their weapons would not be accurate at any great distance, the men awaited Pickett's Charge by removing the large ball from their charges, leaving only the three buckshot. They then combined several of those charges to produce one with as many as twenty buckshot, making their weapons into large and deadly shotguns.

The regiment had two officers and twenty men killed, four officers and eighty men wounded, and nine men declared missing at Gettysburg.

K-21: 108th New York Infantry Monument
39° 48.974′ N, 77° 14.076′ W

The 108th New York occupied this position on July 2 and 3 in support of Battery I of the First United States Artillery during the artillery duel that launched Pickett's Charge. It came under heavy fire

vering during the assault, their officers drew their swords and threatened to use them on any man who dared leave the ranks. None did.

During the fighting, Corporal William Raymond of Company A volunteered to deliver ammunition to the men of Companies A and C on the skirmish line while under heavy fire. When no others volunteered to help, he went alone. His clothing was pierced several times by bullets, but he was unharmed, although he was wounded later at Gettysburg. Raymond would be wounded two more times during the war and captured once, escaping in May 1864. He was awarded the Medal of Honor in 1896 for his actions at Gettysburg.

The monument was sculpted by R. D. Barr, fabricated by Smith Granite Company, and dedicated September 4, 1888. It represents the position the regiment held on July 2 and 3 in support of Lieutenant George Woodruff's battery.

K-22: 126th New York Infantry Monument
39° 48.999′ N, 77° 14.066′ W

In September 1862, the 126th New York Infantry had been in service only two weeks when it was captured with the rest of the 12,500-man garrison at Harpers Ferry, leading to the unfair nickname "Harpers Ferry Cowards." But at Gettysburg on July 2, 1863, the regiment acquitted itself well in an assault along Plum Run, successfully pushing the Confederates back. The next day, it occupied this position and as-

and was unable to return fire against the Confederates. During the charge, the Confederate line came within fifty yards of the 108th before breaking.

One of two New York units known as the Rochester Regiment (the other being the Eighth New York Cavalry), the 108th was commanded at Gettysburg by Colonel Francis E. Pierce, who established the Rochester Military Academy. The regiment had sixteen killed and eighty-six wounded in the battle, most of those casualties coming during the pre-charge artillery barrage.

When some of the troops showed signs of wa-

Overall, the regiment had five officers and 35 men killed, nine officers and 172 men wounded, and 10 men missing out of a force of 455.

The 126th had the honor of seeing three of its members receive the Medal of Honor for their actions at Gettysburg. Captain Morris Brown Jr. of Company A received his for capturing a flag on July 3; his award came posthumously in 1869. Sergeant George H. Dore of Company D was awarded the Medal of Honor for rushing into a crossfire to rescue the colors, which had been struck down by a shell during Pickett's Charge. The third Medal of Honor was awarded to Private Jerry Wall of Company B, also for capturing a flag.

Caspar Buberl sculpted the 126th's monument, which was dedicated October 3, 1888.

K-23: Ninetieth Pennsylvania Volunteers Monument
39° 49.015′ N, 77° 14.061′ W

This monument marks the position of the Ninetieth Pennsylvania Volunteers on the afternoon of July 3. A carved granite drum is topped by a bronze eagle, its wings outstretched. A plaque on the side shows a canteen surrounded by oak leaves. The regiment's motto, *"Non sibi sed patriae,"* or "Not for self, but for country," appears on the front of the monument.

J. M. Cessler carved the monument, which was dedicated September 3, 1888. Astute observers may notice that the monument indicates the regiment was part of both the First and Fifth corps. At first glance,

sisted in repulsing Pickett's Charge. Regimental records noted the capture of five stands of colors and a large number of prisoners.

The brigade commander, Colonel Eliakim Sherill, whose likeness is on the monument, was mortally wounded in this part of the battle. Sherill, a farmer who had served as a United States congressman from 1847 to 1849, had taken command when Colonel George Willard was killed (see K-19). Sherill was still recovering from a wound received the previous September at South Mountain in Maryland when he was wounded again on July 3. He died the following day. The regiment's monument sits where Sherrill suffered his mortal wound.

this seems confusing, but the explanation is simple. In 1864, the First Corps was joined with the Fifth Corps, at which time the Ninetieth became part of the First Brigade, Second Division, Fifth Corps, along with the Thirteenth and Thirty-ninth Massachusetts, the Sixteenth Maine, and the 104th New York. The Ninetieth chose to use the double corps designation on its monument.

The regimental commander, Major Alfred Sellers, received the Medal of Honor in 1894 for his actions on the first day at Gettysburg, when he voluntarily led the regiment to a position where it was able to repel the enemy, all this while under heavy fire. Sellers had replaced Lieutenant Colonel William A. Leech, who was absent due to illness.

The Ninetieth entered the battle with 208 men, of whom 11 were killed, 44 wounded, and 39 declared captured or missing. The regimental chaplain, Horatio S. Howell, was one of those killed (see C-12).

The regiment joined in the pursuit of the Rebel army on July 4.

Two additional monuments to the Ninetieth are on the battlefield. The famous Granite Tree Monument sits on Oak Hill (39° 42.778' N, 77° 14.518' W), while a natural boulder monument on Hancock Avenue (39° 48.372' N, 77° 14.095' W) marks the regiment's position on the evening of July 2, when the men were deployed as skirmishers.

Appendix A

Union Medal of Honor Recipients at Gettysburg

The United States Army Medal of Honor was created in July 1862. To earn the medal during the Civil War, a soldier had only to show "gallantry in action" or other "soldierly qualities." These criteria obviously left room for interpretation. Over the years, they have been made much more specific.

Sixty-three Medals of Honor were awarded for the Battle of Gettysburg, most of them many years afterward. Only nineteen were awarded during the war, and three more in the decade following the battle. By 1880, however, the men who had fought at Gettysburg realized the medal was being awarded and began to overwhelm the War Department with applications. Despite the difficulty in fairly judging the applications, forty-one more medals were awarded between 1880 and 1907. Many of those recipients probably were not deserving, while countless others were denied whose claims had merit.

The most common reason for receiving the medal was the capture of an enemy flag. Such an act was the Holy Grail for all soldiers. Anyone who did it received the utmost admiration of his comrades. The list below shows just how much the act was respected.

One of the medals was specially awarded through an official act of Congress. Corporal J. Monroe Reisinger of the 150th Pennsylvania Infantry received the Medal of Honor in 1907 after Congress reviewed his actions at Gettysburg. There, Reisinger had held on to the colors and rallied his regiment despite suffering wounds to his foot, knee, and side.

Today, Congress is close to awarding the sixty-fourth Medal of Honor for bravery at Gettysburg. Lieutenant Alonzo H. Cushing, commanding Battery A of the Fourth United States Artillery near the Angle, lost his life as he directed fire despite having already suffered severe wounds. With only a skeleton crew left to man the guns, Cushing dragged his wounded body to a gun and fired it. As he prepared to fire again, he was shot through the mouth and died instantly. Now, 150 years later, Congress is reviewing his actions with the idea of awarding the Medal of Honor to the young lieutenant.

Below are the citations for the Medals of Honor awarded for Gettysburg, by regiment.

First Delaware Infantry

Private John B. Mayberry, Company F—"Capture of flag."

Private Bernard McCarren, Company C—"Capture of flag."

Captain James Parke Postles, Company A—"Voluntarily delivered an order in the face of heavy fire of the enemy. (A 600 yard ride carrying orders under intense fire.)"

First Massachusetts Infantry

Corporal Nathaniel M. Allen, Company B—"When his regiment was falling back, this soldier, bearing the national color, returned in the face of the enemy's fire, pulled the regimental flag from under the body of its bearer, who had fallen, saved the flag from capture, and brought both colors off the field."

First Minnesota Infantry

Corporal Henry D. O'Brien, Company E—"Taking up the colors where they had fallen, he rushed ahead of his regiment, close to the muzzles of the enemy's guns, and engaged in the desperate struggle in which the enemy was defeated, and though severely wounded, he held the colors until wounded a second time."

Private Marshall Sherman, Company C—"Capture of flag of 28th Virginia Infantry (C.S.A.)."

First Pennsylvania Rifles

Sergeant James B. Thompson, Company G—"Capture of flag of 15th Georgia Infantry (C.S.A.)."

First Vermont Cavalry

Major William Wells—"Led the second battalion of his regiment in a daring charge."

Third Pennsylvania Cavalry

Captain William E. Miller, Company H—"Without orders, led a charge of his squadron upon the flank of the enemy, checked his attack, and cut off and dispersed the rear of his column."

Fourth United States Artillery

First Lieutenant Alonzo H. Cushing, Battery A—"Despite serious wounds and the loss of most of his guns and men, moved cannon forward to aid in repulsing enemy during Pickett's Charge, losing his life in the process." [Award pending as of this writing. Exact wording of citation to be determined.]

Sergeant Frederick Fuger, Battery A—"All the officers of his battery having been killed or wounded and five of its guns disabled in Pickett's assault, he succeeded to the command and fought the remaining gun with most distinguished gallantry until the battery was ordered withdrawn."

Sixth Pennsylvania Reserves

Corporal Chester S. Furman, Company A—"Was 1 of 6 volunteers who charged upon a log house near Devil's Den, where a squad of the enemy's sharpshooters were sheltered, and compelled their surrender."

Sergeant John W. Hart, Company D—"Was one of six volunteers who charged upon a log house near the Devil's Den, where a squad of the enemy's sharpshooters were sheltered, and compelled their surrender."

Sergeant Wallace W. Johnson, Company G—"With five other volunteers he gallantly charged on a number of the enemy's sharpshooters concealed in a log house, captured them, and brought them into the Union lines."

Sergeant George W. Mears, Company A—"With five volunteers he gallantly charged on a number of the enemy's sharpshooters concealed in a log house, captured them, and brought them into the Union lines."

Corporal J. Levi Roush, Company D—"Was 1 of 6 volunteers who charged upon a log house near the Devil's Den, where a squad of the enemy's sharpshooters were sheltered, and compelled their surrender."

Corporal Thaddeus S. Smith, Company E—"Was 1 of 6 volunteers who charged upon a log house near the Devil's Den, where a squad of the enemy's sharpshooters were sheltered, and compelled their surrender."

Sixth United States Cavalry

Private George C. Platt, Company H—"Seized the regimental flag upon the death of the standard bearer in a hand-to-hand fight and prevented it from falling into the hands of the enemy."

Private Martin Schwenk, Company B—"For bravery displayed on the field of battle in an attempt to carry a communication through the enemy's lines, and for the rescue of a wounded officer of the 6th United States Cavalry from the hands of the enemy."

Sixth Wisconsin Infantry

Corporal Francis A. Waller, Company I—"Capture of flag of 2nd Mississippi Infantry (C.S.A.)."

Seventh Wisconsin Infantry

Sergeant Jefferson Coates, Company H—"For unsurpassed courage in battle, where he had both eyes shot out."

Eighth Ohio Infantry

Sergeant John Miller, Company G—"Capture of two flags (34th North Carolina and 38th Virginia)."

Private James Richmond, Company F—"Capture of flag."

Ninth Independent Battery, Massachusetts Light Artillery

Bugler Charles W. Reed—"Rescued his wounded captain from between the lines."

Twelfth Vermont Infantry

Second Lieutenant George G. Benedict, Company C—"Passed through a murderous fire of grape and canister in delivering orders and re-formed the crowded lines. Benedict was detached from his regiment, which was not on the battlefield, as Aide de Camp to General [George J.] Stannard."

Thirteenth Vermont Infantry

Captain John Lonergan, Company A—"Gallantry in the recapture of 4 guns and the capture of 2 additional guns from the enemy; also the capture of a number of prisoners."

Fourteenth Connecticut Infantry

Private Elijah W. Bacon, Company F—"Capture of flag of 16th North Carolina regiment (C.S.A.)."

Corporal Christopher Flynn, Company K—"Capture of flag of 52nd North Carolina regiment (C.S.A.)."

Sergeant Major William B. Hinks—"During the high water mark of Pickett's Charge on July 3rd the colors of the 14th Tennessee Infantry C.S.A. were planted 50 yards in front of the center of Sgt. Maj. Hincks' regiment. There were no Confederates standing near it but several were lying down around it. Upon a call for volunteers by Major [Theodore G.] Ellis to capture this flag, this soldier and two others leaped the wall. One companion was instantly shot. Sgt. Maj. Hincks outran his remaining companion[,] running straight and swift for the colors amid a storm of shot. Swinging his saber over the prostrate Confederates and uttering a terrific yell, he seized the flag and hastily returned to his lines. The 14th Tennessee carried twelve battle honors on its flag. The devotion to duty shown by Sgt. Maj. Hincks gave encouragement to many of his comrades at a crucial moment of the battle."

Fifteenth New York Battery

Second Lieutenant Edward M. Knox—"Held his ground with the battery after the other batteries had fallen back until compelled to draw his piece off by hand; he was severely wounded."

Sixteenth Vermont Infantry

Colonel Wheelock G. Veazey—"Held his ground with the battery after the other batteries had fallen back until compelled to draw his piece off by hand; he was severely wounded."

Nineteenth Massachusetts Infantry

Corporal Joseph H. DeCastro, Company I—"Capture of flag of 19th Virginia regiment (C.S.A.)."

Sergeant Benjamin F. Falls, Company A—"Capture of flag."

Sergeant Benjamin H. Jellison, Company C—"Capture of flag of 57th Virginia Infantry (C.S.A.). He also assisted in taking prisoners."

Major Edmund Rice—"Conspicuous bravery on the third day of the battle on the countercharge against Pickett's division[,] where he fell severely wounded within the enemy's lines."

Private John Robinson, Company I—"Capture of flag of 57th Virginia Infantry (C.S.A.)."

Twentieth Indiana Infantry

Private Oliver P. Rood, Company B—"Capture of flag of 21st North Carolina Infantry (C.S.A.)."

Twentieth Maine Infantry

Colonel Joshua L. Chamberlain—"Daring heroism and great tenacity in holding his position on the Little Round

Top against repeated assaults, and carrying the advance position on the Great Round Top."

Sergeant Andrew J. Tozier, Company I—"At the crisis of the engagement this soldier, a color bearer, stood alone in an advanced position, the regiment having been borne back, and defended his colors with musket and ammunition picked up at his feet."

Twenty-third Pennsylvania Infantry

Captain John B. Fassett, Company F—"While acting as an aide, voluntarily led a regiment to the relief of a battery and recaptured its guns from the enemy."

Twenty-sixth Pennsylvania Infantry

First Sergeant George W. Roosevelt, Company K—"At Bull Run, Va., recaptured the colors, which had been seized by the enemy. At Gettysburg, he captured a Confederate color bearer and colors, in which effort he was severely wounded."

Forty-fifth New York Infantry

Captain Francis Irsch, Company D—"Gallantry in flanking the enemy and capturing a number of prisoners and in holding a part of the town against heavy odds while the army was rallying on Cemetery Hill."

Fifty-fifth Ohio Infantry

Private Charles Stacey, Company D—"Voluntarily took an advanced position on the skirmish line for the purpose of ascertaining the location of Confederate sharpshooters, and under heavy fire held the position thus taken until the company of which he was a member went back to the main line."

Fifty-ninth New York Infantry

Sergeant James Wiley, Company G—"Capture of flag of a Georgia regiment."

Seventy-first Pennsylvania Infantry

Private John E. Clopp, Company F—"Capture of flag of 9th Virginia Infantry (C.S.A.), wresting it from the color bearer."

Seventy-second New York Infantry

Sergeant Thomas Horan, Company E—"In a charge of his regiment this soldier captured the regimental flag of the 8th Florida Infantry (C.S.A.)."

Seventy-third Ohio Infantry

Musician Richard Enderlin, Company B—"Voluntarily took a rifle and served as a soldier in the ranks during the first and second days of the battle. Voluntarily and at his own imminent peril went into the enemy's lines at night and, under a sharp fire, rescued a wounded comrade."

Eighty-second New York Infantry

Sergeant Hugh Carey, Company E—"Captured the flag of the 7th Virginia Infantry (C.S.A.), being twice wounded in the effort."

Eighty-eighth Pennsylvania Infantry

Sergeant Edward L. Gilligan, Company E—"Assisted in the capture of a Confederate flag by knocking down the color sergeant."

Ninetieth Pennsylvania Infantry

Major Alfred J. Sellers—"Voluntarily led the regiment under a withering fire to a position from which the enemy was repulsed."

Ninety-ninth Pennsylvania Infantry

Sergeant Harvey M. Munsell, Company A—"Gallant and courageous conduct as color bearer. (This noncommissioned officer carried the colors of his regiment through 13 engagements.)"

108th New York Infantry

Corporal William H. Raymond, Company A—"Voluntarily and under a severe fire brought a box of ammunition to his comrades on the skirmish line."

125th New York Infantry

Corporal Harrison Clark, Company E—"Seized the colors and advanced with them after the color bearer had been shot."

126th New York Infantry

Captain Morris Brown Jr., Company A—"Capture of flag."

Sergeant George H. Dore, Company D—"The colors being struck down by a shell as the enemy were charging, this soldier rushed out and seized the flag, exposing himself to the fire of both sides."

Private Jerry Wall, Company B—"Capture of flag."

140th Pennsylvania Infantry

Captain James Pipes, Company A—"While a sergeant and retiring with his company before the rapid advance of the enemy at Gettysburg, he and a companion stopped and carried to a place of safety a wounded and helpless comrade; in this act both he and his companion were severely wounded. A year later, at Reams Station, Va., while commanding a skirmish line, voluntarily assisted in checking a flank movement of the enemy, and while so doing was severely wounded, suffering the loss of an arm."

Lieutenant James J. Purman, Company A—"Voluntarily assisted a wounded comrade to a place of apparent safety while the enemy was in close proximity; he received the fire of the enemy and a wound which resulted in the amputation of his left leg."

143rd Pennsylvania Infantry

Sergeant James M. Rutter, Company C—"At great risk of his life went to the assistance of a wounded comrade, and while under fire removed him to a place of safety."

150th Pennsylvania Infantry

Lieutenant Colonel Henry S. Huidekoper—"At great risk of his life went to the assistance of a wounded comrade, and while under fire removed him to a place of safety."

Corporal J. Monroe Reisinger, Company H—"Specially brave and meritorious conduct in the face of the enemy." [Awarded by act of Congress.]

Independent Pennsylvania Light Artillery

Private Casper R. Carlisle, Company F—"Specially brave and meritorious conduct in the face of the enemy."

United States Volunteers

Major General Daniel E. Sickles—"Displayed most conspicuous gallantry on the field[,] vigorously contesting the advance of the enemy and continuing to encourage his troops after being himself severely wounded."

Brigadier General Alexander S. Webb—"Displayed most conspicuous gallantry on the field[,] vigorously contesting the advance of the enemy and continuing to encourage his troops after being himself severely wounded."

Sources: *Official Records of the War of the Rebellion*, series 1, vol. 27/2 (S#44).
Congressional Medal of Honor Society records
United States Army Heritage and Education Center
United States Army Center of Military History

Appendix B

Confederate Medal of Honor Recipients at Gettysburg

The Confederate government wished to recognize soldiers who fought valiantly. In 1862, it authorized plans to establish a medal for commissioned officers and badges of distinction for noncommissioned officers and enlisted men who showed unusual courage in battle. One recipient from each regiment was to be selected by a vote of the men.

Since the war was in progress, however, metal was needed for weaponry and ammunition, making the production of medals and badges impractical. A Roll of Honor was established instead, with the intent of producing actual medals at some future date. The roll served to publicly recognize soldiers who had distinguished themselves. Initially, only a handful of Confederate units participated, and the rolls listed only name, rank, and unit, offering no description of the men's actions. As only one man from each regiment was selected, many deserving soldiers were overlooked.

For several years, the postwar recovery effort throughout the South pushed the production of medals into the background. That, coupled with differences of opinion over how the honors were to be awarded, further delayed the medals. In 1896, former Confederate lieutenant general Stephen Dill Lee addressed the convention of the United Confederate Veterans. His message was that the history of the South had to be preserved, and that it would fall on groups such as the one assembled to do it. The result was the formation of the Sons of Confederate Veterans.

Gradually, interest in recognizing individual soldiers grew. The United Daughters of the Confederacy established the Southern Cross of Honor to recognize those who had displayed honorable service to the Confederacy. The first medal was issued in 1900. It temporarily satisfied the desire to honor those who had fought. The Southern Cross of Honor, however, didn't actually elevate any particular soldier for his gallantry. Eventually, the need for an official Confederate Medal of Honor was recognized.

The first Confederate Medal of Honor was awarded in 1977. Five have been issued for actions at Gettysburg. They are listed below.

First Texas Infantry

Private Wilson Barbee

Twenty-sixth North Carolina Infantry

Colonel Henry King Burgwyn Jr.

Garden's Battery, Palmetto Light Artillery

First Lieutenant William Alexander McQueen

Garnett's Brigade

Brigadier General Richard Brooke Garnett

Hampton's Brigade

Brigadier General Wade Hampton

Sources: *Official Records of the War of the Rebellion*, series 1, vol. 27/2 (S#44)
Museum and White House of the Confederacy
Clemmer, Gregg S. *Valor in Gray: The Recipients of the Confederate Medal of Honor*. Staunton, Va.: Hearthside Printing Co.

Appendix C

Sullivan Ballou Letter

Sullivan Ballou was born March 28, 1829, and enlisted in the Second Rhode Island Infantry when the war began. Early in the war, he penned this now-famous letter to his wife, the former Sarah Hart Shumway. Many consider it one of the most beautiful love letters ever written.

July 14, 1861
Camp Clark, Washington

My very dear Sarah:

The indications are very strong that we shall move in a few days—perhaps tomorrow. Lest I should not be able to write again, I feel impelled to write a few lines that may fall under your eye when I shall be no more. . . .

I have no misgivings about, or lack of confidence in[,] the cause in which I am engaged, and my courage does not halt or falter. I know how strongly American Civilization now leans on the triumph of the Government and how great a debt we owe to those who went before us through the blood and sufferings of the Revolution. And I am willing—perfectly willing—to lay down all my joys in this life, to help maintain this Government, and to pay that debt. . . .

Sarah[,] my love for you is deathless, it seems to bind me with mighty cables that nothing but Omnipotence could break; and yet my love of Country comes over me like a strong wind and bears me unresistibly on with all these chains to the battle field.

The memories of the blissful moments I have spent with you come creeping over me, and I feel most gratified to God and to you that I have enjoyed them for so long. And hard it is for me to give them up and burn to ashes the hopes of future years, when, God willing, we might still have lived and loved together, and seen our sons grown up to honorable manhood, around us. I have, I know, but few and small claims upon Divine Providence, but something whispers to me—perhaps it is the wafted prayer of my little

Edgar, that I shall return to my loved ones unharmed. If I do not[,] my dear Sarah, never forget how much I love you, and when my last breath escapes me on the battle field, it will whisper your name. Forgive my many faults and the many pains I have caused you. How thoughtless and foolish I have often times been! How gladly would I wash out with my tears every little spot upon your happiness. . . .

But, O Sarah! If the dead can come back to this earth and flit unseen around those they loved, I shall always be near you; in the gladdest days and in the darkest nights . . . always, always, and if there be a soft breeze upon your cheek, it shall be my breath, as the cool air fans your throbbing temple, it shall be my spirit passing by. Sarah[,] do not mourn me dead; think I am gone and wait for thee, for we shall meet again. . . .

Sullivan Ballou was killed a week after writing this, at First Manassas. He was thirty-two years old and left Sarah and two sons, Edgar and William. His wife was twenty-four. She later moved to New Jersey and never remarried. She died in 1917 at age eighty and was buried next to her husband in Swan Point Cemetery in Providence, Rhode Island. They have no known living descendants.

In a cruel twist of fate, Sullivan Ballou never got to mail this letter. It was found among his effects when Governor William Sprague of Rhode Island traveled to Virginia to retrieve the remains of Rhode Island's dead. Although Ballou did not live to fight at Gettysburg, his regiment did, as its monument testifies (see J-3).

Suggested Reading

Bachelder, John. *History of the Battle of Gettysburg.* Edited by David Ladd. Dayton, Ohio: Morningside House, 1997.

Boritt, Gabor S. *The Gettysburg Nobody Knows.* New York: Oxford University Press, 1997.

Busey, John W. *The Last Full Measure.* Hightstown, N.J.: Longstreet House, 1988.

Catton, Bruce. *The Battle of Gettysburg.* New York: American Heritage Publishing Co., 1963.

Coco, Gregory A. *A Strange and Blighted Land: The Aftermath of Battle.* Gettysburg, Pa.: Thomas Publications, 1995.

———. *A Vast Sea of Misery: A History and Guide to the Union and Confederate Field Hospitals at Gettysburg.* Gettysburg, Pa.: Thomas Publications, 1996.

Coddington, Edwin B. *The Gettysburg Campaign: A Study in Command.* New York: Touchstone, 1997.

Frassanito, William. *Early Photography at Gettysburg.* Gettysburg, Pa.: Thomas Publications, 1995.

———. *Gettysburg: A Journey in Time.* Gettysburg, Pa.: Thomas Publications, 1996.

———. *Gettysburg, Then and Now: Touring the Battlefield with Old Photos.* Gettysburg, Pa.: Thomas Publications, 1996.

Gindlesperger, James and Suzanne. *So You Think You Know Gettysburg?* Vol. 1. Winston-Salem, N.C.: John F. Blair, Publisher, 2010.

Petruzzi, J. D., and Stephen Stanley. *The Complete Gettysburg Guide.* El Dorado Hills, Calif.: Savas Beatie, 2009.

Pfanz, Harry W. *Gettysburg: Culp's Hill and Cemetery Hill.* Chapel Hill: University of North Carolina Press, 2000.

———. *Gettysburg: The First Day.* Chapel Hill: University of North Carolina Press, 2010.

———. *Gettysburg: The Second Day.* Chapel Hill: University of North Carolina Press, 1998.

Pierce, Tillie A. *At Gettysburg, or What a Girl Saw and Heard of the Battle.* New York: W. L. Borland, 1889.

Reardon, Carol. *Pickett's Charge in History and Memory.* Chapel Hill: University of North Carolina Press, 2009.

Sears, Stephen W. *Gettysburg.* New York: Houghton Mifflin, 2003.

Trudeau, Noah Andre. *Gettysburg: A Testing of Courage.* New York: HarperCollins, 2002.

Wills, Gary. *Lincoln at Gettysburg: The Words That Remade America.* New York: Simon & Schuster, 1992.

In addition, we recommend several excellent Internet sources:

The American Civil War: The Battle of Gettysburg. 2012. http://www.brotherswar.com/Gettysburg-2s.htm.

Battle of Gettysburg Buff. 2012. http://battleofgettysburgbuff.com.

Draw the Sword: The Gettysburg Monument Project. 2012. http://www.drawthesword.goellnitz.org/blog/.

National Park Service: Gettysburg National Military Park. 2013. http://www.nps.gov/gett/index.htm.

Stone Sentinels: The Battle of Gettysburg. 2013. http://www.gettysburg.stonesentinels.com/index.php.

To the Sound of the Guns: Civil War Artillery, Battlefields and Historical Markers. 2013. http://markerhunter.wordpress.com/battlefields-by-markers/gettysburg/gettysburg-markers-by-location/.

Index

Abbott, Col. Ira C., 147–48
Acheson, Capt. David, 150
Adams County Cavalry Company, 59
Adams County Historical Society, 60
Alabama regiments: Alabama Brigade, 73, 107, 111, 112; Fourth Infantry, 188; Fifth Infantry, 36; Fifteenth Infantry, 181, 188, 190, 195–97; Forty-seventh Infantry, 181; Forty-eighth Infantry, 181
Albert Russell and Sons, 62
Albright, Capt. H. C., 14, 240
Aldie, Va., 213
Alexandria, Va., 148
Allen, Cpl. Nathaniel M., 108–9, 252
Alms House Cemetery, 29, 53
Alsop's Farm, 23
Althoff, Francis, 156
American Bible Society, 95
American Bronze Company, 178
Ames, Capt. Nelson, 123
Anderson, Brig. Gen. George T., 133
Anderson, Daisy, 74
Anderson, Maj. Robert, 154
Anderson's Brigade, 133, 172
Andrew, Gov. John A., 241
Angle, the, 162, 227, 228, 231
Antietam: First Texas casualties at, 119, 230, 241; Second Delaware at, 166; Twentieth Massachusetts at, 234; 125th New York at Harpers Ferry during, 246; 125th Pennsylvania Infantry Monument at, 24; Battlefield Board, 82; Col. Adoniram J. Warner wounded at, 193; Col. Charles Taylor at, 139; Col. Eugene Powell wounded at, 102
Appomattox, 120, 140, 198, 210, 218
Archer, Brig. Gen. James J., 3, 60
Archibald, W. B., 167
Arkansas regiment. See Third Arkansas Infantry
Arlington National Cemetery, 74
Armistead, Brig. Gen. Lewis, 227, 228, 239
Army of Northern Virginia: capture of Harpers Ferry, 242, 246; engages Ricketts's Battery, 71; Ewell's Corps of, 87; field hospital at Culp Farm, 52; Heth's Division of, 3, itinerary tablets, 61–62, 69, largest regiment in, 240
Army of the Cumberland, 49
Army of the Potomac, 3, 16, 62, 139, 140, 243
Army of the Potomac itinerary tablets, 69–70
Avery, Col. Isaac, 47, 50, 52, 65

Bacon, Priv. Elijah, 54, 254
Bailey, Col. Edward L., 121, 122
Baily, Col. William P., 167
Baker, Senator Edward, 238
Baldwin, Capt. Ambrose, 229
Baldwin, George W., 60
Baldwin, Joseph H., 60–61
Baldwin, Lt. Col. Clark B., 109
Ballou, Edgar, 261
Ballou, Maj. Sullivan, 210, 261–62
Ballou, Sarah Hart Shumway, 210, 261
Ballou, William, 261
Ball's Bluff, 233, 235, 238
Baltimore, 49, 136–37, 156
Baltimore cross, 87
Banelt, Maj. J. P., 184
Banks, Gen. Nathaniel, 138
Barbee, Priv. Wilson, 259

Barksdale, Brig. Gen. William: attack of, 111, 115, 117, 128, 220; counterattack against, 111, 114, 117, 128, 246; mortally wounded, 107, 117, 220
Barlow, Brig. Gen. Francis Channing, 29
Barlow Knoll, 28 (map), 29, 47, 51
Barnes, Capt. Almont, 211
Barr, R. D., 17, 126, 160, 248
Bataan, 242
Batchelder, Lt. Col. Nathaniel W., 23
Bates, Mable, 183
Beam, Capt. John E., 126
Beam's Battery, 126
Beattie and Brooks, 55, 246
Beaver, Col. James, 140
Beecher, Rev. Thomas K., 94–95
Benedict, Second Lt. George G., 254
Benning, Brig. Gen. Henry L., 161
Benning's Brigade, 160
Berdan, Col. Hiram: commander of sharpshooter regiments, 112, 198, 217, 241; court-martialed, 217; promoted to brigade commander, 112; qualifications for becoming sharpshooter, 217
Berdan Sharpshooters, 111, 112, 120, 198
Beveridge, Maj. John L., 9
Biddle, Lt. Col. Alexander, 5
Big Round Top: 180 (map); Fifth Pennsylvania Reserves at, 192; Ninth Massachusetts Infantry at, 194; Tenth Pennsylvania Reserves at, 19, 193–94; Twelfth Pennsylvania Reserves at, 191–92; Twentieth Maine Infantry Monument at, 190–91; Twenty-second Massachusetts Infantry at, 145; 118th Pennsylvania Infantry at, 149, 188; 119th Pennsylvania Infantry at, 189; 139th Pennsylvania Infantry at, 152; Federal troops on, 184, 188–94; War Department trail to, 189
Bigelow, Capt. John, 129
Bignall, Cpl. Thomas, 122
Billings, Capt. Charles W., 191
Billings, Priv. Otis, 237
Bing and Cunningham, 93–94
Bingham, Col. Daniel G., 168
Birney, Maj. Gen. David, 92, 109
Bissell, George Edwin, 99
Bliss, Adelina, 55
Bliss Cavalry, 186–87
Bliss Farm: First Delaware skirmishers sent to, 56; Twelfth New Jersey at, 54, 55–56, 246–47; 126th New York captures barn, 55; assault on, 54, 55–56, 238, 246–47; burning of, 54, 56; Confederate sharpshooters in barn, 54, 55, 56; site of house, 55–56
Bliss, William, 55
Boebel, Lt. Col. Hans, 40
Boonesboro, Md., 20
Boston Marble and Granite Company, 213, 235
Bouvier, Lt. John Vernou, 7
Bowdoin College, 190
Bowen, Capt. Edward R., 115
Bradley, Maj. Leman W., 168
Brady, T. M., 147
Brehm, Color Sgt. Henry, 10
Brickyard, Battle of the, 47, 49
Briggs, Adj. Walter S., 67
Brinkerhoff Ridge, 215
Brinton, Lt. Col. William Penn, 185
Broady, Lt. Col. Knut Oscar, 141
Brooke Avenue, 143, 158 (map), 159–78
Brooke, Col. John R., 133–34, 168–69
Brown, Capt. Morris, Jr., 249, 257
Brown, Capt. T. Fred, 235
Brown, Col. Henry W., 215
Brown, Col. Hiram, 170–71

Unknown remains, 73–74
Upton, Col. Emory, 204

Valley of Death, 134, 139, 198, 204
Van Armitage Granite Company, 76
Van Armitage, William, 78
Van Buskirk, Lt. David, 84
Van Gunden, Young, and Drumm, 116
Van Rensselaer, Maj. Walter, 229
Van Slyke, Capt. Charles H., 37
Van Wyck and Collins, 99
Vaughan, Sgt. Henry, 220
Veazey, Col. Wheelock Graves, 221–22, 254–55
Vermont regiments: First Brigade, 222; Second Brigade, 222; First Cavalry, 182, 185, 187–88, 222, 252; Twelfth Infantry, 254; Thirteenth Infantry, 207, 219, 223–24, 254; Fourteenth Infantry, 117, 219–20; Sixteenth Infantry, 207, 219, 220–22, 254–55; Sharpshooters, 222
Vermont State Memorial, 222, 223
Vicksburg, Miss., xvii
Vincent, Col. Strong, 181, 182, 197
Virginia regiments: Fourteenth Cavalry, 21; Seventeenth Cavalry, 59; First Infantry, 230; Seventh Infantry, 230, 256; Ninth Infantry, 256; Eleventh Infantry, 207; Nineteenth Infantry, 255; Twenty-fourth Infantry, 207; Twenty-seventh Infantry, 146; Twenty-eighth Infantry, 231, 252; Thirty-eighth Infantry, 53, 253; Forty-ninth Infantry, 84; Fifty-second Infantry, 84; Fifty-seventh Infantry, 255
Virginia State Memorial, 108
Von Amsberg, Col. George, 30
Von Hartung, Col. Adolph, 31
Von Mitzel, Lt. Col. Theobald, 31–32
Vosberg, J. H., 174

W. E. Spragg Granite and Marble Works, 71
Wade, Jennie, 48, 65–66
Wadsworth, Brig. Gen. James, 17–18
Wagner, A., 169
Walcott, Lt. Aaron Francis, 152
Walker, Brig. Gen. James, 84
Walker, Col. Elijah, 162
Walker, Lt. Col. Thomas M., 89
Wall, Pvt. Jerry, 249, 257
Wallace, Col. James, 100
Waller, Cpl. Francis A., 253
Walz, John, 239
War Department, 69, 82, 138, 156, 189, 196, 201, 223
Ward, Col. George H., 234–35
Ward, Emily, 235
Ward, Lt. Henry C., 234
Warner, Col. Adoniram J., 192
Warner, Maj. L. D., 50
Warren, Brig. Gen. Gouverneur, 181, 182
Warrenton, Va., 209
Washington Artillery, 107–8
Washington, Pa., 150
Webb, Brig. Gen. Alexander, 228, 258
Weed, Brig. Gen. Stephen, 181, 182, 199, 200
Weikert, George, 208, 215
Weikert, John T., 150, 156, 212
Weikert, Sarah, 156
Welch, Lt. Col. Norval, 197
Wells, Lamson and Company, 188
Wells, Maj. William, 182, 187, 188, 252
Wentz, John, 122
West Virginia regiments: First Cavalry, 185, 187–88; Seventh Infantry, 70–71
Westbrook, Lt. Col. Cornelius D., 130
Westminster, Md., 154, 243

Wheatfield: 132 (map); absolution of Irish Brigade, 147; Confederate control of, 133–34; fighting in, 133–34, 140–56, 159, 167, 168, 170, 176, 177, 202, 211, 212; monuments in, 135–36, 139–44, 167; officers killed in, 133, 135–36, 139, 170; trolley line through, 171; wild hogs feed on bodies in, 134
Wheeler, Capt. Charles, 55
Wheeler, Col. John, 165–66
Wheeler, Lt. William, 35
Wheeler Rock, 165–66
Wheeler's Battery, 33, 35
White, Lt. Col. Elijah, 59
White, Lt. Israel, 43
Whitman, Lt. Col. Henry, 233
Whitney, Pvt. Freeman P., 21
Wiebecke, Lt. Col. Charles, 215
Wiedrich, Capt. Michael, 68
Wiedrich's Battery, 42, 51, 68, 69, 70
Wilcox, Brig. Gen. Cadmus, 73, 112, 220, 221
Wilderness, the, 18, 146, 148, 164, 189, 192, 194, 200, 208, 228
Wiley, Sgt. James, 256
Willard, Asst. Surgeon James, 85
Willard, Col. George, 107, 117, 246, 249
Williams, Col. Samuel J., 15
Williams, Lt. Col. Jeremiah, 43
Williamsburg, Va., 122
Williamsport, Md., 192
Willoughby Run, 3, 60, 72
Wills House, 47
Wilson, Vice President Henry, 145
Winchester, Third Battle of, 155
Winebrenner Tannery, 187
Winkler, Maj. Frederick, 40
Winslow, Capt. George B., 144, 154
Wisconsin regiments: Fifth Infantry, 189; Sixth Infantry, 73, 253; Seventh Infantry, 253; Twenty-sixth Infantry, 37, 39–40; Company G, First Sharpshooters, 111–12
Wister, Col. Langhorne, 11
Witness tree, 76–77
Wolf Hill, 82, 86
Wood, Mayor Fernando, 160
Woodruff's Battery, 248
Woodward, Lt. Col. George A., 138–39
Woolsey, Capt. Henry, 113
Worchester, Mass., 234
Work, Lt. Col. P. A., 184
Wrangham, Pvt. Thomas J., 86
Wray, William J., 93
Wright, Brig. Gen. Ambrose, 219
Wright, First Lt. William P., 237

Yellow Hill Cemetery, 53
Yorktown, Va., 234
Young, Adj. P. F., 42

Ziegler's Grove, 129, 228
Zook, Brig. Gen. Samuel, 133, 135, 177